Frank Norris Remembered

AMERICAN WRITERS REMEMBERED
Jackson R. Bryer, Series Editor

Frank Norris Remembered

Edited by
JESSE S. CRISLER
and
JOSEPH R. McELRATH JR.

THE UNIVERSITY OF ALABAMA PRESS
Tuscaloosa

The University of Alabama Press
Tuscaloosa, Alabama 35487-0380

Manufactured in the United States of America

Typeface: AGaramond

Cover photograph: A publicity photo of Frank Norris released by Doubleday, Page, and Co., to advertise Norris's newly released novel *The Octopus* in April 1901. Courtesy of The Bancroft Library, University of California, Berkeley
Cover design: Michele Myatt Quinn

∞
The paper on which this book is printed meets the minimum requirements of American National Standard for Information Sciences—Permanence of Paper for Printed Library Materials, ANSI Z39.48-1984.

Library of Congress Cataloging-in-Publication Data

Frank Norris Remembered / Edited by Jesse S. Crisler and Joseph R. McElrath Jr.
pages cm — (American Writers Remembered)
Includes bibliographical references and index.
ISBN 978-0-8173-1795-9 (trade cloth : alk. paper) — ISBN 978-0-8173-8672-6 (ebook) 1. Norris, Frank, 1870-1902. 2. Norris, Frank, 1870-1902—Friends and associates. 3. Novelists, American—19th century—Biography. I. Crisler, Jesse S. II. McElrath, Joseph R.
PS2473.F67 2013
813'.4—dc23
[B]

2012040554

For James De Hart, gentleman and scholar

Contents

List of Illustrations

Acknowledgments

For services of various kinds, all of which immeasurably contributed to our research, we thank the following: Anthony Bliss, curator, Rare Books and Library Collections, and Susan Snyder, head, Public Services, The Bancroft Library, University of California, Berkeley; Sara S. Hodson, curator, Literary Manuscripts, Natalie Russell, library assistant for Literary Manuscripts, and Lita Garcia, Manuscripts Department, The Huntington Library, San Marino, California; Andrea Reithmayr, curator, Rare Books and Special Collections, Rush Rhees Library, University of Rochester, Rochester, New York; Sean Casey, curator, Rare Books and Manuscripts Department, Boston Public Library, Boston; Robert Parks, director of Library and Museum Services, The Pierpont Morgan Library, New York; Katherine Chandler, reference librarian, and Paul Artrip, assistant department head, Rare Book Department, Free Library of Philadelphia, Philadelphia; Ruth Van Stee, Grand Rapids Public Library, Grand Rapids, Michigan; Susan Abbott, Old Military and Civilian Records, National Archives and Records Administration, St. Louis, Missouri; Eugene T. Neeley, university archivist, Swirbul Library, Adelphi University, Garden City, New York; Richard T. Yanco, Worcester Academy, Worcester, Massachusetts; Max Lombardi, Records, Graceland Cemetery, Chicago; and Ti'Ata Sorenson, ILL Services, Brigham Young University, Provo, Utah.

We also thank the staffs of several other institutions: Passport Applications, National Archives, Washington, DC; Reference, Palo Alto Public Library and Palo Alto Historical Association, Palo Alto, California; Special Collections, Charles E. Young Research Library, University of California at Los Angeles; Special Collections, San Diego State University Library, San Diego, California; William Andrews Clark Memorial Library, University of California at Los Angeles; and the Robert Frost Library, Amherst College, Amherst, Massachusetts.

A number of people supplied useful and needed assistance to us as well, for which we extend our gratitude: Wendy Cloutier, P. Lance Crisler, Charles Crow, Donna Danielewski, Richard Allan Davison, Benjamin F. Fisher, Donald Foss, Joel Myerson, Jessica Peters, Gary Scharnhorst, Jo Scofield, and the late James D. Hart. Besides these, we have benefited in countless ways from the generous experience of our series editor, Jackson R. Bryer, Professor Emeritus, University of Maryland, College Park, and Daniel Waterman, Editor-in-Chief and Joanna Jacobs, Assistant Managing Editor, the University of Alabama Press, Tuscaloosa. For financial support we are indebted to the National Endowment for the Humanities; the American Philosophical Society, Philadelphia; and the College of Humanities, Brigham Young University, for monetary grants, which in part funded our research, and, likewise, to the Department of English and College of Arts and Sciences of Florida State University and the Department of English of Brigham Young University.

Linda Webster, indexer of this and our biography of Norris, worked diligently and quickly, making both books not only better but far more useful than they would have been without her astute efforts.

Finally, our wives, Sharon McElrath and Lou Ann C. Crisler, never fail to offer us extraordinary good cheer and continued encouragement.

Chronology

1870	Born in Chicago, Illinois, and baptized at Trinity Episcopal Church.
1876	Enrolls at Allen Academy.
1882	Enrolls at Harvard School.
1885	Moves to San Francisco; enrolls at Belmont Academy.
1886	Enrolls at Boys' High School and then California School of Design; confirmed at St. Luke's Episcopal Church.
1887	Begins study in the William Bouguereau studio at Académie Julian in Paris.
1889	Sees publication of his first article, "Clothes of Steel"; returns to San Francisco from Paris; prepares for admission to the University of California.
1890	Begins studies at University of California; composes *Yvernelle: A Legend of Feudal France.*
1891	Becomes a member of Phi Gamma Delta fraternity; publication of *Yvernelle*; short stories begin to appear in regional magazines.
1894	Completes four years at the University of California; begins two semesters of study at Harvard College.
1895	Drafts portions of *McTeague* and *Vandover and the Brute* while at Harvard; collection of his short stories accepted for publication by Lovell, Coryell, and Company, but never published; accepts a *San Francisco Chronicle* assignment to write descriptive articles about South Africa and there witnesses the "Jameson Raid."
1896	Serves the British cause in South Africa and is deported by the Boer government; accepts a position on the staff of the San Francisco *Wave* weekly magazine; becomes a member of the Bohemian Club.
1897	Completes but never sees book publication of a collection of recently composed short stories to have been titled

	"Ways That Are Dark"; completes the composition of *McTeague.*
1898	Serialization of *Moran of the Lady Letty* in *The Wave*; receives employment offer from the editorial offices of S. S. McClure and moves to New York City; serves as a *McClure's Magazine* correspondent in Cuba during the Spanish-American War; book publication of *Moran*; begins composing *Blix* and *A Man's Woman* while recuperating from malaria or dengue fever in San Francisco.
1899	Publication of *McTeague*; serializations of *Blix* and *A Man's Woman*; book publication of *Blix*; English publishers Grant Richards and William Heinemann decline the manuscript of *Vandover*; Norris travels to California to begin research for *The Octopus*; Jeannette Black and he announce their engagement.
1900	Leaves the employ of S. S. McClure to work as manuscript reader for Doubleday, Page & Co.; marries Jeannette at St. George's Episcopal Church in New York City; book publication of *A Man's Woman*; recommends Theodore Dreiser's *Sister Carrie* for publication; completes the composition of *The Octopus.*
1901	Conducts research for *The Pit* in Chicago; Jeannette and he visit San Francisco in April when *The Octopus* appears in print; returns to New York City where he completes *The Pit*; the success of *The Octopus* results in his being invited to write a significant number of literary essays and short stories for periodicals.
1902	Birth of daughter Jeannette "Billy" Norris; a version of *The Pit* serialized in the *Saturday Evening Post*; following their daughter's baptism at St. Andrew's Dune Church at Southampton, Long Island, the Norrises move to San Francisco; prepares to begin research on the novel that will complete the "wheat trilogy"; dies from peritonitis three months before the book publication of *The Pit.*

Frank Norris Remembered

Introduction

When the distressing news of the premature death of Frank Norris reached his uncle in Lincoln, Nebraska, on November 22, 1902, William Alfred Doggett delivered a brief summary of his impressions of his nephew as a youth to a reporter: "The boy was inclined to be melancholy. At times he was full of activity and animal spirits, but ordinarily he was slow and thoughtful" ("Lincoln Man" 1902, 16). Nearly three decades later, on October 14, 1930, Lucy A. H. Pownall Senger, wife of Joachim Henry Senger, Norris's tutor for his 1890 entrance examinations to the University of California, limned an even more truncated portrait of twenty-year-old Norris, newly returned from studying art in Paris and eager to begin a new phase of his life as a college student: "I remember him as a quiet young man, very polite." Twenty years thereafter, a classmate of Norris's at Berkeley, Edwin Milton Wilder, who on August 26, 1952, characterized himself as a "green boy . . . from [a] country high school," recalled Norris with a possible touch of suppressed envy as "a blasé, patronizing, indifferent man, not of the world, but from another world."

What these fleeting comments reveal is a lack of real familiarity with their subject, Frank Norris, in life one of America's most popular novelists. Even half a century after his death, Norris was still alive enough in the memory of a classmate (though hardly an intimate—Wilder admits, "Although I sat in class with [Norris] for five years, I never knew him well") to evoke vivid, if inaccurate, memories of him. For far from being "slow and thoughtful," "quiet," or "blasé, patronizing, indifferent," the Frank Norris known and loved by a wide circle of family members, fraternity brothers, college friends, employers, professional colleagues, fellow writers, and even critics belies the faulty memories of these more distant acquaintances.

Born in Chicago on March 5, 1870, Norris as a teenager moved to San Francisco in 1885. The privileged son of a father grown wealthy as a highly successful jeweler and a mother with finely tuned cultural and social aspirations, he matured in comfortable ease in their house at 1822 Sacramento, and embraced his new state of California so wholeheartedly that even early in his career he unabashedly informed newspaper critic Isaac F. Marcosson that he "was 'bawn 'n raise' in California" (Crisler 1986, 57). When a broken arm ended his tenure at a succession of elite college preparatory academies in both Chicago and the Bay Area, Norris persuaded his parents to allow him to explore a talent for drawing at the California School of Design, then under the able direction of Virgil M. Williams. As a regimen of art whetted Norris's appetite for a more intensive program, his parents accordingly took him to Paris to continue his studies at the famous Académie Julian. But when Norris's impatient father realized a seemingly inexplicable penchant for literary pursuits had supplanted his son's earlier interest in painting, he promptly summoned his errant boy home, where the younger Norris devoted himself to shoring up gaps in his formal education in order to gain entrance to the University of California in the hope of learning the rudiments necessary for writing successful fiction.

A thorough delight in college life notwithstanding, Norris failed to realize his fondest dream while at Berkeley; save at only a handful of American colleges, instruction in what is today termed *creative writing* was simply unknown at institutions of higher learning during the last decade of the 1890s. One such, fortunately for Norris, was Harvard College, which he entered as a "special student" in 1894, having received no degree at Berkeley, despite four years of college courses heavily slanted to British and French literature and history. Norris's year at Harvard at last yielded the fruit he had desired to pick at Berkeley: taught by Lewis Edward Gates, Norris learned much more than the basics of effective writing, as his extensive work in Gates's courses on two novels, *McTeague* (1899) and the posthumously published *Vandover and the Brute* (1914), indicates.

Hoping now to enter the ranks of professional writers but simultaneously aware that he needed more direct engagement with his chosen craft, Norris parlayed modest success as a cub reporter for the San Francisco *Wave* to an assignment from the *San Francisco Chronicle* to travel to South Africa in October 1895. Conflict there was brewing between Boers, who claimed the area by right of descent from Dutch colonists settling there over two centuries earlier, and British newcomers bent on solidifying their emerging but shaky authority in the region. What ensued for Norris was more thrilling than any fiction he might have concocted. For his part in the famous raid agent provocateur Leander Starr Jameson led, Norris was arrested by the Boers and summarily exiled, though not before contracting a mysterious, debilitating fever. Upon his return to San Francisco, he cemented earlier relations with *The Wave*, which hired him first as full-time writer and later as assistant editor under John O'Hara Cosgrave.

After two years of furious authorship for that magazine, Norris came to the notice of the enterprising publisher S. S. McClure, whose firm offered him a joint position as manuscript reader and contributor to its flagship publication, *McClure's Magazine*. A new professional opportunity before him, one even more propitious because of its potential for national exposure than had been possible with his work for the regional *Wave*, Norris understandably saw life as good. As he wrote his college fraternity brother, Harry M. Wright, "I've moved up a peg" (Crisler 1986, 50).

Life became even better a month later when McClure dispatched him to Cuba with a veritable fleet of journalists to cover the Cuban war. Once again, Norris's exploits in Cuba, both as reporter and participant, exceeded his wildest imaginings, making a reality of his complaint two years earlier in "An Opening for Novelists": "We don't want literature, we want life" (Crisler 1987h 7). Unfortunately, however, his fever recurred in Cuba, and he traversed the North American continent to recuperate once again in San Francisco.

Having met and courted subdebutante Jeannette Williamson Black during his days with *The Wave*, Norris, now a convalescent, continued to woo her. Meanwhile, his novels began appearing at a dizzying pace—*Moran of the Lady Letty* (1898) just after McClure hired him, *McTeague* early in 1899, *Blix*, a thinly veiled autobiographical idyll of his courtship, later that year in September. *A Man's Woman* was published in February 1900, only a month after he and Jeannette had at last married. Their wedding took place following the year Norris had spent alone in New York, save for three months in the spring of 1899 when he returned to California to research *The Octopus* (1901), the novel he considered his grandest yet. As a couple, he and Jeannette were a splash, meeting and entertaining the likes of such luminaries as the Hamlin Garlands; the Collis P. Huntingtons; Robert Louis Stevenson's widow, Fanny, and her entourage; and Katherine Herne and her daughters, who were prominent in America's dramatic circles. *The Octopus*, the first of a projected trilogy concerning wheat production, distribution, and consumption, fared well in sales, and research in Chicago in 1901 was successful enough to allow Norris not only to complete his next novel, *The Pit* (1903), by mid-1902 but also to capitalize on contacts there, as well as in New York, to extend his earlier journalistic experience by becoming a flourishing newspaper and magazine columnist.

Following by now established routine, Norris was laying plans for yet another fact-finding trip, this time to India, for the novel planned as "The Wolf," which would complete his Trilogy of the Wheat, when tragedy struck. A visit in late July 1902 to San Francisco to purchase a mountain retreat from Mrs. Stevenson and to arrange for the care of his eight-month-old daughter, Jeannette Williamson Norris, with her grandmothers, ended with his wife suffering from appendicitis but ultimately recovering via an operation. Ironically, two weeks later Norris then died on October 25, 1902, from peritonitis resulting from a burst appendix.

This unanticipated loss to American letters led to an outpouring of sentiment, most of it predictable keening over "one of the cruelest blows of fate" ("Norris"

1902), but a good many articulate responses from close friends—former classmates, fellow authors, and even employers. These constitute the first body of written remembrances of Norris, yet their ephemeral nature—hastily written letters to his shocked wife or as precipitately composed articles for daily newspapers—often led, if not to their complete loss, then at the least to near obscurity. Indeed, when Franklin D. Walker, a young graduate student at the University of California, in 1930 settled on Norris's life as the subject of his doctoral dissertation, that subject, despite the appearance of a lavish edition of Norris's complete works two years earlier, had virtually receded into literary insignificance, his life little appreciated, his novels largely unread, his shorter works nearly unknown, his influence all but negligible. Seeking to redress this lamentable situation, Walker embarked on a laudable program to track down anyone who had known Norris, writing to many and interviewing others. His success was notable, generating a second batch of reminiscences in the form of nearly twenty interviews and as many letters written in response to his invitations for recollections of Norris.

This was well, since prior to Walker's attempt to acquire accounts of Norris's life, only three biographical sketches of him existed, each of them as fanciful as it was factually misinformed. The three perpetrators were Denison Hailey Clift, Charles Caldwell Dobie, both California journalists, and Norris's brother Charles, who had also supplied Dobie with often-specious information. Thus Walker's 1932 biography of Norris drew upon information not available to Clift in 1907 for "The Artist in Frank Norris," Dobie in 1928 for "Frank Norris, or Up from Culture," and Charles Norris also in 1928 for his introduction to the tenth volume of *The Argonaut Manuscript Limited Edition of Frank Norris's Works.* But even Walker larded *Frank Norris: A Biography* with flagrant speculation, demonstrably erroneous interpretation, and in some cases outright falsehood. He also failed to capture the spirit of the accounts of those who either wrote him or with whom he conducted interviews, such as the generous persona informing the comments of Norris's roommate at Berkeley, Albert J. Houston, the foreboding mystery of fellow artist Bruce Porter's description of Norris's final days, or the perceptive poise reflected in a letter from Dulce B. Davis at whose ranch Norris stayed while researching *The Octopus.*

A third spate of memoirs on Norris came in 1952 when James D. Hart, then professor of English at the University of California, Berkeley, and later director of its Bancroft Library, was informed by Robert D. Lundy, his graduate student, that the Bancroft numbered no Norris manuscripts in its voluminous collections nor for that matter much else relating to him. Determined to remedy what he viewed as woeful neglect of a native son of the university, Hart founded the magnificent Frank Norris Collection, a treasure trove of primary Norris documents as well as more letters, memoirs, and other accounts of him. When, nearly a half-century later, we began assembling our findings from more than thirty years of research on Norris to write *Frank Norris: A Life* (2006), we discovered yet more remembrances of a man whose colorful life had made an indelible impression on those who knew him. Like Walker before us, however, we realized we could report the facts of that life, in many instances filling in noticeable gaps, but we could not begin to weave into our biography all the information contributed by Norris's contemporaries at his death, amassed by Walker during his research, extended in turn by Hart, and finally collected by ourselves.

Even the most meticulous biography cannot hope to present the complete record of its subject, but a collection of reminiscences such as those printed in this volume, when viewed as a companion to our biography, gives not just flesh to Norris's stark body but also dresses him in the impressions of friends and family, regardless of their personal biases or sometimes possibly imperfect memories. Certainly, it puts into proper perspective the faulty, even less charitable comments of people such as Norris's uncle, William Doggett, his tutor's wife, Lucy Senger, and his college acquaintance, Edwin Wilder, all of whom knew him not under the circumstances revealed by the contributors to this collection but at a considerably more distant remove.

Thus the primary reason for such a collection as this is not to demonstrate what everyone already knows about the profound difficulty encountered in reconstructing the past; rather, it is to make available a substantial body of recollections and perceptions meriting full attention from anyone seriously interested in understanding Norris's life, the personality that informs interpretation of his writings, and what both reveal about the character of the time and cultural conditions in which he passed that life. A second reason is that we are certain that readers will find these remembrances inherently interesting not only for what they tell about Norris but also what they divulge regarding the personalities of the correspondents, interviewees, and memoirists, many of whom are noteworthy as literary or historical figures in their own right. Finally, the personal statements gathered here reveal details of Norris's appearance, character, beliefs, literary likes, even prejudices, for example, Norris's conflict with the military science department as a college student, a situation about which many sources comment. Assembling these and other surviving sources in a single volume fills such biographical lacunae by providing a rich assortment of material previously accessible for the most part only either as quickly written letters of condolence to Jeannette, Walker's inexpertly typed notes, letters to both him and Hart, or articles that appeared in unfamiliar periodicals such as *Phi Gamma Delta Quarterly* and *University of California Chronicle.*

Both a desire to present an unembellished portrait of Norris and a concomitant wariness of duplication have driven the final arrangement of this collection.

Even so, some repetition occurs: for instance, among Norris's brothers in Phi Gamma Delta, his college fraternity, some of his more famous antics and the arcane memorabilia gracing his private quarters ascended over time to the realm of legend, stories that all of those brothers felt compelled to relate, if only through cursory allusion. These and other common memories characterize many of the reminiscences, coalescing in a multifaceted yet harmonious image of Norris as genial acquaintance, generous friend, playful teaser, worldly flaneur, dutiful son, ardent husband, delighted father, assiduous observer, and, most significantly, discriminating writer, for, clearly, above all else, that was how Norris saw himself, as these contributions make abundantly clear.

Although the content of the reminiscences marks four discrete periods in Norris's life—his boyhood phase, his college years, his writing apprenticeship, and his professional career—a strictly chronological arrangement ultimately proved infeasible; for example, Norris encountered virtually all of his college friends, certainly all of his fellow fraternity members, at the same time, that is, his freshman year at Berkeley. Instead, each period comprises reminiscences written by those who first met Norris during that period but ordered alphabetically by their last names. Had the writers confined themselves to recalling only memories from the time when they were introduced to Norris, the result might have seemed more synchronized, though perhaps more bland, than it is, but the reality is that they did not, ranging throughout the years of their association with Norris, often with little thought to chronology, rather than addressing only a specific time of his life. As a case in point, Gelett Burgess, an instructor at Berkeley when Norris attended the University of California, met Norris because of their mutual interest in drama, but Burgess later involved Norris in the avant-garde activities of his literary coterie, Les Jeunes, in San Francisco, and later still accompanied him to meet William Dean Howells in New York. Similarly, Jeannette's interviews with Walker demonstrate much more than passing familiarity with her husband's life prior to their meeting in 1896 that only she could have derived from Norris himself.

In addition to an explanation of the nature and arrangement of these selections, a few other clarifications are in order. While previously published sources required little editorial attention, that was not the case with those that were handwritten and typed. Our conservative policy was to correct indisputable misspellings and provide absolutely essential punctuation in cases when confusion for the reader threatened. Published sources did not require editorial emendation of words intended to receive special emphasis by means of italicization, but the underlining of words in handwritten and typed sources did. They appear in italics in this volume. Finally, bracketed ellipses in sources indicate editorial omissions, while ellipses without brackets occurred in original sources.

The volume contains sixty-seven contributions—fifteen previously published—by fifty individuals; besides the published pieces, represented are letters of condolence to Jeannette, letters to Walker, his interview notes, letters to Hart, Hamlin Garland's diary entries, excerpts from Albert Houston's autobiography, and three letters to other recipients. A brief commentary introduces each section; headnotes identify contributors and contextualize their relationship with Norris; endnotes explain literary allusions, identify figures mentioned in various sources, and present other information deemed useful for interpreting the sources themselves; and both a list of the reminiscences included and another list of all known reminiscences of Norris complete the volume. Full information for contributions in the former list appears in the source notes preceding reminiscences.

1. Frank Norris at ten years of age as a student at Allen Academy in Chicago. Courtesy of The Bancroft Library, University of California, Berkeley.

1
Childhood and Youth
Chicago, San Francisco, and Paris, 1870–90

Frank Norris's infancy and youth, spent amid sumptuous surroundings in Chicago, are documented in census reports, academic catalogs, city directories, school texts, newspaper articles, personal books, church records, and even dance programs. He was clearly born to the manner. But aside from meager comments by his mother's older brother William Doggett, who lived several hundred miles west in Lincoln, Nebraska, no one in Norris's immediate family or among his classmates at Allen Academy, Harvard School, and Bournique's Dancing Academy left even the briefest written testament reporting his years as a youngster—that is, no one save his brother Charles. True, Charles, eleven years Norris's junior, is hardly an unimpeachable source for those years. True as well, whatever Charles learned about that period in his brother's life was perforce filtered through the lens of a doting mother and a father who may have been hypercritical. True finally, Charles himself inarguably distorted what little he did know, augmenting it with what he felt he could legitimately imagine. Following his brother's death, Charles became not only his ever-loyal publicist and the energetic executor of his literary estate but also, for this early period in Norris's life, the most important source of information about him.

As to Norris's early years in California, Charles's is not the only voice, although the chorus is a relatively small one. But Norris begins to assume fuller definition as a young man and promising artist in the reminiscences of Philip King Brown and M. C. Sloss, Norris's classmates at the Belmont School for Boys; Louis W. Neustadter, a near neighbor after the Norrises moved to San Francisco in 1885; and Ernest C. Peixotto, a fellow student at both the California School of Design in 1886 and later in Paris at the Académie Julian.

1 / Philip King Brown

A native Californian, Philip King Brown (1869–1940) was a member of the first class to graduate in 1886 from Belmont School for Boys, which Frank Norris also attended for a short time in 1885. Belmont's founder, William Thomas Reid (1843–1922), a former teacher at Boys' High School in San Francisco, retired as president of the University of California and opened the semimilitary institution to prepare young men to gain admission to Harvard College. Located south of San Francisco on the former estate of banker and industrialist William Chapman Ralston (1826–1875), Belmont immediately attracted the interest of wealthy San Franciscans with aspirations for their male offspring. Fulfilling Reid's vision, Brown did matriculate at Harvard, where he received his MD in 1893, afterward becoming a progressive physician, specializing in treating diseases of the heart and lung. As is the case with other reminiscences, Brown's response to Franklin Walker indicates the impact Norris apparently had upon those he met, many of whom, like Brown, could recall in surprising detail their sometimes slight association with him not only after many years but often also after a fairly brief acquaintance.

Source: Philip King Brown to Franklin D. Walker, letter, October 7, 1930, Franklin Dickerson Walker Papers, BANC MSS C-H 79, The Bancroft Library, University of California, Berkeley.

Dear Mr. Walker,

The Belmont School was founded by W. T. Reid, formerly president of the University of California, in 1885 & opened that fall at the old Ralston place at Belmont with about 25 scholars. Frank Norris didn't join till later & was not in my class as he was somewhat younger. The first class was made up of M. C. Sloss, Summit Louis Hecht, F. L. DeLong & myself. The next class was made up of A. L. Bancroft, Charles Adams & Frank Norris together with a few others whose names I do not now remember. There was thus 1 year's difference in preparation for Harvard & U.C. & all the first class went to Harvard.[1]

Frank Norris broke his arm playing football & I brought him to town. He lived on Sacramento St., north side, between Van Ness & Franklin. His mother was a very brilliant woman & for years in her later life was the leader of the Browning Society. The father was a successful business man—a jeweler I think.[2] Mrs. Norris, the mother, was a patient of mine for many years & until his death I kept up some relation to Frank. He was brilliant as was the mother, very quiet, full of dry humor & eccentric rather aiming to draw fire for the sake of arousing acute discussion. He was indifferent to all that did not interest him & gave the impression of being physically lazy. He had great charm & was popular. I was away most of the time after that first year till about 1896.

You could get some facts from Bruce Porter, Santa Barbara, & Gelett Burgess whose present whereabouts I do not know. J. O'Hara Cosgrave, Porter Garnett (Berkeley), Willis Polk (now dead) all belonged to the later group of literary lights who met occasionally at dinner.[3] I think I could find a menu of a birthday dinner to Gelett Burgess ("Purple Cow," Goops, *The Lark*) served by the crowd. If I can uncover it I'll send it to you provided it is promptly returned.[4]

Yours truly,
Philip King Brown

2 / Louis W. Neustadter

As a boy, Louis William Neustadter (1873–1968), whose family were wealthy members of San Francisco's Jewish community, lived at 1701 Van Ness Avenue, just around the corner from Norris's family. When he was only eighteen, Neustadter entered employment at his father's firm, Neustadter Brothers, purveyors of fine men's furnishings, and later became a prominent civic leader in the Bay Area.

Source: Louis William Neustadter to James D. Hart, letter, March 22, 1954, James D. Hart Papers, BANC MSS 81/107c, The Bancroft Library, University of California, Berkeley.

Dear Jim,

Yours of the 20th will, as are all your letters, be preserved for future generations when the name of Dr. James D. Hart will be listed with other greats of the literary world.

Now re the Norris era; I am not certain about a cable car on Polk Street when McTeague operated there, nor can I recall a gold tooth above the post office, the which was located on Polk, between Bush and Pine Streets, on the north west corner of Polk and Bush Streets was the Roberts Candy Store, presided over by a good looking brunette, she dispensed other dainties besides candy, but because she had a deformed right thumb, she did not appeal to me, I still think that a deformed thumb detracts from the sex appeal of any gal. Was there a "resort" a few doors below a drug store not far from the corner of Sutter and Kearney Sts.? I really do not know, my mother did not permit me to visit "resorts" at that time, the drug store was there, complete with live snakes the which were fed with live rats for the entertainment of those who enjoyed watching the said reptiles absorb the poor rodents.[5]

The Norris family lived on Sacramento Street, a few doors from our ancestral home, Norris mère was a dragon like character who bossed Hell out of both her sons, Frank and Charles, the latter was called "Doc,"[6] don't ask me why, I don't know, I attended the Urban School with these Norris

Boys,[7] who were very much afraid of their Mamma, I would have bet on the old gal against a Grizzly bear.

As for the locale described by Frank Norris in his *McTeague*, his descriptions are accurate, the only discrepancy was the reference to Joe Frenna, who if my memory serves me correctly, was the owner of a barber shop; I can recall him very well, a dark, short guy, not at all handsome.[8]

It might interest you to learn that Erich von Stroheim made a movie of *McTeague*, it was called *Greed* and had to be severely cut for American production, the entire film was sent to South America, Von Stroheim has a filthy mind, one of the scenes which were cut out was a toilet full of rats; the deleted American version was rather tame and not too much like the book.[9]

When writing to you I recall so many authors now forgotten, F. Marion Crawford who wrote *Saracinesca*, followed by *Don Orsino*, etc. I also read his *Mr. Isaacs* with great interest, George Eliot in *Adam Bede*, etc., Thackeray and Dickens of course, Galsworthy and the long family sagas,[10] now these all appear to be ancient history, their characters knew nothing of the blessings of H-bombs and other modern comforts; they dwelt in ignorance if not in bliss.

Speaking of drug store snakes, I remember Elsie Venner who was I believe a somewhat reptilian character;[11] yet these ancient books hold a certain charm altogether absent in modern literature; perhaps I am getting old, my interest in women has become, as I formerly remarked, impurely academic; don't ever get old, it is one Hell of a mess.

Be good, it won't get you anywhere.

With love to you and Ruth,[12] I am as ever,

Louis

3 / Charles G. Norris

The unexpected death from diphtheria of their brother, Albert Lester Norris (1877–1887), in part accounts for a closeness between Norris and his surviving brother, Charles Gilman Norris (1881–1945), that under more normal circumstance would most likely not have obtained: with eleven years between them the two surely had little in common. But Norris seems genuinely to have cared for Charles; the family journeyed to Europe soon after Lester's death to enroll Norris in the celebrated Académie Julian in Paris as an art student, and though B. F. returned to San Francisco fairly soon, Charles and Gertrude remained with Norris for nearly a year, during which time he entertained his brother by mounting elaborate campaigns with him of lead soldiers and regaling him with fabricated stories of one Gaston le Foix and his nephew, the latter predictably named Charles Gilman Norris. After Norris's untimely death, Charles became his de facto literary executor and maintained friendly relations with his sister-in-law, Jeannette Williamson Norris, for many years. Thus his recollections of his brother as a college student and subsequently as a successful writer were unequalled.

Source: Charles Gilman Norris to Jeannette Williamson Norris, letter, [August? 1903], Frank Norris Collection, BANC MSS C-H 80, The Bancroft Library, University of California, Berkeley.

My dearest sister,

I cannot exactly recall the date but I'm quite sure that it was about the time you will get this letter, that a year ago we celebrated all together your last birthday. I have hesitated about writing and reminding you but I am anxious that you should know I remembered and that on this birthday I was thinking of you and wishing with all the heart of me, that it were possible for you to be as happy again this year as you were last. Oh—it seems so very, very long ago and I seem to feel that we were all very different people. Surely we are not the same as those four happy persons that had dinner in the private room on that day in the Poodle Dog Restaurant.[13]

Thank God none of us could look forward and have seen ourselves as we are today and so blight the happiness of that one supreme night. Do you remember how afterwards we took Mama to the Sutter street cars and then the three of us went down town, again to see the sights? Some convention was there and later we went up to Café Zinkand.[14] Oh, Jeannette dear, it all comes over me with a rush. It's so hard to go on and keep back the tears and try to forget. I *can't* forget. Would to God, he were here now and whispering to me—"good man." But my grief dwindles away to nothingness when I think of the emptiness and the bareness of what I know your life must be. Dear JB, would that I could suffer more and lessen your great grief or in some way fill the vacant place if only with my love. And may I presume to say that were he here today I know how proud he'd be of his wife. I can't tell you, Jeannette, how nobly I think you have acted and it's a comfort for me to know that he picked the one woman in the world who could bear his name, and bear it as she should.

If devotion, pride or love could send you with this letter some spark of happiness on your birthday, let my heart send it and believe me now and always until death reunites one of us with him that's gone, your devoted brother

Charley.

Source: Charles Gilman Norris. Interview notes by Franklin D. Walker, May 16, 1930, Franklin Dickerson Walker Collection, BANC MSS C-H 79, The Bancroft Library, University of California, Berkeley.

As this was a luncheon engagement I failed to take notes on a considerable part of it. Says that he is very willing to cooperate in working out the book and will try to place it in New York. Has collected a considerable amount of material which he keeps in Saratoga.[15] Believes a book of about 40,000 the best, with emphasis on the formative period. His letters were burned as well as the South African notebook and "Robert d'Artois."[16] Wants me to come down to the ranch on Tuesday, May 27th, his secretary, Mr. McCollough to meet me at the train which reaches Palo Alto at noon.

He doesn't remember much about Frank before he was sixteen (1886) but has a good many things about childhood which he will be able to give.

When they went to Paris Frank would do everything he wasn't supposed to do. Absent-minded; poorly kempt; terrible complexion; took castor oil every day. Was speaking rotten French and mother used to read Fénelon's *Télémaque* every night to him.[17] Ernest Peixotto a good friend.

He remembers "Robert d'Artois" as a simply impossible story. No good at all, from a promising writer. More later.

After Frank returned from Paris (thinks it was in the Spring of 1890) he began writing *Yvernelle* and had strong ambition to join state militia.[18] Does so but does not get a horse. Later, when he was suspended from military in the University there was a grand blow-up and he dropped the militia.[19] Get more on this.

University of California. Not many kind words for faculty. Hated Armes. Very fond of Le Conte and Paget.[20] Never passed entrance math. When first in college stayed with somebody [Senger.[21] See Samuels's letter, chapter 21 this volume]. Most of his time was spent with Wolf and Samuels, two Jews.[22] When he was initiated into the frat the boys asked him first whether he was a Jew. Used to draw pictures on Haggerty's [*sic*] saloon.[23] Suspended from military.

Harvard. Reason for going. Had been a plan before the separation of parents. Hence carried it out. Mother and Charles lived in Cambridge; he stayed in Grays.[24] Course with Gates the only one which he took. Charles has some of his papers; he took a straight A.[25] When *Vandover* was to be published he wrote to Gates for a foreword;[26] the latter wrote back a most heated letter declaring that it should not be published. Thinks he has gone sour.

Vandover. Had to leave out some details which were too revolting. Added about five thousand words before it was in shape to publish.[27]

Separation of parents. Father a most unusual man. A good Presbyterian; smoked only cigars, did not drink. Had a Sunday school class. Used to spend all of his evenings at home where his wife would read to him. All at once got a bug for travel and wanted to go around the world. Wife did not want to so he went alone. On the trip he met a woman, a widow (1893), and became enamored of her. On arriving in Chicago he filed suit for divorce, much to the astonishment of his wife. Mrs. N. filed counter-suit and won by default. His father, sixty years old, remarried and left his money to his second wife.[28] He used to send Frank checks but Mrs. N. did not like to have him accept them; remembers him tearing one up. Probably started returning them while at Harvard.

Wave. The Wave was started in order to advertise the Del Monte Hotel, which was owned by the Southern Pacific, as well as the railroad to it.[29] Cosgrave was bull-headed. Charles calls him nothing but a stuffed-shirt. He fired Frank once from *The Wave* because he said he could not write. Told him to go into the jewelry business. Later Frank got him his job with *Everybody's*.[30] Ran into luck later.

At this time, women were always crazy about Frank. He was not a chaser. Remembers that he got in a mess over a girl named Viola Rodgers.[31] Feels that when Jeannette went east, Frank was more in love with her than she was with him.[32] He went up to the Big Dipper mine. Mardi Gras incident to be written up for *The Wave*.[33]

McTeague. Is sure that he started it at U.C.[34] Thinks that Dobie made up the murder in the kindergarten.[35] Used to turn in some of *McTeague* at Harvard.[36] See Waterhouse. Had no strong sympathy for working classes; cursed Russian revolutionists. Aristocrat at heart. Holbrook Blinn made it into a fine movie, *Life's Whirlpool.*[37]

Militia. Love of horses. Admired Remington's horses a great deal. Put action in them.[38]

Moran was not copyrighted. Hence no return on the movie.[39]

Moulson helped a good deal with *The Pit.*[40] Says that he rigged up the Bull and Bear game for them.

Interest in football in college intense. All broken up when Hunt broke his leg.[41] He learned part of Jocasta (Creon?) for *Oedipus* in the Greek.[42]

His nickname while young was Skinny Well-fed. (Used in *Vandover.*)[43]

He considered Henry Lanier to have had a very bad influence on Frank. Interested in sales of his books. Was due to him that we have the triangle in *The Pit.* Frank would not have written it that way. Curse Lanier.

Of friends. Houston, Gibbs, Waterhouse. Believes artists knew him best; Porter, Burgess, Peixotto. Doesn't like Wright; apparently has had letter from him since I started writing book.

Jimmy White. Old football player. Was in house when Frank was there although he had graduated. Used to drink a great deal; suddenly stopped without another drop. Frank admired his strength; became close friends. Remembers seeing a letter which Frank wrote to Jimmy on all kinds of paper, including toilet paper.[44]

Tells of how Haggerty came to see Charles while the latter was mowing lawn in front of Fiji house.[45] Tears in his eyes. Talks of old spree together.

Formula for Maria Macapa an old one mother used to hear.[46] Ask about this.

Source: Charles Gilman Norris. Interview notes by Franklin D. Walker, June 9, 1930, Franklin Dickerson Walker Papers, BANC MSS C-H 79, The Bancroft Library, University of California, Berkeley.

This was at Saratoga and a good deal of the time was spent in giving me the material which I brought away and showing me the pictures on the walls.

Belmont school; one of the charter members. Then under W. T. Reid, formerly president of University of California. Stayed only a part of a term when he broke his arm playing football. Returned home; sent to the Boys' High School (Lowell High School).[47] Didn't like it and begged to get out. Folks took him out and sent him to the Virgil Williams Academy which later became the Mark Hopkins Acad.[48]

The armor article for the *Chronicle* was sent to mother from Paris. Note date on notes at hand is June 20, 1889.[49]

Archibald. They met him some time on the train coming east [*sic*] from N.Y. and he became much interested in Ida Carleton.[50] Used to call at the house frequently and he and Frank became well acquainted; together much of the time until the latter went to U.C. Later he met him in Cuba; disliked him in many ways. On return from Santiago, Archibald had to appear in full get-up.[51]

Remington once came running up in his shirt tails to warn them to get out of the way of gun-fire. They laughed at him.

Cuba. Mother met him in Coronado where he tried for some time to recuperate.[52]

Life in Paris. Two years.

The first year the family spent in Paris after one month in London. They got an apartment in the back of the Opéra about 100 Blvd. Haussmann, after first staying at the Continental Hotel. This apartment had been used by some explorer and was full of interesting relics. They ate wretched meals out at the American Hotel. His father was very restless and decided to go back to America. Sometime later his mother and Frank went off on a trip to Italy and Charles stayed with the Quatremain family (probably on left bank).[53] Also a Mme. Desseau and a Marguerite—in the family; the latter Frank's first love. (No. 1, Rue de Lille, left bank. [. . .]) [See Peixotto, chapter 4 this volume.]

After the family returned to America (they spent Easter on the boat), Frank stayed in Paris with the Quatremain family. He had made a close friend of Peixotto and several others. Had been attending the Julian Academy but was disappointed in not getting into the Beaux Arts;[54] he really didn't work very hard at it. It was necessary to do a daily oil; one day he did a picture of his mother's black cat on a cushion which was "hung on the line" to his surprise and gratification. Bouguereau would come in once a week to inspect the drawings.[55] Also thinks Lepage was there at the time.[56] He was mad about *Trilby*.[57]

He was quite mad about the opera and got a job in the claque, paying $1.50 and getting 75¢ back. He did this more for the lark than need of money. He knew nothing of German music or symphony but heard and re-heard the operas; they could hear them from their lodgings. Fond of *Les Huguenots* and *Le Prophète*; remember once going to hear Gounod lead the opera at a matinee.[58]

Before they had gone to Paris Frank had begun to be interested in the lead soldiers and would spend a great deal of his time telling stories about them. He divided them up between Romans and Spartans, having all kinds of heroes and anachronisms. He had no American heroes as they were too close to home. He became so engrossed in these stories that he forgot that it was only a game. After they went to Paris the games continued and Charles would take back the jam glasses, get *sous* and buy lead soldiers packed in fig tins. Charles would spend all day long in setting them up for the time when Frank came home.

After Charles' return to S.F. Frank continued to send the installments by mail. It was the story of Charles Gilman Norris, nephew of the Duke of Burgundy. He had had a good deal of trouble due to getting drunk and killing a man. Gaston le Foix banished him to Saxony and there he had to escape in sixty days. He had a companion with a glass hat; à la Stockton. Marcelle appears as one of the figures; suddenly tells the story of the lady and the tiger.[59] Also the frozen voices of Bulwer-Lytton.[60] These installments of 6–7000 words, profusely illustrated, came for months. One contained a picture of a bony horse, "full of points." They finally get over into Saxony and Charles becomes an attendant in an insane asylum. He views Gaston le Foix attacking from his vantage point on the roof and the big insane man appears and insists that they jump off. Charles, ever keeping his head, offers to go below and jump up. Finally he is locked in signal tower with the heroine attached to the switch.[61] His father decides that this is enough and sends to him to come home.

Return in 1889. He returned some time this year and spent the following year preparing for the entrance examinations with Senger of the German department (with whom he lived on first entering the university). Writes *Yvernelle.* Is very much interested in two girls, Lulu Fargo and one other.[62] Also the French maid. Is sure that he had been initiated into the mysteries of sex in Paris. He always radiated sex and the women were very conscious of it. This he inherited from his mother who was quite outspokenly interested in it.

"Robert d'Artois." He had this with him when he returned and kept it quiet; later became ashamed of it. It was all about the figures in the *Chronicle* of Froissart;[63] a rotten novel even to a boy of Charles's age. He remembers a whole chapter written just to get the concluding sentence; I ask for bread and you give me a stone; I ask for an egg and you give me a scorpion.[64]

It was at this time that he became enthusiastic for a horse and joined the National Guard. Doesn't know whether he got the horse or not. His mother bought him the banjo to keep him at home. He used to play it quite well, particularly at Harvard.[65]

In Paris they came out of the opera with about forty of the colorfully dressed cuirassiers in the street to control traffic. On hearing a cab horn toot, one of the horses jumped, and Frank said "He hears the call to battle" quite seriously. (Street-car horn.)

The *Collier's* article on student life in Paris was written by request at the time of a student riot and he refused to do it for $100; said $200 and was surprised to get it.[66]

He doesn't know much about his life at Chicago. A wealthy family with sleigh, etc.[67] Dancing school.[68] Has picture of him. Started keeping a diary at five. Went to Europe at eight [1878] and spent some time at Brighton.[69] "The hour for departure has come."[70] Charles has a picture of him at five; also when he was at Lowell High School.

He didn't like Harvard very much because he failed to make friends.

Charles says he was reading Zola on return from Europe and believes that he began *McTeague* before entering the University.[71] Does not think that he did anything after getting in with that bunch of Fijis.[72]

Vandover. Mrs. Preston had the MS. all of the time and was slow about getting it to him. The story about the fire, etc. was all a lot of hooey. Charles added about five thousand words.

Source: Charles Gilman Norris. Interview notes by Franklin D. Walker, July 8, 1931, Franklin Dickerson Walker Collection, BANC MSS C-H 79, The Bancroft Library, University of California, Berkeley.

Rode down to Saratoga with him and spent the day there.

Given portrait of Gertrude Doggett, copy of *Bellman* for May 27, 1916, containing article by Randolph Edgar.[73]

Also Mr. Norris says he will try to get me copy of Mrs. Alister's address;[74] suggests writing to Miss Comstock, Nelson Doubleday's secretary, and says that Mr. Dan Longwell, editor of Doubleday, will be out for grove play (Aug. 1) and he will invite me out to meet him at that time.[75]

Samuel Doggett had nine children who aided in taking care of the ranch in Mendon, Mass. Most of them were killed or scattered during the war and the ranch went broke. If anyone, he was prototype of Magnus Derrick.[76] Long line of Doggetts—probably Unitarians—buried at Taunton, Mass.[77] Believes that Priscilla was in family tree—mother thought so.[78] English stock from early settlers. Much more aristocratic than father's.[79] Mother was very set on stage career and only gave it up after first child was born,[80] father had brain fever, and mother milk breasts.[81]

Gertrude's mother's father was a ship captain and carried slaves; at one time he brought home a little negro girl from Africa for her to play with; the little girl would do nothing but hide under the bed and jabber—had to send her home.[82]

Does not know much about father's family—only that they were Michigan farmers.[83] Father had a pretty hard struggle of it at first but was an extremely active man—thought a man to amount to anything should have a fire-cracker up his ass. Does not know how he came from New York to Chicago, but he was just getting a start when he met his mother. (Gertrude.) He picked up Alister as a young immigrant from Scotland, made him cashier and then partner, and Mrs. Norris engineered a marriage with her niece, the sister of Ida Carleton. Charles thinks Alister told him there was $800,000 left to his second wife. He was heavy set, broad shouldered. Long grey mustache; very white hair. Limped noticeably. Brown eyes. Wore nose glasses. Was very direct as business man. Never swore. Straight English stock. Knows nothing about Spring Valley Co.[84] He followed Gertrude to Cincinnati to get her to marry him. They first lived in a room over a photographer's shop.[85]

Grace, the daughter born before Frank, died of spinal meningitis at three months. The second daughter, Flora, born after Frank, died a year old from cholera infantum, which also nearly killed Frank.[86]

The father's business was burned out during the fire; one of the assistants loaded a good deal of jewelry into a trunk and wheeled it out with a wheel-barrow; it was the stock with which Norris started back on the up-grade.[87] Brick-kiln.

Picture of Frank at four in heavy red or black overcoat with wide white trimming, snow cap, standing very erect with arm on chair, one foot twisted behind him. Hands look plump. Very attractive face, dark with dark hair, determined little chin and firm cheeks.

The family must have been getting along very well because they had six horses, a coachman, a French maid.[88] Father very fond of driving; mother in a sleigh accident.

Mother was intensely ambitious for Frank; always a driving force. Note *Yvernelle* incident.[89]

Father's expression, "Get there, Eli."[90] When building a house in S.F. he was so impatient at a delay in delivering a cornice that he carried it up himself. He was always up at 8 and had no use for laziness.

Lived for a year at Lake Merritt.[91]

Picture while at Lowell High. Looks very much as Vernon Bryson would with dark hair.[92] Pompadour. Upper lip slightly protruding. Eyes a bit squinty. Slender. Erect posture.

He was being fed cod-liver oil, not castor-oil.

(Paris.) Remembers that his mother read *Télémaque* to counteract the *atelier* French. Frank hated it. They enjoyed the trip to Italy as if it were a honeymoon—brought back many things. Mother took him to a French doctor and gave him more cod-liver oil. Charles remembers that he was working on a piece of writing about the commune; barricaded streets—note short sketch of man killed in

1870 while playing the piano—a remnant.[93] Sure he read Froissart in French; remembers the book. Learned quite a bit of Old French.

Yvernelle period. Mother pushed this poem; note her determination.

Still emphasizes fustian episode. Does not think that Grettir stories were written at this time.[94]

Zola. Thinks *La Terre* was one of greatest novels—was also a favorite of Frank's. Zola greater than Flaubert; note poor construction of *Madame Bovary*—starts with hero, then goes to heroine.[95]

Frank lazy during this period—also at Harvard; only when married did he get energetic.

Physically fairly strong. Enthusiastic about fencing, football, poker, horseback riding, fishing.

Not sure whether he knew Gates or not. Gates gave him very good criticism on *McTeague*; remembers when Gates told him to picture how cat looked to others and not what was inside of her mind.[96]

Frank ate at Memorial hall.[97] Note the writing on his banjo. Found Harvard cold. They lived near what is now Dana Street. Miss Bates and Old Grannis were at the boarding house (Mr. and Mrs. Welch's) next door.[98] They were in love with each other; subject for gossip. (See *Trilby*.)

Vandover ms. lost by Doubleday. Chap. 3 was a disgusting picture of a drunk; also cut out sections describing parlour used in *Blix*. Quite clear that he did not intend to revise it. Doesn't know where he got shipwreck.[99] Saw father at distance on return trip to Chicago.

Wanted to get regular writing job with *Harper's* but failed.

Hoover not a friend.[100] Viola Rodgers—quite a serious case. Believes that he went up to Big Dipper to get away from her. He was dippy about Jeannette, but she played around most of the time he was in N.Y. Millicent Cosgrave a good friend.[101] Salary $20 a week. Is sure Cosgrave fired him. Likes Cosgrave much better now.

Believes *McTeague* was finished up to Big Dipper incident before leaving Harvard. Agrees that the sixth sense instinct was possibly due to Porter; also possibly Svengali.

He and Frank went to see first American production of *Trilby* in Boston. Very enthusiastic.[102]

How much did Frank rewrite *McTeague*?[103] Note the unity of it.

Moran feuilleton fashion—had to remember early part.[104] Cf. Gaston le Foix.

Phillips, not McClure, was responsible for discovering Frank. McClure was crazy—everybody knew it. Does not know about syndicate stuff.[105]

P. 106. Was under the impression all of first edition included the page. Reviewers objected. Thinks that Doubleday wrote out suggesting change.[106] Does not know where Taylor got his story.[107]

Doubleday now has sleeping sickness.

Nothing. Note letter on sale of El Caney.[108]

Sister Carrie. Believes first issue was limited to 500 copies.[109] Dreiser a man of little manners.

Doesn't remember Sewards. Frank made trip to San Joaquin but not to Miller and Lux ranch.[110] Porter and Vanamee.[111]

Reading. Liked *Anna Karenina*—all his Russian. Very fond of Daudet's *Jacques*. Always saying to him, "Well, life is not a romance."[112]

Write to Miss Comstock about books sales. Thinks *Octopus* sold 25,000.

The Pit sold 150,000.[113]

Gilroy place cost $500. Jeannette sold it back to the Stevensons.[114] Frank stayed in S.F. for the football games. He and Jeannette came over and stayed for a week at the frat house. He was to receive $3000 from *Saturday Evening Post* on *The Pit*.[115] Hoped possibly to get a yacht.

No reason why he changed name of "Wolf." Nothing further on other novels.

"Cock-eye Blacklock" had been with *Century* for two years.[116]

Jeannette and Mrs. Strong compiled the bibliography.[117]

4 / Ernest C. Peixotto

Possibly Norris's oldest friend, Ernest Clifford Peixotto (1869–1945) met him when they were both students at the California School of Design in 1886. A mutual love of horses led them to the Presidio, where they spent hours perfecting the rudiments of drawing from life by sketching them there. Nor did their budding friendship end when Norris left San Francisco the next year to continue his artistic studies in Paris, for a year later Peixotto also enrolled at the Académie Julian. Peixotto remained in Paris somewhat longer than Norris, yet the two kept in touch. At Berkeley Norris maintained contact with Peixotto through the latter's sister, Jessica B. Peixotto. Later, they both became members of San Franciscos exclusive Bohemian Club. When Norris moved to New York in early 1898, Peixotto was still in San Francisco, though for only a short time; not long thereafter, he and his wife, Mary Glasscock Hutchinson (1869–1956), herself a painter who had studied at the School of Design and then the Académie Delecluse in Paris, arrived in New York. They settled, like Norris, on Washington Square South, where the three were on intimate terms.

Source: Ernest Peixotto, "Romanticist Under the Skin," *Saturday Review of Literature* 9 (May 27, 1933): 613–15.

Though thirty years have elapsed since his death, the place of Frank Norris, in the field of American letters, remains assured. The precursor, the forerunner, as he was, of the now firmly entrenched American school of realism, he, perhaps more than any one else, set the pace for the much discussed group of writers, whose work is so loudly acclaimed or so sharply criticized, according to the tastes and standards of the reader. But it has always seemed to me that Frank Norris, despite his very evident realistic tendencies, his exhaustive compilations of facts, his Zolaesque methods, betrays, beneath all this outer skin of realism, the romantic spirit that colored all his early life and his earliest works, and therein lies the basic difference between him and some of his most brilliant successors.

His start in life, for a man of his subsequent achievement, was strange enough, and, as it is so little known, I am glad to be able to tell of it. I feel qualified to do so, for, in his early life, I was one of his few intimate friends and his life at that time and again a very few years later, was quite closely interwoven with my own.

When first I knew him, Frank Norris was a tall, good-looking lad of seventeen, studying art, as I was, in the Art School in San Francisco. For again it is not generally known that, before he began to write, he set out seriously to become a painter. During these early student days, his particular interest seemed to center in the study of animals, and [. . .] he had already mastered a fairly good pen and ink technique and knew his animals well. We often went together, he and I, out to the Presidio Reservation, and there, in the cavalry barracks, we used to sit by the hour, and sketch the heads and rumps, the knee joints, and flexible fetlocks of the restless horses.[118]

He had been brought up in a family circle that was distinctly well-to-do, if not indeed wealthy, and his home, at that time, was a large "double" house with spacious, comfortable rooms, in a then fashionable neighborhood, on Sacramento Street near Van Ness Avenue. His mother, who presided over it, was a stately lady of commanding presence with a crown of white hair curled high upon her head in the fashion of the day. Of literary propensities, she played a prominent part in the local Browning Club and other artistic activities of the city. His father was a business man of whom I saw but little and his younger brother, Charles (who was, later, also to become a well-known novelist), was then but a boy of six.

In 1887, it was decided that Frank was to continue his art studies abroad and his parents took him to Paris. The family remained about a year and then left Frank ensconced in a French family in a large rather bourgeois apartment house that still stands on the Left Bank, near the river at the corner of the Rue de Lille and the Rue des Saints-Pères.[119]

By that time, I had followed him to Paris and, during the winter that ensued we saw much of each other, both in the Académie Julian, where we both were studying, and out of it. He became violently interested in medieval armor and we used to go together to the Artillery Museum in the Hôtel des Invalides and gloat over the glorious coats-of-mail there displayed. We studied the beautiful chased arms and armor; we hefted the jousting helmets to test their weight; we sketched the lances and bucklers and corselets and the Italian suits-of-mail, as well as the rich trappings of the horses.

Indeed he became so interested in all this, that he started to paint a huge historical picture of the "Battle of Crécy"![120] The preliminary sketches were made and he even "drew in" the large canvas that took up one entire end of his *pension* room. But one evening, when a friend, Guy Rose,[121] and I called upon him, he told us that he was thoroughly discouraged and had definitely decided to give up the picture, and to prove it, he offered us the big canvas and stretcher, a precious quarry indeed for a couple of impecunious young Latin Quarter students.

The canvas, however, was so big it could not be taken down the stairs, and we had to lower it out of his window out into the courtyard beneath. It was a blustery winter's night with a high wind blowing, and Rose and I, at each end of the great canvas, were swept back and forth around the corners and across the streets, like a ship at sea, reeling home, as best we could, with our prey. And that was the end of the "Battle of Crécy"!

Its abandonment was symptomatic of Norris's general attitude toward his work and, soon after, he decided to go home. When I returned to California the following year, I found, much to my surprise, that he had given up painting, was attending the University of California, and had begun to write.

His first story, "The Jongleur of Taillebois," which I, by the way, had the honor to illustrate (one of my very first commissions), appeared in the Christmas number of *The Wave*, a local weekly, in 1891.[122] As its name implies, it was a medieval tale still replete with echoes of what he had seen in France, and, early in the next year, he published (or, rather, his mid-Victorian mother proudly had published for him) a long, romantic poem, à la Walter Scott,[123] called *Yvernelle* [. . .] richly bound in white and gold and illustrated by some of the leading painters of the day: Dielman, Shirlaw,[124] Church, Will Low, and others.

It is now a rather rare literary curiosity, I am told, and I have still in my possession one of the few copies extant autographed by the author, dedicated "à mon ami," etc., recalling the days in Paris. So, of course, does the poem, itself, filled as it is with pictures of knights in armor and scenes of medieval chivalry, as witness the following excerpt from Sir Caverlaye's ride that gives a notion of the lilt and meter of the poem:

> Cast off his sword, his helm, and targe,
> Unlaced his haubert and his gorge,
> Threw off each tasset, cuissott, greave,
> Naught weighty on his limbs did leave.[125]

But it must be remembered that Frank Norris was still a student at Berkeley, writing and making illustrations too, for *Blue and Gold*, the college paper, of which he was one of the editors.[126] At the end of his few years there he went to Harvard and had a rather thrilling year with Professor Gates, who at once recognized his literary ability and gave him his first real encouragement. Under this stimulus, he began work on *McTeague*, which, later on, when it was published, he dedicated to "L. E. Gates of Harvard University."

Back in San Francisco again, thanks to the perspicacity and literary discernment of John O'Hara Cosgrave, then editor of *The Wave*, Norris became assistant editor of that periodical and his contributions to it have recently (1931) been collected and published in book form.[127] They consisted of essays on various topics and stories that gradually evolved from the romantic vein of his first works to tales of adventure and bits of realism that he picked up, with reportorial precision, in Chinatown, along the picturesque waterfront, which always fascinated him, and in the old Latin Quarter of San Francisco. His restless spirit of adventure, however, was always seeking new outlets and took him at this time to South Africa where he fell into the Uitlander insurrection.

On his return to California, he became acquainted, on the cliffs overhanging the Presidio, with an old sea-dog (a "buccaneer" he called him), whose salty talk and jargon of the sea, delighted him, and to him he dedicated his first published book, *Moran of the Lady Letty*, a rattling good tale of adventure off the California Coast.[128]

This story was being printed serially in *The Wave*, when it attracted the attention of an Eastern publisher and Norris was invited to come to New York and read for the house of Doubleday & McClure. This offer he gladly accepted.

He had been in New York but a few months, however, when the Spanish-American War broke out, and again his restless spirit got the better of him and he managed to be sent to Cuba as a war correspondent. In many ways, it is too bad that he did so, for his experience there left him broken in health and sick at heart, as is evident from the following graphic excerpts from a letter he wrote me soon after his return:

> 10 West 33rd St., New York:
>
> My Dear Ernest:
>
> I had your very kind little note day before yesterday and would have replied sooner were it not that I've been down with fever ever since leaving Santiago.
>
> The thing got a twist on me somewhere between Daiquiri and San Juan and laid me out as soon as we got inside the city. J. F. J. played out also and was not off his cot once during the voyage home.[129] I am very much tempted to accept your invitation to Chadd's Ford and very probably would if I did not think there was a chance for me to go out to San Francisco for three or four weeks. I need a rest very badly and a bit of a change for a while and a good opportunity to forget a good many things I had to see during the war. Now that I can stand off and as it were get a perspective of the last three months the whole business seems nothing but a hideous blur of mud and blood. There is precious little glory in war, if the Santiago campaign is a sample, and when you try to recall the campaign it's only the horrors that come to you, the horrors and the hardships and nothing of the finer side. I have made a roof for myself to sleep under, out of boards that were

> one glaze of dried blood, though I didn't find it out till morning, I have seen men, who were shot in the throat stretched out under the sun at the Division hospital who had been for forty-eight hours without water, food, sleep, shelter or medical attendance, I have seen a woman of seventy trying to carry on her back another of ninety-two and at Caney I was the first to discover—in one of the abandoned houses the body of a little girl—Ernest, I don't believe she was fifteen—who had been raped and then knifed to death just before the beginning of the battle.
>
> I want to get these things out of my mind and the fever out of my blood and so if my luck holds I am going back to the old place for three weeks and for the biggest part of the time I hope to wallow and grovel in the longest grass I can find in The Presidio Reservation on the cliffs overlooking the Ocean and absorb ozone and smell smells that *don't* come from rotting and scorched vegetation, dead horses and bad water.

He did go out to the cliffs over the Presidio but he was never able to get the fever out of his blood, those treacherous malarial fevers that recurred from time to time and had, I have always thought, a direct bearing upon his untimely end.

During his stay in California, he finished *McTeague* and wrote *Blix*, the latter somewhat autobiographic, its final chapter being a fairly accurate account of his own romance that culminated, in the following year, in his marriage to Jeannette Black.

But it was *McTeague* that definitely stamped him for what he was and in it he struck his great gait. Always an admirer of Zola and his methods, he once and for all made up his mind that, in this school of realism, lay his own true means of expression. So, priming himself with all the facts and collecting a mass of infinite detail, he set out to classify this material and build his story about it.

I well remember McTeague's Dental Parlors on Polk Street over a branch Post Office and just around the corner from Frank Norris's own home. Hanging out the window was the "huge gilded tooth, a molar with enormous prongs, something gorgeous and attractive," just as he describes it.[130] The book was a daring effort for its time, was much discussed, was praised, but was also much criticized, and his publishers felt constrained to print the following sort of apologia, symptomatic of its time, at the end of the first edition: "It may as well be stated at the outset that this is a harsh, almost brutal, story. It deals with a class of people who are beyond question 'common,' and the author is far too conscientious an artist not to depict them as they really are."[131]

During the winter that followed its publication, we were much together, living in adjoining houses in South Washington Square, me in Number 62, he in Number 61. Being on the same floor, we could rap on the brick wall that separated us and, by sticking our heads out of the windows, talk to each other and make rendezvous. Naturally a proud man, he would no longer accept a cent from his mother's purse and was living, very stintingly indeed, uniquely upon his meager editorial salary.

He made few friends and went out very little, though his personality would quickly have gathered about him a host of people, for he was strikingly handsome and attractive. Tall and slender, he was always carefully dressed, and his abundant hair, at the age of twenty-six or twenty-eight, had prematurely turned white, adding greatly to the distinction of his appearance.

Well do I remember at this time, one winter's evening when our doorbell rang violently, and, mounting the stairs two steps at a time, he burst into our room in a perfect fever of excitement, exclaiming "I've got it; I've got it. A trilogy. Three books, one after the other. 'Wheat. Wheat. Wheat.'"

This was the inception of his idea to write a trilogy of "Wheat" and this was the big task that he now set himself—his magnum opus:—first *The Octopus*, the growing of wheat in California and the grasp of the railroads; then *The Pit*, depicting the manipulations of the Chicago wheat pit, and finally the third of the series (alas, never written), to follow the marketing of wheat throughout the world.

In the following spring, we sailed for Europe, my wife and I, to be gone, as it afterward proved, some years.

So it seems to me that I can not do better here than to quote, almost *in extenso*, two letters that he wrote us at this time, one upon the eve of our sailing and the other a little later. Neither has ever before been published and they are couched in such characteristic language that they give, better than any account that I could devise, a most graphic picture, not only of him and his doings and aspirations, but of his exuberant temperament that rose to bursts of enthusiasm one moment, only to nosedive into despair the next.

The first was written from San Francisco and was dated Sunday, May 7, 1899.

> My Dear Oleman and Mrs. Billy Magee:
>
> I wanted to write you aboard your steamer to say bon voyage but of course I have forgotten the boat's name, though you told me often enough. . . . It's a wonder I don't forget me own name these days I'm having such a bully good time. Feel just as if I were out of doors playing after being in school for years. Jeannette and I spent the whole afternoon on the waterfront yesterday . . . among the ships (*on* and all over *one* of them) came back and had tea and pickled ginger in the balcony of our own particular Chinese restaurant over the Plaza and wound up by dining at Luna's *Mexican* restaurant "over in the Quarter." . . . The Wheat stuff is piling up B.I.G.

Everybody is willing to help and McT. is soon to be perpetrated in England.[132] I suppose by the time I get your answer to this you both will be playing out of doors yourselves and having *your* own particular good time. I don't dare think of going back to Washington Sq. with you people away. New York can never be a *very* lovely place to me but New York minus Mr. & Mrs. Billymagee—well we won't think much about that just yet. I may be here longer than I first expected, mebbe till late in the fall, and I donno why I should not write my immortial worruk at a wheat ranch *anyhow.* I think it will come to that. . . . Had two long letters from Frank Burgess the other day apropos of *Blix* and The Dentist—both very encouraging. Do you expect to see him? If you do tell him I'm full of ginger and red pepper and am getting ready to stand up on my hind legs and yell *big.* . . .

I have seen Hodgson—my buccaneer chap, and I have gone (naturally not alone) out to The Presidio Reservation, and sat down and wallowed in the grass on just the spot I told you about and done everything just as I had planned we should, and I'm just having the best time that ever was—*voilà tout.* . . .

Goodbye. When will we all be together again, and will I ever forget how much you both helped to make this hard winter of '98–'99 easy for me? What I should have done without you I honestly don't know, because there were times when the whole thing was something of a grind, and it didn't seem worth while to go on at all. Well somehow one does pull through—with such help as yours. . . . I'm not good at saying the things that would be appropriate here, but please consider them said and believe me when I tell you that I owe you both more than I can ever express.

Goodbye—or *au revoir*—whichever it is to be.

This letter was never signed and its last sentence has always seemed to me strangely prophetic, for, though we both were under thirty, I never saw him again.

The second letter was written early in the following year, and reads as follows:

Sunday morning
Feb. 16

My Dear Billymagee & Mollypeixotto,

I don't know how much of this is old news to you by now, but if you have heard anything about anything before you can consider this as "official." I'm ashamed of myself that I have not written you in all this long time, but never mind. I guess we are all good friends enough to write each other how and when and where we jolly well please.

The fact of the matter is that Jeannette and I were married here in New

York very early last Monday. I do hope you have not heard because I want to surprise you. It don't seem quite real yet, but there's a good long time to find it out in. It sure does seem strange to remember last winter and to think how very far away it looked then.—Remember all the thousand and one times I used to come to see you of an evening? I knew perfectly well I was terribly under foot at times, but it was so bully good of you to let me come. Fancy, Jeannette and I are in your old rooms at the Anglesea, and we are having a *rather* good time of it. Wish you people could be here. When are you coming back? Write "us" all about it, and yourselves and how you have been doing. As for me, *on fait son petit chemin tout doucement*,[133] though you might have gathered that from the fact that I can afford to be married. The books have done fairly well this year, well enough, so that we have quite a bit ahead in case of emergency, wh. is bully. *MacTeague* is in his twelfth thousand—ain't it gloryhallejujah—though a good part of that is a paper edition,—and the last book wh. was published on the third sold out its first edition before publication date.[134]—hear me toot my toot—but I shall expect you—and *want* you to toot yours loud and long. [. . .]

I could go on writing things now that I'm started till the cows come home. [. . .]

Goodbye until next time, and be sure to write early and often.

Yrs. forever,
Frank Norris.

Only two years later, his brilliant career was ended, cut short while he was in San Francisco again, where he was seized by an acute attack of appendicitis, was operated upon, and died a few days later at the age of thirty-two.

Such, in brief, is Frank Norris's story as I knew it,—a gallant life, if ever there was one, so full of promise and so full of achievement, especially when one stops to consider that, in the short span of four years between 1898 and 1902, he was wafted on the wings of fame from an assistant editorship on a California weekly to front rank among American novelists.

He was always writing of his art, his beliefs, his methods of work, and his artistic creed, I think, may be summed up in a paragraph from his "The Need of a Literary Conscience": "the place of high command . . . shall come to you, if it comes at all, because you shall have kept yourself young and humble and pure in heart, and so unspoiled and unwearied and unjaded that you shall find a joy in the mere rising of the sun . . . a pleasure in the sight of the hills at evening."

5 / M. C. Sloss

Like Peixotto and Neustadter, Marcus Cauffman Sloss (1869–1958) was a member of one of San Francisco's prominent Jewish families. First acquainted with Norris at Belmont School for Boys, where he was in its first graduating class, Sloss later consorted with Norris at gatherings of both the group of bons vivants known as Les Jeunes and the Bohemian Club, which Sloss joined in 1893, a few years before Norris. Sloss's wife, Harriet "Hattie" Lina Hecht Sloss (1874–1962), a cousin of her husband's Belmont classmate Summit Hecht, and a fellow member of the Browning Society with Norris's mother, dedicated *Certain Poets of Importance: Victorian Verse Chosen for Comparison* (1929) to Gertrude. After graduating from Harvard Law School in 1893, Sloss returned to San Francisco, where he enjoyed a distinguished career as a jurist and philanthropist.

Source: M. C. Sloss to James D. Hart, letter, December 3, 1952, James D. Hart Papers, BANC MSS 81/107c, The Bancroft Library, University of California, Berkeley.

Dear Jimmy:

Mrs. Sloss tells me that you are gathering material for a book about Frank Norris, and that you had heard that I had been a schoolmate of his and might recall some incidents that could be useful to you.

I am glad to give you the following scattered recollections although I do not believe that you will find they have any special value for your purpose.

In 1885 William T. Reid who had been principal of the Boys' High School in San Francisco, and subsequently President of the University of California, decided to start a boarding school for boys at Belmont, California. He acquired an estate which had, I believe, belonged to William Ralston, the banker, and established his school, opening in the fall of 1885. Together with three of my classmates at Boys' High School, who intended to go to Harvard, I entered Reid's school. At that time the Boys' High School did not, on graduation, quite meet the entrance requirements of

Harvard College. It was in order to make up this gap that we went to Belmont School to take one year in place of the last year at the high school.

The school opened with some 25 or 30 boys. In addition to those who, like myself, were in the senior class, preparing for college, there was a number of younger boys. One of these was Frank Norris who, as I recall, was about twelve years old.[135] He was a quiet, unaggressive boy who, at that time gave no indication of the great talent which he displayed later. I recall one incident of no great significance. The boys in the school were playing football one afternoon. Frank Norris was running with the ball and was tackled and thrown. When he arose his left arm was broken above the wrist in both bones. He left the school for the necessary treatment and I think did not return during the school year. Whether he came back in the following year I do not know as I was no longer there.

I have, however, other recollections of him at a somewhat later period. When I returned after going through Harvard and Harvard Law School, I began practice in the law office of Chickering, Thomas & Gregory.[136] This was in the fall of 1893. Soon after my return my associate Gregory, who was a few years older than I, and I were asked to join a group of young men who were interested in literature and the arts and who used to meet at dinner [. . .] from time to time. I do not know how Gregory and I got into this company as neither of us had any claim to literary or artistic ability. The young men who met at that time included several who afterwards attained considerable note. One was Bruce Porter whose varied accomplishments are no doubt known to you. Another was Frank Gelett Burgess who passed away not very long ago. Among the number, also, was Ernest Peixotto who gained international fame as a painter, illustrator and writer. His brother, Sydney,[137] was also one of those who used to meet on those occasions. Finally the company included Frank Norris. He was then in his early twenties, but had already begun to attract attention by his short stories which appeared in local magazines. I think he had not then published any of his long novels which later became famous. Despite his youth, his appearance was notable for the fact that his hair was prematurely gray.

One thing that occurs to me is that these young men, Porter, Norris, Burgess and Ernest Peixotto were among those who had cooperated in founding the little magazine called *The Lark*, which made quite a splash during its relatively brief career.

I am talking about events that occurred well over fifty years ago and my memory may not be very accurate. My wife has suggested to me that Mrs. Norris, Frank's mother, who was the literary leader of the Browning Society here was an intimate friend of Mrs. Ralph C. Harrison. Mrs. Harrison is no longer living but it is possible that some information or some writings relating to her connection with Mrs. Norris or her son Frank may be in the possession of her step-son Robert W. Harrison.[138] He is still practicing law here and has an office in the Merchants Exchange Building; his telephone number is SUtter 1–1150. Perhaps you might get something worth while by communicating with him.

I hope your projected work will come out soon as I am sure I would like to read it.[139]

With best regards, I am

Sincerely yours,
M. C. Sloss

2. Frank Norris with members of his college fraternity, Phi Gamma Delta, at the University of California, Berkeley, in 1893. Norris is the one in profile in the front row with his foot resting on Monk, the chapter's mascot. Courtesy of The Bancroft Library, University of California, Berkeley.

2
College Years
Berkeley and Cambridge, 1890–95

As formative of Norris's character as his childhood, if not more so, were his college years at the University of California. There he embarked on a fairly traditional four-year course of study followed by a year at Harvard College, with neither experience resulting in a degree. Nevertheless, if the recollections of fraternity brothers, college classmates, and university professors can be trusted, he benefited both intellectually and socially from his time in cloistered academe. Steadfastly loyal, generously unselfish, dependably congenial, unfailingly polite, always fun loving, and mildly rebellious, he was the perfect fraternity buddy, as attested by the comments of eight fellow members of Phi Gamma Delta who remembered both his pranks and his friendship fondly. But Norris also figured prominently in the memories of those he met outside his fraternity, such as Stanly A. Easton, who knew him through a college dramatic society, Louis Bartlett who in the student cadet corps commanded Company F, of which Norris was a recalcitrant member, Eleanor M. Davenport, a serious student interested in Norris's literary bent, Hull McClaughry, who, though a year ahead of Norris, cherished their acquaintance not only at Berkeley but also at Harvard and even later, and Maurice V. Samuels, whose friendship with Norris in their freshman year he recalled three decades later as one of the boons of a lifetime. Nor did Norris neglect the other side of college life. Never a superior student and bedeviled by mathematics, he fared better in literature and history. Three of his professors left affectionate tributes to their former student, while a fourth, Gelett Burgess, just four years older than Norris, counted him as a lifelong friend.

6 / Thomas R. Bacon

As an associate professor at the University of California and former Congregationalist minister, Thomas Rutherford Bacon (1850–1913) taught Norris in four history courses, in none of which he distinguished himself, receiving a 2 or B as a second-semester sophomore in Nineteenth-Century History, a 3 or C the previous semester in European History, a 4 or D in English History, taken the second semester of his freshman year, and during his first semester in college a "condition" in Middle Ages History, meaning that he had to pass additional requirements in order eventually to convert his grade to another 3 (see Norris's transcript, University Archives n.d.). That record might well have eroded any ground between most students and their professors, but such seems not to have been the case for Norris and Bacon. In May 1899, five years after Norris left the university without having been awarded a degree because he had never completed a requirement in mathematics, he petitioned for an "honorable dismissal," which the faculty committee on student affairs voted to grant, and which Bacon, then serving as a member of that committee, signed, duly granting Norris's belated request (Crisler 1986, 81–82). Two years after that, the 1901 *Blue and Gold* printed the poem "A Reply," which Norris had forwarded its staff in answer to a request for a contribution to the yearbook from him; in it Norris jokingly recalls his less than sterling record by having "flunk[ed] in Tommy's class," a direct result of "When T. Bacon called on me / To recite in history / And I mumbled 'I am not prepared today'" (Norris 1900a, 174). Just as Norris remembered with apparent fondness his history professor, so Bacon's tribute to Norris indicates that he had not forgotten his former student. Indeed, the next year Bacon reviewed *The Pit* in an article titled "The Last Book of Frank Norris" (Bacon 1903).

Source: Thomas R. Bacon, "University Loses Distinguished Son," *Daily Californian*, October 27, 1902, 1, 3.

The early and sudden death of Frank Norris must recall to those who were his teachers during his college course one fact of peculiar interest. He had made up his mind, before entering the university, what his life work was to be. It was because he had so determined that he came to college at all. He wanted to fit himself to be a writer of fiction. To this he bent all his energies, and subordinated almost every other interest. Those studies which he did not think would help him in this respect he did not care for and was apt to neglect. Perhaps his judgment as to what would help was not always sound, nor such as he would have made when he was matured by greater experiences. But such as it was he followed it unswervingly. There was nothing in his literary work while in college which gave to others the assurance of success in his chosen pursuit which he felt himself. It did not seem to promise more than that of many students who try experiments in literature. What distinguished him from such was his unfailing confidence that he had the capacity for literary success in him, and his dogged determination to bring it out, using all possible means to that end. His later study at Harvard, his travels, every occupation of his life, were subordinated to this single aim. What intelligence and industry could do to make an author out of himself, he did with his might.

His earlier novels attracted attention, as they could not fail to do; and they called forth a great deal of criticism, much of which was richly deserved. Even the critics who seemed to see most of merit in his work were apt to doubt whether the author would ever be able to overcome such grave literary faults as were conspicuous in his books. Nor did his method of receiving even the friendliest criticism seem to promise well. He seemed to regard it as an attack, and to defend himself with resentment, or even to ignore it altogether, which is worst of all. But in the depths of his heart he knew that he had not done the best of which he was capable, and probably the criticisms from without affected him more than he knew himself. Certainly there was a steady improvement in his work, due to the same unflagging purpose by all means to do his best, until he triumphed in his novel, *The Octopus*. Critics might find fault with it, but not one of them denies its power and literary skill, the spacious breadth of the canvas, and the fine workmanship of the details. The death of Norris is a loss, not because it removes a successful author in his prime, but because it takes from us one who showed in his most successful work an almost unlimited capacity for improvement. This fulfillment of earlier promise was only the making of a new and larger promise—now never to be fulfilled.

Those who knew Norris know how good this later promise was because they know the unfailing determination and industry which had brought him thus far and which would have taken him much farther had the opportunity of longer life been given him. Whether he had a single talent or ten talents it would be idle to discuss now. The treasure committed to him he did not bury in the ground or hide in a napkin,[1] but faithfully put it out to use and made it greater. He had opportunity and to those who thus do a regard is given.

7 / Louis Bartlett

Louis de Fontenay Bartlett (1872–1960), though he only knew Norris slightly at Berkeley, seems, like many of those who came in contact with him during his college years, nonetheless to have remembered him, and not just in passing. What is interesting about Bartlett's unsolicited letter to Walker is that having just completed a reading of Walker's biography of Norris, Bartlett would take time from a busy career as an attorney to write Walker regarding two matters of slight consequence to anyone after the passage of nearly forty years; as well, Walker at that point could do little about any mistakes he might have made in the biography. Even more surprising is the nature of the "two points" about which Bartlett wrote: Norris as an inept cadet under Bartlett's command, and when, if at all, Norris encountered Zola in courses Félicien V. Paget taught. Despite what Bartlett surmises, according to Jessica B. Peixotto, a classmate of Norris's and a student in Paget's courses with him, Norris apparently did not read Zola in any of many courses he took from Paget.

Source: Louis Bartlett to Franklin D. Walker, letter, April 29, 1933, Franklin Dickerson Walker Papers, BANC MSS C-H 79, The Bancroft Library, University of California, Berkeley.

My dear Mr. Walker:

I have just read with great pleasure your biography of Frank Norris. It is an extremely interesting and vivid portrait, very well done. I knew Norris at the University of California, and am writing you this memorandum concerning two points in your biography, with one of which I agree heartily and about the other of which I think you are somewhat in error.

I was in the class ahead of Norris, and was the unfortunate corporal charged with the duty of managing the most incorrigible awkward squad, to which he and Ben Weed belonged. At that time his antagonism to the drill was most pronounced, and his early interest in tin soldiers, disclosed by your book, came as quite a surprise to me. It seemed impossible for him to keep step, and fortunately for me he very kindly absented himself from the formal reviews. Ben Weed, who ordinarily was as hard to drill, very loyally bucked up the rest of the squad so it made a good showing.

I think you are mistaken about the date of his interest in Zola and Flaubert. Professor F. V. Paget, who was the head of the French Department and a man of wonderful literary appreciation and intuition, gave a number of lectures in French on French literature and one course was devoted to those two writers and a few others. Norris was not in this class with me. Juilliard, who was two years my senior, took some of Paget's lecture courses in French with me, but I think not the one discussing Zola.[2] I think Norris must have had the course the year after I did, for his views, as so well expressed in your book, coincide so closely with those of Professor Paget that it would seem to me extraordinary if he had not reached some of them in classroom discussions. Zola's books most discussed in class were *L'Assommoir* and *Nana*, and we made a careful critical study of *Madame Bovary* and *Salammbô*.[3] I have a hazy recollection, though I am not sure of this, of discussing Zola with Norris, and I know that he was popularly supposed while at college to have had a good knowledge of the modern French novel, and that meant Zola in those days.

In closing let me repeat that you have produced a very just, interesting and sympathetic portrait and one that might well have been written by a contemporary and an actor in the events related. It is a real contribution to the history of American letters.

Sincerely yours,
Louis Bartlett

8 / Gelett Burgess

Although an instructor in topographical drawing at the University of California (1891–94) when Norris first met him, Frank Gelett Burgess (1866–1951) in many ways acted the part of student rather than faculty member. His diaries record frequent late-night dinners with various students, "hours of nonsense" with others, visits to the Phi Gamma Delta house on several occasions, and iconoclastic romps such as toppling the grandiose drinking fountain erected by temperance crusader Henry Daniel Cogswell (1820–1900) (see Wright, chapter 26 this volume). He coauthored, with Norris's classmate Maida Castelhun (see Jessica Peixotto, chapter 18 this volume) and aid from Norris and others, "Vehmegericht," the first play ever performed in what would become the renowned Greek Theatre at Berkeley (Weed 1913, n.p.), inaugurating the tradition of a Senior Extravaganza put on by those graduating; and he studiously cultivated the friendship of certain students, most prominently Norris. After quitting his teaching post in 1894, having been summarily dismissed for his part in the Cogswell escapade (Dillon 1967, n.p.), Burgess continued his exploits in a more literary vein by successively founding *The Lark* in 1895, *Le Petit Journal des Refusées* in 1896, and *Phyllida* in 1897, promoting the formation of Les Jeunes, joining the Bohemian Club in January 1895, and writing its 1896 Christmas Jinks, "The Christmas Nightmare." When Norris made his second trip to the Big Dipper Mine in March 1897, Burgess succeeded him as subeditor of *The Wave* for two months before he went to New York, where he and Norris later renewed their friendship, when Norris also crossed the continent the next year.

Source: Gelett Burgess to Claude Fayette Bragdon, excerpt from letter, May 18, 1899, Bragdon Family Papers, A.B81, Department of Rare Books, Rush Rhees Library, University of Rochester, Rochester, New York.

Me Deer Clodd;[4]

[. . .] Have you read Frank Norris's *McTeague*? He is, you know, one of *les jeunes*, though he never wrote for the Bird.[5] I am amazed by this book of his. As a work of art it is a masterpiece, and the way he has handled his construction, his secondary situations and characterization seems to me to put him out of the possibilities into the probabilities. The way the thing hangs together, the way it grows, the original method, and the humour, not subtle, yet keen and incisive, all this has aroused my admiration. He has curiously enough missed everything distinctive of San Francisco life, and he has not written the romantic side, that we all want to have shown up, but he has made the book jump, jump and yell. I am awfully glad for his success. Frank, naturally lazy, has won it with years of hard persistent effort. "Blix" in the *Puritan* is naïve and almost amateurish, a jumble of incidents, and not nearly up to this. [. . .][6]

Forever your friend,
Gelett

Source: Gelett Burgess to Jeannette Williamson Norris, letter, October 29, 1902, Frank Norris Collection, BANC MSS C-H 80, The Bancroft Library, University of California, Berkeley.

My dear Mrs. Norris:

To write you what I feel about losing Frank is impossible and I could not do it without using the same words that so many must have used. Sorrow and shock and wonder we have all felt before but there has been something so uncanny and almost malign in this terrible adventure that sets it off from anything in my experience—and the feeling is universal—everyone says "why had this to be?"

Frank was so much more intimately connected with his work than most writers, that his loss comes on his whole acquaintance upon everyone who knew him, but only his friends know what beside his power of work is gone. I count it a great privilege to have known him when, to be sure of his ultimate success was coincident with calling him friend. To have been able to watch that ambition and that almost foolhardy will of his unfold—and seeing it grow stronger with everything he touched, to prove one's own judgement—that has been one of the warmest and most satisfactory things in my life. And to keep him for a friend through it all and to have influenced him in ever so slight a degree was a delight.

Somehow, though I don't feel the catastrophe as mocking as some do—to lose him as a friend is terrible, but Frank, if he had not accomplished his aim had already proven beyond jawsaying, what was in him.

I doubt if anyone will ever question his power in conception, will, and capacity. From an idle boy—and a dreamer he has pulled himself together in the most magnificent way a man could do. He was on the road, and he was moving steadily onward—and how few can say that.

Not the least interesting thing in his life was to watch your influence over him—it was evident to me in many little things—in the addition of "wood" to his orchestra when he had been content with the animal force of "brass" and the stinging emotion of "strings"—more and more he changed after he was married. He never knew women till he knew you, I am sure—I can remember one definite topic we discussed when he first came to New York, and he confessed he had changed afterwards.

Frank was a natural story teller, and to my mind that faculty is infinitely higher than style or poetry—His imagination was creative in every circumstance he found himself in. Where an ordinary man, even a writer, sees two different incidents in turn, Frank was always tying them together in his brain with the thread of his fancy.

You know all this—I don't know why I write it. But better that than any maudlin sentiment or perfunctory condolence. I have pride: and I think I do not need to tell you how fiercely this blow has struck me. I confess I was badly hurt that he did not seem to need to see me—that I seemed to have slipped back to a second or third place. But there was never a trace of bitterness in that and if there had been there could not be now. I know, from last time, how your time was taken, and though had he sent me the most informal word I would have gone gladly to him—please do not feel badly, for I am as sure as ever of his friendship—my sensitiveness has no doubt come from a feeling that Frank thought that I was stinting my work or had not, at least, made good—No one knew that better than I.

I am glad I had the chance to do what was in my power at the last—I am glad that Frank died in San Francisco—but I did not dare to go to him or to you or to offer what no doubt I should have done. I threw into his grave some violets I had bought in front of the *Chronicle*[7]—on the sidewalk in the heart of this dear city of his—and I am sure,—aren't you?—that Frank would have preferred the cheap flowers of the street at Lotta's Fountain[8]—to any others?

I shall come and see you as soon as I think, or hear, that you are ready—and if I can do anything to help—and you have no one better fitted to assist—I hope you will let me know—

I know that in 1897 Frank had collected a lot of his short stories for publication and I have no doubt D. P. & C. would be glad to publish them.[9] I would advise it, for some of them are models of story telling. If you have not all of them I have a file of *The Wave* covering the whole time that he wrote on it.

I hope you will pardon the personal element in this letter and believe me on both Frank's and your own account

Faithfully your friend,
Frank Gelett Burgess

Source: Gelett Burgess to Claude Fayette Bragdon, excerpt from letter, December 5, 1902, Bragdon Family Papers, A.B81, Department of Rare Books, Rush Rhees Library, University of Rochester, Rochester, New York.

My dear Claude;

[. . .] Frank Norris's death was a terrible shock to all of us here and it has been brought home to me more by some work I have been doing. Mrs. R. L. S. is to build a sort of memorial seat on his place at Gilroy next to hers (he bought it just before he died), and this I designed.[10] Two weeks ago I went down there to pick out the site, found a good one, and got a block of sandstone and myself carved this inscription:

FRANK NORRIS
1870 1902
SIMPLENESS AND TEN
DERNESS AND HONOR AND
CLEAN MIRTH

I found it in Kipling's poem to Wolcott Balestier when he died and I think it suits Frank's character so well as anything could.[11] Now I am helping Mrs. N. in the construction of a tombstone. She wants a single slat of bronze with the name and dates. Mrs. N. gave me Frank's meerschaum pipe which I am this minute smoking. I could not have been given anything I would rather have had. [. . .]

Your old pal:
[Burgess's chop mark][12]

Source: Gelett Burgess to Franklin D. Walker, letter, October 18, 1930, Franklin Dickerson Walker papers, BANC MSS C-H 79, The Bancroft Library, University of California, Berkeley.

My dear Mr. Walker:

I hasten to answer your letter asking information about Frank Norris, although I am afraid that, with my poor memory, I can help you but little with exact information. But I will try, at least, to answer some of your questions.

GENERAL IMPRESSIONS. Frank Norris always impressed me as my ideal of the aristocrat. I imagine him always, with all his modernity, as having a title. By aristocracy I mean absolute self-control and objectivity. Repression of feeling and expression of thought. This was heightened by his ironic humor, it gave him, with his picturesque appearance, a kind of Mephistophelean touch, tempered with kindness. One anecdote of him in New York, 1897, will illustrate this:

IRONIC HUMOR. After *The Lark* had ended publication, I went to New York, and found, when I arrived, a card of William Dean Howells who had thought I had already arrived. As Frank was already acquainted with Howells (whom Frank admired) we decided to call on him together. I was then living at the Benedick,[13] Washington Square East, and on the evening of the call, Frank came for me. I was dressing. We were to call in evening dress. Frank watched me dress with that ironic, devilish smile of his on his lips the while. It was not until we had been in Mr. Howells' drawing room for almost an hour that I discovered to my horror, that instead of having put on my tail coat, I had, by inadvertence put on my "cutaway" coat with my evening vest and trousers. Frank had known it all the time, and had said nothing to me, letting me make a fool of myself, and enjoying my embarrassment and mortification to the full.

THE WAVE. I replaced Frank as sub-editor on *The Wave* and he almost immediately left for New York. This must have been in 1896 and so I saw little of him for a year or so. I never contributed while he was sub-editor.

UNIVERSITY OF CALIFORNIA. I am not sure that Frank was at the University of California while I was there as Instructor (not Professor). He may have been for a little while, for I certainly did see him at the "Fi-ji" house. But I am quite sure that he had not, at that time, started *McTeague*. He was writing stories for the *Overland Monthly*. He used to talk about *McTeague* later to me, while I was editing *The Lark*, and especially about that one episode in it that was, at that time, a most daring detail. (The boy wetting his pants at the Orpheum.[14]) He used to describe it with great glee—it was the nearest he ever came to his adored Zola. I remember seeing the notes for *The Octopus*, too, his Dramatis Personae, with the biographies of the different characters, complete to the last detail.[15] Also some of the MSS., he used, as I remember, very broad right hand margins, for corrections. All, of course, in long-hand. Frank had two handwritings, as I recall, one for letters of almost microscopic characters, the smallest writing I have ever seen except Kipling's. At other times he would write large. He was at the age when one has affectations and indulges one's self. (I myself in those late 90's used to wear a carnation in my button-hole, with a stem a foot long or more.) You could get a rise out of Frank by mentioning his *Yvernelle*. He seemed extraordinarily ashamed of it. But it shows how one can swing between wide extremes. I doubt if Frank got any real help or even literary encouragement at the University of California, from what I know of it. You know they fired Rowland Sill[16]—and me.

THE LARK. No, Frank had little interest in *The Lark*, he was for more monstrous aims than the Joy of Life. He thought it mere play of kids I suppose.[17]

JOHN O'HARA COSGRAVE. It would surprise me to hear that the relations between Jack and Frank were ever anything but most friendly. We all liked Jack Cosgrave, and his only fault was that he could pay us but little. I refer to Frank, myself, Bill Irwin and Jimmie Hopper, and also Geraldine Bonner[18] and Juliet Wilbor Tompkins (Pottle). I doubt if Frank was ever "fired."[19] He did splendid work, didn't need the money, would do what he pleased, and Jack was only too glad to get his work. *The Wave* wasn't the kind of office where one was fired. We were like brothers. Frank would even do the "whitemailing" occasionally (write-ups for pay). We all regarded it as a lark, *The Wave*, we had such freedom. We were learning to write. "Jack" had fine taste, great appreciation, and he was as generous as his means allowed.

Write to Cosgrave, (The Players, 16 Gramercy Park, New York City) he ought to have a lot of information.

PARIS LIFE. When Frank studied art in Paris, he was most intimate with Ernest Peixotto. (Write to him, also [care of] The Players.)

MRS. NORRIS. I think that Jeannette was ambitious for him, but, like so many literary men's wives (not including mine) she was hardly an intellectual companion. Frank had few mental friends. He did his thinking alone. I doubt if Mrs. Norris made him "more serious and ambitious" except that she naturally liked him to be "famous."

McCLURE'S. I know little of him at McClure's, except that they were all hunting inchoate geniuses and Frank enjoyed the hunt, from his vantage point of Editor. I saw little of him in N.Y., he was just married and I was running the intellectual gauntlet and doing the little "salons." I lived next door to the Norrises at one time, 61 Washington Sq., and saw them occasionally. He was absorbed in Jeannette. I was absorbed in another. Have you written THEODORE DREISER?

JESSICA PEIXOTTO, Ph.D., of the University of California, knew Frank pretty well, too, why not see her? Also Dr. Millicent Cosgrave. I think she lives in Syracuse. (Jack's sister.)

MISS VIOLA RODGERS, Lardy, Seine-et-Oise, France, knew Frank in N.Y. (Don't mention my name, please, though.) She was on the *American* daily.[20]

LETTERS &C. Unfortunately the few letters I have of Frank's are in storage with my things in N.Y. I may return in January, though. There are only two or three.

WILL IRWIN, as you know, wrote an introduction to a book of Frank's stories. He knew Frank little, though, I think. Address The Players.

MILDRED HOWELLS (married? dead?).[21] W. D. H.'s daughter might remember something about him. Perhaps one of the Doubledays—who was on *McClure's*. Walter, I think, don't know.[22] Perhaps also William Morrow (publisher, N.Y.).[23] Is S. S. McClure alive?

So sorry I can give you nothing but these scraps.

Yours sincerely,
Gelett Burgess

9 / Eleanor M. Davenport

Norris had much in common with Eleanor Mack Davenport (1874–1941): they both began their studies at the University of California as "special" students, meaning that they had not yet declared a course of study; both eagerly sought the rewards of an active college social life; and both manifested an interest in things literary. While Davenport was a year behind Norris, the friendship they formed at Berkeley, beginning in 1891, the year that she and her family moved there from Redlands, California, continued after their college years, which her article on Norris in the *University of California Magazine* in November 1897 discloses (Davenport 1897), as do surviving letters from Norris to her and her mother, Elizabeth Hewitt Davenport (1849–1912), a social force in her adopted state. As a student, Eleanor Davenport served as vice president of her class when she was a sophomore, recording secretary for the Bushnell Union Debating Society, founding member of the Ciccada Club, formed to advance an appreciation of music among students, and associate editor of the 1895 *Blue and Gold*.

Source: Eleanor M. Davenport to Franklin D. Walker, letter, October 5, 1930, Franklin Dickerson Walker Papers, BANC MSS C-H 79, The Bancroft Library, University of California, Berkeley.

My dear Professor Walker:

I am very much interested to know that you are writing a biography of Frank Norris and shall be glad to furnish you with any material in my possession. I presume that you know that Charles G. Norris, a younger brother of Frank's, lives near here. His address is 1247 Cowper Street, Palo Alto, California.

Mrs. Benjamin Franklin Norris was born in Mendon, Massachusetts, and her maiden name was Gertrude Doggett. She seldom spoke of her stage career, which, I believe, terminated when she was married and went to Chicago to live. Mr. Norris was in the jewelry business. I think that they moved to California for the health of the children, but am not sure.

I first met Frank Norris when he was at Berkeley in the class of 1894 and a Phi Gamma Delta, and he introduced his mother to my mother and me. Apparently she had been divorced for some time and I have always heard that Mr. Norris wanted her to go to Europe with him, which she refused to do because her children were young and that he then eloped with her niece.[24] I do not remember hearing Mrs. Norris refer to her divorce but once when she said, "I was more sinned against than sinning." She was a marvellous elocutionist and the finest Browning scholar I have ever met. She was tall and very stunning and she adored Frank. She lived in a very handsome house here when Frank was in college and appeared to have a very large income. She founded and supported the Lester Norris Kindergarten for many years.[25]

So far as I know both Charles and Frank Norris refused to have any thing to do with their father.

Frank was extremely witty and quick at repartee. One incident I remember was in the early nineties, the day of the "Willie-Boy coat" and silk hat, when Mrs. Norris had outfitted both her sons in the finest of these garments and they were walking on Van Ness Avenue here before the fire, when it was still a street of handsome residences. Frank looked at Charlie and then at his own clothes and remarked solemnly: "The management has spared no expense."

I have two or three notes, which Frank wrote to me or to my mother, but I doubt whether they would interest you. However, if you would like to have them, let me know and I will send you copies.[26]

Are you writing this article for publication?

If you care to ask any questions about Frank Norris or his work, I should be glad to answer them to the best of my ability.

Very truly yours,
Eleanor M. Davenport

Source: Eleanor Mack Davenport to Franklin Dickerson Walker, letter, October 19, 1930, Franklin Dickerson Walker Papers, BANC MSS C-H 79, The Bancroft Library, University of California, Berkeley.

My dear Professor Walker:

In reply to your letter of October 14th I am enclosing copies of the letters from Frank Norris, which I have preserved.

From the morbid character of some of his books it is difficult to imagine him as the cheerful, joke-loving man, whom I remember. I do not recall ever having seen him depressed or ever out of sorts. He was a loyal friend and, I believe, a really great novelist.

With best wishes for the success of your thesis—

Sincerely yours—
Eleanor M. Davenport

10 / Stanly A. Easton

Stanly Alexander Easton (1873–1961) graduated from the University of California in 1894. In different college fraternities—Easton, like Hull McClaughry and Frank M. Todd, was a member of Delta Kappa Epsilon—Norris and Easton seldom crossed paths socially in college, but they would certainly have known each other and not merely because the student body of the University of California at this time was still fairly small. Both were members of the dramatic society, Skull and Keys, which Norris helped found as a junior, writing, according to Todd, the society's ritual and acting in at least two of its productions, *Our Boys* (1875) by Henry James Byron (1835–1884) in 1893 and the next year *Engaged* (1877) by Sir W[illiam]. S[chwenck]. Gilbert (1836–1911).

Source: Stanly Alexander Easton to James D. Hart, letter, July 19, 1957, James D. Hart Papers, BANC 81/107c, The Bancroft Library, University of California, Berkeley.

Dear Dr. Hart:—

As an Old Time Friend of the University of California Bancroft Library I am pleased to learn from your letter of the ninth of its project the Great Frank Norris Collection.

Chas. Weck is right.[27] Norris and I were 1894 classmates, and members of Skull and Keys.

Because I was in the College of Mines Norris and I had little in common in our College Work. Still with every one on the Campus I greatly prized the association I had with Norris, but especially in Skull and Keys. I seem to recall Frank had a part in preparing its ritual, and wrote the skit that S and K put on during commencement week.[28]

I do not remember that Norris was interested in sports; he was inclined to be casual physically. Norris easily dominated any group he happened to be in by his charming personality, his clever and witty flow of bright conversation.

Frank Norris liked all people, he apparently always enjoyed listening and talking to every one he happened to be with.

Gentleness and kindness were implied by his every action.

I left for the booming mine fields of the North West and Canada, shortly after graduating and have worked and lived here ever since, thereby losing many associations with college friends. So I do not have a single thing to add to the Great Frank Norris Collection, which I greatly regret, except these words of sincere appreciation.

Faithfully Yours,
Stanly A. Easton

11 / George C. Edwards

George Cunningham Edwards (1852–1930) was the last of a trio of professors at the University of California who wrote tributes to their former student, immediately following his death; of these only his and that by Thomas R. Bacon qualify as reminiscences, while in the third William D. Armes treats Norris's literary output rather than his life (Crisler 1997, 81–83). Although Norris failed algebra under Edwards during the second semester of his junior year (see Norris's transcript, University Archives n.d.), affection between the two seems not to have waned, as revealed by both Edwards's memory of the impression Norris made on not just him but on all, professor and student alike, who came in contact with Norris, and Norris's comment, "To [Pierce's] class you come back, if you miss the Col's section" in his untitled poem, beginning "I took my girl to Schuetzen Park," appearing in the 1894 *Blue and Gold* (Norris 1894a, 252). A student failing trigonometry under Archie Burton Pierce (1867–1951), as Norris had the previous semester, must repeat the course, once again under Pierce's tutelage, unless he were fortunate enough to be placed instead in the section taught by Edwards, whose reputation was somewhat less fierce (Crisler 1990, 124, n. 21). Having served as commandant of cadets at the university for several years, Edwards was fondly dubbed the "Col." by generations of students.

Source: George C. Edwards, "University Loses Distinguished Son," *Daily Californian*, October 27, 1902, 1, 3.

[. . .] We stand with bowed heads and quick-beating heart. A comrade has fallen. The suddenness of it!—Can it be possible that he who so delightfully entertained us at our family meeting barely a moon ago has slipped away to the higher reward?[29]

Frank Norris—do I remember! I should say I did. When he entered the University as a Freshman, above the average in height, slender and bright-eyed, he would attract the attention of any one who was an observer of young men. He was a good fellow among good fellows. As he advanced from step to step of his college career his particular makeup which had attracted to him a host of student friends developed into the genius of the man, who had within him the power to work out his own destiny. He was not a college "dig."[30]

There was very little about algebra that attracted him. He was a keen observer of men and women as he saw them and interpreted their lives—their longings, their foibles, their loves, their truthfulness and their shams. It was thus he became a mirror showing us to ourselves. And after fulfilling his part in college life he went out into the larger life of the world, better equipped and stronger to do for humanity that which he had so well done in the smaller academic life. He did his part well.

As we stand, reverent, and expressing the hope that it is well with him we loved, we repeat to ourselves the old Welsh saying: "Work as though we were to live always; live as though we were to die tomorrow."

12 / Wallace W. Everett

As a freshman Fiji during Norris's senior year at Berkeley, a writer for *Sunset* extolling the virtues of motoring in such far-flung locales as northern California and the Rhine Valley, a publisher of an esoteric newspaper with the unlikely title of *Lumber Journal*, and a fruiterer in California's famed Napa Valley, Wallace Washburn Everett (1875–1943) seems a curious source for an article on Norris's exploits with Delta Xi, the University of California chapter of their college fraternity. Even so, the two did know each other briefly in college. In "The Exile's Toast," a poem in humorous German dialect Norris sent to his fraternity chapter on November 20, 1900, in place of his own presence at the traditional "pig dinner" preceding the annual "big game," Norris playfully observes that "Wallie Every-bit . . . alle-ways knows ut alle" (Crisler 1986, 129). More to the point, Everett, who would naturally have heard tales about one of his chapter's more flamboyant members, likely had little trouble recalling both Norris's antics and his personality.

Source: Wallace W. Everett, "Frank Norris in His Chapter," *Phi Gamma Delta* 52 (April 1930): 561–66.

It is far easier to talk about Frank Norris than it is to write about that paragon of true fraternity men. It is not as a successful novelist that we think of him nor is it to bring up for consideration his powerful influence upon our country's literature, when we speak of Norris; we who knew him in the early nineties, love to just *feel* that we were with him and we are happier because of that lovable contact.

Some time ago, a graduate member of one of Yale's junior societies had luncheon with me at the Fiji chapter-house at the University of California. I remember well his remark: "Didn't your fraternity have any other literary light but Frank Norris? You seem to advertise him as such and make a lot out of him!"

Such a man as this who had not lived four years with a fellow fraternity man like Norris; who had been simply a member of a club in Yale could not appreciate how we of the old guard felt towards this member of the class of 1894 in Delta

Xi chapter. It is Norris the Fiji—Norris the Lovable Fellow—Norris the Man whom we remember and not Norris the Novelist.

After his return from Paris, Frank Norris went to a small preparatory school—Urban Academy—in San Francisco in the latter '80s and entered the University of California in the fall of 1890 with the class of '94. He lived in a house on the north side of Bancroft Way, just east of Dana Street and around the corner from the first Fiji House on that latter street. He was a tall, gaunt, sallow-complexioned young fellow, yet strikingly handsome and distinguished in his general appearance, according to Brother Ralph L. Hathorn, '93, to whom and to Brother William Penn Humphreys, '92, I am indebted for this description of the young freshman of twenty.[31] Eccentric in his dress and still possessed of some French mannerisms from his early student days in Paris, Norris entered college as a special in English literature. For the first five months, absorbed in his work, he kept closely to himself making but few acquaintances and no close friends. All the fraternities were unaware of the measure of the man who had come into the college life of Berkeley.

As befitted the man, his introduction to a member of Phi Gamma Delta was intensely interesting. Some time in December of 1890, a heavy storm had driven a large vessel ashore below the Cliff House in San Francisco.[32] Thousands of spectators journeyed out to the beach to view the wreck, braving the raging wind and driving rain to witness the heavy seas and great combing breakers pound the ship to pieces on the shore before them. Ralph Hathorn, late that afternoon, saw a young fellow standing near him in the chill of this winter's afternoon without overcoat or protection from the rain or wind and invited the drenched and shivering youth to share his umbrella with him. With this stirring drama of the sea as a setting, there started here the basis of a cherished friendship which lasted through the life of the pair, for the wet, bedraggled youngster was Norris the freshman.

Hathorn and Norris had dinner that same evening in the men's grill of the old Palace Hotel and the menu probably was thick juicy fillets for which the hotel was famous then as now; French fried potatoes, bowls of lettuce salad, with a couple of bottles of Chevalier Cabernet accompanying—all, as Hathorn fondly remembers, for a trifle over a dollar per.[33] Somehow or other, we lived in those days.

Immediately afterwards, Frank's name was proposed for membership in Delta Xi Chapter of Phi Gamma Delta. Discouraging opposition and complete indifference upon the part of a few was met by immediate enthusiasm upon the part of other members. One senior and one junior refused to make the slightest effort either to see the youngster or to come to any decision after they had met him. This indifference almost lost the prospect and other fraternities started to rush Norris. Gradually his irresistible charm and magnetic personality won over the opposition, and, on June 10, 1891, Benjamin Franklin Norris signed the roll-book of Delta Xi Chapter of Phi Gamma Delta.

A little later on, the "Benjamin" became "B." and was later completely dropped from his signature and the strong, simple name became Frank Norris and as such the world knows him. His early signatures to art works and stories are modes of interesting chirography.

It was but a short time after his initiation in the fraternity when Frank Norris came into his own and became one of the most popular and beloved men in the entire college. One of his confreres writes of him:

"My mental picture of Frank the freshman (I a junior) is that of a likeable fellow of patrician blood, living in a Continental rather than an American atmosphere. Bohemian in social inclinations, responsive to the beautiful and imaginative in art and life yet disorderly and unsystematic in personal habits and mental attitude. He was restless and bored with the routine of college discipline."

Yet withal, his brilliant literary ability, his congenial good fellowship and his intense enthusiasm for whatever he did, made him one of the most distinguished leaders in the life of the University of California of his time.

Shortly after his initiation, Norris moved his belongings into the Fiji House on Dana Street near Bancroft Way and entered immediately into the spirit of the chapter. He lived there for the remainder of his college life. With him in that sterling class of '94 were H. M. Wright, Edward A. Selfridge, Jr., Harry Rhodes and J. M. Gilmore,[34] all of whom have been successful in their chosen fields of endeavor.

Frank's room in the old Dana Street house was a curiosity and never to be forgotten by those who looked in through the ever-open doorway. There was not a space upon the wall where you could put the palm of your hand—covered as it was with souvenirs of his life in Paris and of those occurrences which had interested him in his active past. The old chair in which he sat while studying has a hole in the right hand arm rest where he used to keep tapping away with a small pen knife blade.

Brother Humphreys distinctly remembers one night when Frank Norris returned at a late hour from San Francisco. He went to his room and closed the door. During the night loud sounds emanated from Frank's room but no one paid any attention to them. The sounds were still continuing the next morning when the Fijis were going down to breakfast so Humphreys opened the door to see what caused the disturbance. There was Norris asleep upon the bed and the room was a wreck. The decorations were in a heap upon the floor and, in the midst of the chaos, was the monkey which afterwards became quite notorious about Berkeley. The companion of the night before upon the ferry trip across the Bay was the cause of all this havoc.

The first pig dinner came after class day of the class of '93 and was held in the old Fiji House on Dana Street in Berkeley. Norris wrote a mock ceremonial for the introduction and treatment of the roast suckling. From this small dinner of those days when Delta Xi had less than fifty members upon its roster, has come the Norris Dinner of all Fijidom to symbolize the spiritual ideal of good fellowship in the fraternity so perfectly exemplified in Norris the Man.

"An Exile's Toast" was written by Frank Norris in 1900 when he was living in Roselle, New Jersey. With the approach of the annual big game with Stanford, Frank found himself lonely and craving for the good times we Fijis used to have at this period with the result that the toast was written and mailed so that it was read at the annual Fiji dinner. We who heard Brother H. M. Wright read the verses utterly failed to realize what would be the future of "An Exile's Toast." In fact, it is a wonder that the original was ever saved for posterity.

These Fiji dinners occurred annually on the night before the big game and were always held at the Old Poodle Dog restaurant, then located on the southeastern corner of Sacramento and Dupont streets in San Francisco. This habit continued up to the time of the great fire in 1906 but the dinners of the latter '90s were limited to University of California Fijis of whom there were less than a hundred, not one of whom would have missed the dinner. And I want to take this time to say that, while the heartiest of good fellowship reigned and cocktails and red wine were to be had at all times for the asking, there were no evidences of over-indulgence to be found at these dinners. We were there for a good time and we had it but the morning found us ready for the big game rally and all the excitement attendant upon this annual event. That was the Fiji attitude of those days.

Frank Norris took part in the college dramatics and would have made a name for himself upon the professional stage had he chosen that branch of art for his future career.[35] He wrote the ritual and other ceremonials for Skull and Keys—the junior-senior society at the University of California—which still ranks as an honor society. If I am not mistaken, Norris was the originator of the plotting of football plays for the daily press.[36] It is easy to remember him, moving up and down the side lines during the games, cane hung upon his left forearm, pencil busy on a reporter's pad while he sketched the plays of the afternoon. He was always a conspicuous figure wherever he went but this came naturally to him and never for a moment did he ever seem to strive for individuality. His was a personality which needed no false embellishments, no bizarre settings to make him occupy the position his latent abilities entitled him to possess.

There are many phases of the life of Frank Norris in old Delta Xi chapter which we who knew him could dwell upon but I have used too much space as it is. In closing permit me to say that the regard and affection which Frank Norris created amongst those fortunate enough to have known him in those and the latter days of his life have lasted through the subsequent years and we all feel better and happier for his having been amongst us.

He was the embodiment of true college fraternity life. He idealized its associations and believed in them. Phi Gamma Delta is better because of that freshman of 1890, and, as the ranks thin of those who knew and loved Frank Norris, even perhaps the demand for present-day efficiency in our fraternity to the contrary, perchance the influence of Frank Norris may help to place true idealized brotherly love above the lesser qualifications attendant upon membership in Phi Gamma Delta. Heaven help the 2 x 4 whose shelves may be weighted down with efficiency cups, whose bosom bulges with scholarship medals but whose heart has never felt the increased pulse from the hearty handclasp of a Frank Norris. And Phi Gamma Delta is blessed with many such; so the youngster of today had far better believe that his associations of today will certainly outlast the fervor of youth and ornament the environment of the future—better an error in addition than that life in Phi Gamma Delta should pulse to the clatter of an adding machine.

13 / George Gibbs

Unlike the majority of Norris's classmates at the University of California, George Gibbs (1871–?) hailed not from California but from the Midwest, listing Chicago as his hometown at his graduation from the university in 1895. Owner of Gibbs Steel Company in Milwaukee ("Ode on a Grecian Yearn" 1963, 17), he first worked in Chicago, where during Norris's research for *The Pit* he attempted to assist Norris in mastering the mechanics of buying and selling short on the stock exchange. As students and fraternity brothers, Norris and Gibbs, though he was a year behind Norris, were close friends, joining two other members of Phi Gamma Delta, Albert J. Houston and Harvey W. Corbett, for hikes in the High Sierras. In 1893, Gibbs had also traveled to Chicago with Norris, Charles, Gertrude, Norris's cousin Ida Carleton, and another fraternity brother, Ralph L. Hathorn, to attend the World's Columbian Exposition. Gibbs later visited Norris and Jeannette in New York in 1900. The plan had been for him to stay with the Norrises in their apartment; but it proving too small to accommodate three adults comfortably, Gibbs took a room at the Judson Hotel, not far from them on Washington Square South.

Source: George Gibbs to Franklin D. Walker, letter, June 10, 1930, Franklin Dickerson Walker Papers, BANC MSS C-H 79, The Bancroft Library, University of California, Berkeley.

My dear Mr. Walker:

Your good letter of May 11th should have been answered some time ago but I delayed purposely owing to the fact that Mr. Harvey W. Corbett,[37] a class mate of mine at the University of California was on his way from California to Chicago and I wanted to talk to him about Frank Norris and see if he could add any other points besides the ones that I had thought about, but after talking with Mr. Corbett, he decided that he had nothing extra to offer.

Frank Norris was in the class above me, but was a fraternity brother of mine and I saw a good deal of him, not only in college but later on both in New York and Chicago, regularly up to the time of his death.

While in college he took considerable interest in all of the various sports, especially football, and he never missed one of the major games and was often down on the side lines watching the squads go through their drills.

In regard to his studies, he was a great student, especially in the subjects in which he was interested. These studies were especially English, French and history. But he was not at all interested in mathematics and had no conception of higher mathematics, and in fact he failed in his class in mathematics and on this account the University of California would not give him his degree and he was compelled to go on to Harvard where he could secure his degree without the necessity of passing an examination in mathematics.[38]

We never had much correspondence. It was generally just a short letter advising that I was going to be in New York or Chicago, and his replies were just short notes saying "come up, be mighty glad to see you." I have practically all of his books with his autograph, but that is all.

I remember one time shortly after the publication of his *A Man's Woman* that when he was criticized about this story, he replied by saying that he was simply trying to write a book which would make people talk and create a discussion as he felt that by creating considerable talk and getting people to take various sides in regard to his writings it would help him in the sale of future books that he might write.

While he was in Chicago securing the necessary information in regard to the book called *The Pit* I was with him constantly and he was unable to understand the short side of the market and how anybody could sell a thousand or a million bushels of wheat when he did not possess them. I tried in many ways to make this question clear to him, but it was many weeks before he could gain the right conception of short selling in the wheat market.[39]

During the year 1900 after my return from the Paris World Fair I was in New York with him and his wife about six weeks. They had an apartment on Washington Square and on that account I remained at a hotel close to them and we had many picnics together and also many meals in their little apartment. It was always a special joy to have this warm friendship with Frank and his wife.

During the Boer War he was sent from California as a special correspondent and while he was in Africa on this mission he wrote constantly to his dear mother of whom he was extremely fond.[40] In fact, I think one of his outstanding characteristics was his wonderful admiration for his mother. I often called upon her while Frank was away and she would always read his letters to me and together we would talk them over very fully.[41]

After he left college he was extremely fond of playing poker although he never played for high stakes, just a small limit, but I know of nobody enjoying the game more than he did, although he was an extremely poor player and generally managed to lose.

Together he and I formed what we called the only and original Thirteen Club, which consisted of thirteen members of the Fiji graduates. We often had one of the famous dinners in one of the old French restaurants. We would meet in the private dining room and have a real jolly evening, feasting and drinking and telling stories and going over incidents that had happened to any of the various fellows that we knew at that time. These were always extremely jolly dinners and Frank was generally the leader in these gaieties.

I do hope these few paragraphs may be of some interest to you.

His death was a special loss not only to me but to his many friends as he certainly was an outstanding fellow and a man with a wonderful future ahead of him.

If there is any further information that I might be able to give you, please consider that I am at your service.

Yours very truly,
George Gibbs.

14 / Ralph L. Hathorn

Having been impressed with Norris when the two first met in December 1890, during Norris's first semester at Berkeley (see Everett, chapter 12 this volume), Ralph LaForest Hathorn (1870–1943) attempted to generate enthusiasm for his election to Phi Gamma Delta. Failing to muster enough support for his candidate, Hathorn continued his campaign with ultimate success, when Norris pledged the fraternity at the end of that academic year. Hathorn and Norris became fast friends, both having a hand in the origin of the "pig dinner," now termed the Norris Pig Dinner, an annual affair in the chapter houses of Phi Gamma Delta. Hathorn, as class dispensator, delivered an oration at Class Day in 1893; he was also, like Norris, a founding member of Skull and Keys and played on the university's tennis team. He continued his education at Harvard Law School, where he took his LLB in 1897 (Crisler 1986, 33, n. 3), afterward returning to San Francisco to set up a law practice. According to fellow Fiji Seymour Waterhouse, Hathorn was spending time with Waterhouse at his family's mining operation, the Big Dipper Mine, in Iowa Hill, California, in the late summer of 1896 when Norris visited there.

Source: Ralph L. Hathorn. Interview notes by Franklin D. Walker, April 15, 1930, Franklin Dickerson Walker Collection, BANC MSS C-H 79, The Bancroft Library, University of California, Berkeley.

Hathorn was largely responsible for getting Norris into fraternity and was first of frat boys to meet him. He left a year before Norris; went to Harvard and spent three years in law school; returned S.F. in 1897. Lived in S.F. and used to go up to Norris's house during vacations and also spent one in Santa Cruz and part of one in Chicago.

Harvard. He was more or less out of touch with Norris at this time. Remembers him being there—living in college. Harvard was grind for them all—outsiders. Rarely saw each other.

Remembers seeing him afterwards in S.F. and meeting his girl, Jeannette, who was a beauty. Norris liked to play around with women in a casual manner but as far as he knew had no other serious love affair.

Pudding episode. He and Marsh decide to put goop in beds of Norris and Waterhouse while they were out fishing.[42] Norris comes home and gets in bed—swearing. Waterhouse discovers his and leaves the house for two weeks. Remembers Norris's black silk underwear, covered entire body.

Summer in Chicago. Went east about June 1893. Travelled with the Norris ménage, Mrs. Norris, Charles, Miss Carleton, and Frank. Spent thirty days in Chicago.[43] Then the Norrises went off up into the Wisconsin lakes somewhere. George Gibbs also in party.

Also remembers spending one night with Norris in their house in the city. Frank got up during the night, turned the gas on, and failed to light it. Nearly asphyxiated. Had been drinking. Norris liked to drink and frequently drank too much so that the boys had to look after him. Also liked to play blackjack—never lost very much.

15 / Albert J. Houston

Possessed of funds ample enough to dress like a fashionable boulevardier, increasingly successful as a writer of both serious and more whimsical works, a favorite with not only his fellow Fijis but also students generally, liked by many professors even when he did not fare well in some of their courses, Norris cut a broad swath at the University of California, but the popularity he enjoyed did not prevent his taking a typically generous interest in an innocent and impecunious sixteen-year-old from northern California by way of St. Louis. When Albert Joshua Houston (1874–1951) was elected to Phi Gamma Delta, Norris promptly took him under his wing as his roommate in the chapter house, succeeding Seymour Waterhouse in that capacity. Following his mentor's lead, Houston quickly proceeded to leave his own mark at Berkeley, involving himself in a variety of campus activities and endeavors, which culminated in his being named editor of the 1895 *Blue and Gold*, making full use of Norris's talents as an illustrator for that volume. After his graduation that same year, Houston remained in the Bay Area as a student at Cooper Medical College in San Francisco, from which he was graduated in 1898, the first step in an eminent career as an ear, nose, and throat specialist. Their clearly divergent interests did not, however, seriously undermine the friendship Houston and Norris continued to maintain. Norris secured Houston a short-lived position with *The Wave*, commented on his marital prospects in a letter to Eleanor M. Davenport (Crisler 1986, 45), dedicated *A Man's Woman* to him, thereby recognizing the medical expertise Houston had supplied for that novel, and then inscribed a copy of it the day after its publication to "my best man friend—in remembrance of our common college days and the Fiji Fraternity and in token of my earnest affection and admiration" (Crisler 1986, 219). For his part, Houston visited Norris and Jeannette at their new home in Roselle, New Jersey, and in later years unstintingly acknowledged Norris's hand in shaping a raw and inexperienced freshman.

Source: Albert J. Houston. Excerpts from unpublished autobiography, BANC MSS C-D 5067, The Bancroft Library, University of California, Berkeley.

[. . .] Before the end of my freshman year I was asked to live at the fraternity house and when they understood the reason I could not, they arranged for me to be house manager. My duties were to collect the board, buy the supplies, hire the help, arrange the menus, etc., in return for which I would get my board and room. As a result, from the beginning of my sophomore year I lived at the fraternity house. There was quite a lot of work involved in keeping the books and managing the affairs of the house. An expenditure had to be kept with the limit of about $30 a month for board & room. It took an especially stout heart when they all began to kick at once about having cornstarch pudding five times a week. Frank Norris, who was my room mate, was one of the loudest in his complaints as he had a particular aversion to anything "gooey." As a result, with the type of humor prevalent with healthy boys, they placed a dish of it in his bed one night so arranged that when he crawled in he would plant his foot right into it. This naturally started a war of reprisal. Frank, thinking that Seymour Waterhouse had done it, carefully put a pint of honey between Waterhouse's sheets the next night. Waterhouse who had not been a party to the original crime was so incensed that he left the house and sought board elsewhere. He later returned, much to our sorrow, for he came home with a bad habit, smoking five cent cigars. The brand was known as "Knapsack" but we called it Snap back, and the stench was so terrible that we finally had to clear out a storage room on the first floor for his personal use.[44] Many of us smoked—mostly pipes, with an occasional cigarette hand rolled of Bull Durham. Although it is a very fragrant, if cheap tobacco, it was unanimously conceded that those five cent cigars were too much for us.

Living with Frank Norris was one of the most interesting experiences of my life. Frank had just returned from two or three years' study in Paris where he had studied art in Julian Atelier. He was, therefore, both older and more sophisticated than most of us. At the age of 23 his hair already was turning gray. He wore a small mustache and small side burns, of the variety usually known as "fire escapes." The first time I saw him he was wearing a long English travel coat, very wide and almost touching the ground, and a fore and aft shooting cap of the sort Wm. Gillette used as Sherlock Holmes.[45] To say the least he was spectacular, resembling an English sporting Lord rather than a Sophomore at a western college. His clothes were always beautifully tailored and he wore them well, being tall and slender. People always looked twice at him, although he was always dressed in the best taste. He did not mind it because he had a sense of the dramatic in every thing he did. I have never known any one with as great a zest for life. It was all good to him. Always he saw something interesting and dramatic in the slightest event. He had a brilliant mind but it would only work in the direction in which he was interested. For example, he never could do mathematics. He would try for a few minutes, throw up his hands in despair, swear it was useless, and automatically draw a mental curtain on the whole subject. It was not that he was not bright enough but his mind just was not disciplined to do work he disliked. In fact, if I remember rightly, he did not get his degree on account of his mathematics, but was later given an honorary one.[46] He always worked very hard at his drawing and his studies in literature. Already he had written a book called *Yvernelle*, a long ballad after the style of *The Lady of the Lake*,[47] beautifully illustrated and bound in full red morocco at great expense. It was not very good, but already showed the creative ability he displayed when he was interested. At the time he was in College he was interested mostly in drawing and spent most of his time at it. Although occasionally he wrote something for one of the College periodicals, he did not really get interested in writing until he got interested in Zola. Zola had a special appeal for him and influenced his early writing greatly.

It was, however, as a companion and friend that I was mostly interested in Frank Norris, and our friendship became very close indeed. Why I should have been favored with such a rich friendship I have never been able to understand. He was travelled, cultured, and talented, and had plenty of money and savoir-faire, while I had no money, no talent, no social grace, and was still wearing my first made-to-order suit of clothes which had been made by Nicholl the tailor at a cost of $25.[48] It made no difference to Frank, he was no snob; if he liked you he liked you and it was his business why. He not only befriended me at college but took me home with him on weekends. The Norrises lived in a large double home at 1822 Sacramento St. which seemed a palace to me. His mother was a tall queenly woman with snow white hair. She was always beautifully dressed and groomed and never off her guard. I think she had been an actress at one time and she always dressed as a queen and acted as one. She loved Frank and always had dinner parties for him to which she invited beautiful women. To me the whole thing was a bit of fairy land.

I entered his world a raw modest provincial youth and came out a finished gentleman of the world—with considerable limitations, you understand. There was never a dull moment with Frank. He was always starting some lark,—a midnight raid on a neighboring chicken roost, a trip down to Oakland for a poor dinner with a lot of cheap claret, a midnight party at the sub rosa saloon of Mr. Dennis Haggerty, where we brewed a punch and sang songs until morning, or a game of vingt-et-un which was Frank's favorite game.[49] We would sit up all night and win or lose possibly fifteen cents.

I remember one day Frank and I "picked up" two beautiful girls on the ferry boat and made a "date" with them to have a picnic lunch the next day in the Botanical Garden.[50] When we got home we bought champagne and pâté and prepared a beautiful al fresco lunch. The next day we started for the Botanical Garden with our lunch basket and high hope. But no girls appeared and by three in the afternoon we were so discomfited that we decided to eat what we could of the lunch. We drank all the champagne and got back to the fraternity house about six o'clock very nicely illuminated and of the opinion that we had a much better time than if the girls had appeared.

Later it was Frank who got me my first job after I had graduated, and who dedicated one of his earliest books *A Man's Woman* to me, and who rousted me out of bed one night to tell me that he was engaged to the most wonderful woman in the world, upon which we adjourned to the old Zinkand Cafe and opened a bottle of champagne to her, walked through Golden Gate Park to the Cliff House and home again, which was the length of time it took Frank to tell me of it. Altogether he was the perfect friend and I think that some of the joy that I have had in the adventure of life was due to Frank's enthusiasm. A strong character always leaves his mark upon his associates. [. . .]

Source: Albert J. Houston. Interview notes by Franklin D. Walker, April 30, 1930, Franklin Dickerson Walker Papers, BANC MSS C-H 79, The Bancroft Library, University of California, Berkeley.

Dr. Houston had been a close friend of Norris throughout his life, but unfortunately, his memory is not at all satisfactory. Particularly faulty is it in the matter of chronology. He destroyed all of Frank's letters at the times when they arrived. His opinions of Frank are quite frank and appear to be little biased.

Owns part of MS of *McTeague*; has given a section to Oscar Sutro, who was also a friend of Norris.[51]

Remembers when he first saw Frank the latter was dressed in a long coat and two-peaked Sherlock Holmes cap which he had picked up abroad. He was always an actor, as was his mother.

Used to go home with him to S.F. house where his mother always entertained extensively; young ladies, Miss Ida Carleton, Louise Boyd,[52] etc. They would go up to sleep in the huge mahogany bed and Frank would throw his best suit in the corner, as usual, don dirty night-gown—he never wore pajamas—and go to bed with his hair unwashed. This he usually perfumed to avoid washing it. Was fond of perfume. Very bad skin always.

Visited Frank and Jeannette once in Roselle. Found them installed in an old-fashioned double framed house. From there Frank would commute to N.Y.[53] They had little money then: had previously lived in an apartment in the city.

The evening that Frank became engaged to Jeannette he came home and found Bert, took him to dinner, and walked to the Cliff-House and back, telling him of this wonderful girl. He was very enthusiastic.

He was Frank's roommate at Berkeley: Waterhouse they put out in the penthouse because of the vile five-cent cigars which he smoked. Frank was always working on his drawing, with a board and mirror for perspective. Does not think that he was much interested in writing at the time; is sure that he was not working on *McTeague*. Frank passed the math. course, because all of the boys helped him crib it.[54] He just never could get his mind to work on it—always gave it up as a bad job. Houston has the copy of Horace;[55] Frank was always fond of poetry.

He did not have a deeply religious nature; not really religious at all. Liked Episcopalianism for its aesthetic qualities. Mother was a staunch formalist, had prayers in the home every evening before retiring; read the Bible aloud to group twice a day. He was not introspective and tended to take things as they came.[56] Does not believe that he felt deeply about separation of his parents; always treated his mother well but never showed deep affections.

In the Goop incident, Waterhouse suspected Frank of having put the stuff in his bed, after finding it in his own. Hence he was angry with Frank. He was too luxurious and fond of ease to take any interest in sports.

When Bert left college, Frank got him a job on *The Wave*. Paid him 12 dollars a week, and Cosgrave fired him after a month's work because he wasn't worth it. Cosgrave a close friend of Norris. Frank would work hard on *The Wave*, but very sporadically. He was always temperamental about working. Thinks Cosgrave would have correspondence.

Miss Ida Carleton was with his mother, and he thinks that trips were made to San Diego, where Miss Carleton had relatives in the Navy, Carleton or Thompson.[57] Mrs. Norris was fairly well off for a time, but was investing money in houses without business acumen. Madison and Burke were her agents.[58] Things went pretty badly, but Charles helped clear things up as he grew older. Bert pulled Mrs. N. out of her hotel during the fire;[59] she had several trunks of stuff and would not leave without it. He got out one trunk, but the rest burned. Spoke of wigs.

Frank discussed *A Man's Woman* with him, getting all the medical details checked up. Does not think it was while he was on *The Wave*, and yet it was in San Francisco. He was in medical school, 1896–8.

He also talked over *McTeague* with him. In *Octopus* he had little sympathy for people; he was an aristocrat by nature. The S. P. became a great dramatic ogre.[60]

He went to South Africa as correspondent for the *Chronicle*, expecting trouble before he went. Received many letters from him at this time; all destroyed. He was in the thick of the business at S. Africa and believes the dispatch riding was OK.

Frank never worried, but was inclined to be happy-go-lucky. With his writing he had almost a frenzy and would keep at it constantly and incessantly, except for temperamental fluctuations. He never seemed to care anything about the monetary returns, nor does Bert think that he was interested in fame. Just the dramatic passion for love of writing.

16 / H. Hull McClaughry

Different in many ways, Harry Hull McClaughry (1870–?) and Norris nonetheless developed a vital friendship in college. A year ahead of Norris, McClaughry, as captain of Cadet Company A, evidently approached Berkeley's military science requirement more seriously than did his friend. President of his class during the second semester of his senior year, he also took greater interest in college politics. Yet both McClaughry and Norris were fraternity men, the former a member of Delta Kappa Epsilon; both were also members of Skull and Keys; and both went on to Harvard for further education, though Norris enrolled as a special student, as he had at the University of California, while McClaughry graduated from Harvard Law School in 1896. McClaughry also figured in contributions by Norris to two volumes of the *Blue and Gold*. The yearbook for 1894 contains a drawing by Norris of a tall, slender, suited young man with his arm around a much shorter fellow sporting mutton chops; labeled "Election Day Makes Comrades of Us All. McC- - - -y & J. D. H- -g- -ty" (*Blue and Gold* 1893 [1894], 194), it jibes at McClaughry who used Heagerty's saloon as a place to garner votes from his college peers. In Norris's untitled poem, beginning "I took my girl to Schuetzen Park," printed in the next year's annual, he refers to a "friend of mine" whom he calls "Mr. Man" (Norris 1894a, 252), the nickname, according to McClaughry, Norris reserved for McClaughry himself. Noted Philadelphia book collector, Alfred Edward Newton (1864–1940), to whom McClaughry wrote concerning Norris, was closely associated with Bay Area collectors and fine printers.

Source: Henry Hull McClaughry to A. Edward Newton, letter, May 12, 1931, Ms.Am.101, Rare Book and Manuscripts Department, Boston Public Library, Boston, Massachusetts.

Dear Sir:

Your recent interview in the *San Francisco Chronicle* has made me think that perhaps I have a first edition of Frank Norris' *Octopus*. If I have I do not desire to sell it but would be glad to give it to some bibliophile who would appreciate it.

I am a contemporary of Frank and was a college mate of Frank's both at Berkeley and Harvard. I went into the law and retired about fifteen years ago. I have what I consider a well selected reference library in my home but when I pass on in the near future my books will probably be unappreciated and if I should happen to have any book of value it would probably be lost. It is for that reason that I would like to see this book in the hands of a real lover of books if it should prove to be one of value.

Frank and I ate at the same table in Memorial Hall, together with other boys from California, and after dinner it was our custom to gather in my room, which was large and located near the Hall, and there enjoy our after-dinner pipe. Frank smoked a common white clay T-D which he prized very highly.[61] He dropped it one evening and broke the stem. He took it into Boston and had it carefully mended with a silver band.

Many of the incidents mentioned in *Vandover and the Brute* took place in my room at Harvard, for instance, his introduction to Crème Violette. We "discovered" this liqueur in Boston one night and thereafter always kept a bottle of it in my room for an "after dinner." The stove, "the famous tiled stove with flamboyant ornaments," so vividly described by Frank in *Vandover*, was one that he bought second-hand for exactly six dollars and installed in his room in Grays Hall.[62] He never tired of extolling the virtues of this stove and never lost sight of the fact that he bought it for six dollars.

When he disappeared from Cambridge and went to South Africa he was lost for some time both to his college mates and his family as well. Even his mother tried to locate him through the boys in Cambridge. One cold winter night, snow on the ground, a tap on my door, a curt "Come in," and there stood Frank, back against the door, a soft "Hello, Mister Man"! He was dressed in a long feather-weight cape overcoat and a straw hat. True, he had been with Jameson but "the damned scoundrels" had made a cook out of him.

When I retired some years ago and gave up my home in Berkeley I destroyed a number of group photographs taken at Harvard. I am very sorry now that I did not send these to Frank's brother.

Just between you and me, I am sorry that *Vandover* was ever published. I do not think that Frank ever intended to let this work see the light of day. It may have added materially to his estate but not, in my humble opinion, to his fame.

To return to the subject of *The Octopus*: Sometime in the late nineties

I met Frank one morning in the old - - - - Hotel in Stockton.[63] I have forgotten the name of the hotel but it was quite famous in the day. We had breakfast together and he told me that he was just up for a day or two from the San Joaquin Valley where he was gathering material for a book. I think that was the last time I ever saw Frank.

There is nothing in my copy of *The Octopus* to indicate, that is, to me, whether it is a first edition or not. My dear old mother[64] has pasted on the fly leaves some newspaper clippings, a picture of Frank, a notice of his death and an account of his life. One of these clippings is dated October 23, 1902. The copyright date is 1901. I feel quite sure that I must have purchased the book immediately upon its first appearance. Perhaps you could tell me some way in which the edition could be identified. If you wish, I would be glad to send the book to you merely upon the assurance that the book would be placed in the hands of an appreciative owner, it if should prove to be of value. I would be glad to do this not only for Frank's sake but also for that of my dear mother who so lovingly placed the clippings in the book.

Trusting that I have not bored you, I am

Yours very truly,
Hull McClaughry

Upon reading this letter over I am rather ashamed of it. I might add, however, that Frank was very ungrammatical in his speech and I am quite sure all of his writings had to be carefully edited.

17 / Ariana Moore

One of fewer than twenty-five women in Norris's college class, Ariana Moore (1870–1963) from Carpinteria, California, entered the university in the literary course of study. A scholar of some distinction, she received a Phebe Hearst Scholarship, one of two given in 1894, the year the award was established by Phebe Apperson Hearst (1842–1919), the philanthropic feminist perhaps better known as the mother of publishing magnate William Randolph Hearst. Moore spoke at the university's commencement exercises, accepting the gift of a portrait of Mrs. Hearst by her protégé Orrin M. Peck (1860–1921), to be hung in the library as acknowledgment of her annual gift of three hundred dollars for scholarships for deserving "young women" (Jones 1895, 151). By her junior year, Moore had begun to embrace other aspects of college life when she was elected second vice president of her class; the next year she joined both the Bushnell Union, a campus debating club, and the college chapter of the Young Women's Christian Association. Her interests in literature brought her into regular contact with Norris.

Source: Ariana Moore to Franklin D. Walker, letter, April 1, 1930, Franklin Dickerson Walker Papers, BANC MSS C-H 79, The Bancroft Library, University of California, Berkeley.

My dear Mr. Walker,

I have your good letter which deserves a good answer; this it will not have.

All that I could tell you about Frank Norris would be included in what Jessica (Dr.) Peixotto has told you, or will tell you; or the men of his fraternity, Phi Gamma Delta, (the medalist of our class was one,[65] and loved Frank Norris as all the men in his fraternity did).

Frank Norris was, when he matriculated, a slightly slim figure in the Freshman class; he was no older, but seemed so because of French maturity and French grace; at the same time oddly irresponsible and childlike in the prosaic matters in which sensible young Americans are so competent.

When we met to decide on plans for our first dance (called the "Freshman Glee") he rose to suggest that it be conducted as a cotillion. We knew that we were not socially experienced enough, or anywhere near it to have our dance as a cotillion; it would have been ridiculous; yet we were not angry; no one thought Frank was putting on "side." We knew in some way that the dark youth who bore himself so easily and was so unembarrassed was as friendly and likable as he was different.

One of the Phi Gamma boys told me—when we were no longer freshmen—that Frank was pretty terrible about keeping appointments—so utterly undependable that it took a lot of patience not to blame him; but nobody ever did blame him, or resent it at all. He had no capacity for keeping money, so they just looked out for him and loaned it when necessary, though he might never think of paying it back—generous and affectionate though he was.

I think he had a certain amount of pride and pleasure in *Yvernelle*. I thought it trash. But Jessica Peixotto did not think so. She was much more able to understand an artist than anyone in the group; not so unformed and countrified. She could see how he turned with delight—for the time—to the color and lavish ornament of a medieval fantasy without ceasing at all to know that he had to be a realist and that realism was the really beautiful thing.

I don't know where he found mental mates, if he had any. Not in our class. Not in his fraternity,—I'm sure. Not in the student body, probably; yet he may have had sometimes, with a student and a faculty man, or two, or three, hours that were delightful. Mr. Syle was in the faculty then; so was Professor Gayley.[66] I know Mr. Syle was not important; he was a half-failure, sensitive, of uneven brilliance, rather cynical and non-conformist; as my instructor he fascinated me more than did his superiors. I should think he and Frank Norris must have been stimulating to each other, but I don't know it.

The play that Frank Norris wrote for one of our class enterprises, and in which Jessica Peixotto and Will Denman and two other handsome people took part, was very poor.[67] It was an awful blend of French sophistication—which he had half forgotten—and American college wit—which he never fully learned.

I think he must have had a bad time with mathematics.

As to science I don't know at all. It is my belief that he ignored it, to all intents; a much simpler thing to do then than now. I doubt if he perceived, then, that realism in art has close relation to what science may have revealed about life and the world. And science then, if already sovereign, was still a youthful one, and had not yet spread her inflexible rule over all the continents of thought. This is nothing; but it may help you to continue to look elsewhere.

Yours,
Ariana Moore

18 / Jessica B. Peixotto

Although Jessica Blanche Peixotto (1864–1941) was several years older than Norris, she did not enter college until 1891, a year after him. As a young woman, she had followed her family's suggestion that she not pursue further education beyond high school, but her acquaintance with Norris, friend of her brother Ernest, soon radically changed her thinking as well as her later career, when he convinced her to enroll as a student at Berkeley, where she managed with his encouragement to complete her studies in three years. After her graduation, she, like Norris and Ernest before her, traveled to Paris, where she studied at the Sorbonne before returning to the University of California to enroll as a graduate student in sociology, which in turn led to a PhD, the second awarded to a woman by the university. Taking an overload as an undergraduate gave her less time than most of her peers had to participate in extracurricular activities, the lone exception being her accepting the role of Mrs. Faversham in Norris's "Two Pair" opposite William Denman.

Source: Jessica B. Peixotto. Interview notes by Franklin D. Walker, May 28, 1930, Franklin Dickerson Walker Papers, BANC MSS C-H 79, The Bancroft Library, University of California, Berkeley.

Miss Peixotto was a very good friend of Frank's. She met him first in her home in San Francisco after his return from Paris about the time Ernest returned.[68] They had been pals when abroad and remained so after returning. Frank was very much of a dilettante in those days and loved to appear as a man of the world. He was writing *Yvernelle*, painting, preparing for exams, etc. Older than the boys in the university and inclined to look upon them as children. He persuaded her to enter the year after he did and then figure it out so that she could graduate in 1894. He did not graduate because he could not do trigonometry.

When he entered the university he was imitating Kipling in his writing.[69] She seems to think that he contributed much to *The Berkeleyan*.[70] In his senior year, or later, he became very enthusiastic about Zola. They took the realistic course in French Literature under Paget together; Paget was a classicist and had no use for the realists. He didn't mention Zola. At that time people did not tolerate Zola. When she later went to school in France she mentioned him at the dinner table, only to be asked, "Do young girls read Zola in America?"

Frank's chief interests were economic and sex cross currents. He was at heart always something of a reformer. So with *The Octopus* his chief desire was to put the truth before the public.

Ernest he called Little Billie after Du Maurier's novel.[71] When he met her he already had a few gray hairs. He would write in a bare attic room in their home in S.F. Scrupulously polite with the ladies; he met her on the campus while smoking his pipe and put it in his pocket. She smelled it burn. He liked independent women and admired her when she led a movement to shorten skirts to shoe tops to scandal of faculty. He persuaded her to take a part in the farce to the opposition of Bill Denman who did not approve of it. They were always good pals, nothing more.

They took many English classes together. He was particularly fond of Chaucer and admired Bradley very much.[72] He didn't like Armes. Doesn't remember about Gayley.

Maida Castelhun, now Mrs. Darnton, can be reached through the University Woman's Club, New York.[73]

Mrs. Sloss's *Victorian Poetry* was inspired by Mrs. Norris and is dedicated to her.

19 / Harry W. Rhodes

Like many of Norris's friends in college, Harry Willet Rhodes (1870–1947) belonged to Norris's fraternity, which provided a ready field in which an association between them could take firm root. Rhodes's recollection of a limerick Norris wrote in one of "Uncle Joe" Le Conte's classes preserves an early example of his playful wit. As a civil engineering major, Rhodes had little literary inclination, but he did lend his business acumen to *The Berkeleyan* as its business manager when he was a senior. He had previously been involved in the Young Men's Christian Association and helped in the arrangements for his class's Junior Day exercises. Rhodes entered the lifesaving service after leaving the university, serving as supervisor of California's Eighteenth Lighthouse District for many years (Noble 1997, 99).

Source: Harry W. Rhodes. Interview notes by Franklin D. Walker, April 20, 1930, Franklin Dickerson Walker Papers, BANC MSS C-H 79, The Bancroft Library, University of California, Berkeley.

Rhodes is a lighthouse inspector in S.F. and had done a good deal of sea-faring. His opinions seem to be very reliable and to indicate considerable insight into personality, although he has little literary background.

He knew Norris only when he was at college. Saw him once afterwards when he came through from Alaska and had dinner with him and Houston. (1900.) Said little about personal affairs. Norris was a true Bohemian and a good fellow; he spoke always in metaphors. He was not at all reserved with his friends but always rather dramatic. Reserved with strangers.

College life. It is his impression that Norris was physically lazy. The boys often tried to persuade him to take up a sport but he did not care to. This may have been partly due to a rather weak physical makeup and sensitivity but chiefly to that type of laziness. Remembers nothing about his fencing.

Remembers nothing about his vacations. Does not think that he was interested in camping and hiking.

Always inclined to be dramatic. Remembers first football game when the fraternities had stage-coaches on the side-lines. Frank excited, yells "Why don't they catch that son of a bitch?" The flying wedge was a play brought out from the east. Wedge got started down the field with the ball carrier in the center.

In the house he was inclined to be temperamental and somewhat moody—but as a whole could be called cheerful. He was rather sensitive about his art and writing and was continually joshed about it. The boys of the fraternity did not appreciate it and would try to razz it out of him. Especially his drawing. As a result he kept very quiet about his work. Rhodes considers him a dilettante in art and partly in literature—cites his frequent failure to get accurate details, such as Moran reading the sextant on her back.[74] A good many minor details in *Moran*. Used to josh him about it. Assumed he was too lazy to check up on details. He was sensitive about *Yvernelle*—written under Scott influence. He remained very fond of medieval painting and writing. Joshed him for Brunhilde picture.[75]

He was very fond of dogs. Monk, the battle-scarred bull dog in the fraternity, he took under his wing.[76] Always nursed him after his fights.

He would frequently startle the freshmen by bombastic questioning and accusations at the dinner table. He was very fond of pranks. He took part in the famous back-stop rush and always talked about it.[77]

Science. Interested in Uncle Joe's class. Always saw the dramatic possibilities in anything. Wrote limerick on Geology.

There once was an ichthyosaurus,
Who live when the earth was all porous
When he first heard his name,
He fainted from shame,
And departed a long time before us.

"Lauth" would be quite typical of the dramatic possibilities he saw in anything.

Possibly he got something out of astronomy that interested him.

The junior farce was lots of fun. A little shocking. Agrees with Ariana Moore.

He was always in on the gambling.

In the separation of his father and mother he was quite bitter towards his father but said little about it. He always seemed to be independent financially while in college and quite prodigal about money—always had to keep on his trail about house dues so that he would not spend it somewhere else. That the family was in straits later is indicated by Kathleen Norris's accounts of their struggles in N.Y. just after their marriage. (That is, struggles of Charles and Kathleen.)

No correspondence.

Friends. George Gibbs (Minnesota) and Waterhouse his closest friends—might know the inner man. The latter roomed with him.

Fred O. Johnson, L.A., O. T. Johnson Bldg. In house for short time.[78] Good friend.

Selfridge. Foreign and Domestic Commerce.

W. B. Rountree, 2444 Virginia, Ash 4627.[79]

George D. Blood, S.F., was Fiji and superintendent of the Big Dipper Mine.[80]

20 / Leon J. Richardson

While Leon Josiah Richardson (1868–1964) never officially taught Norris at Berkeley, as a teaching assistant he often acted as a substitute instructor in courses taught by his cousin, George Morey Richardson (1859–1896), from whom Norris took three courses in Latin, two as a freshman and the last as a sophomore, in all of which he received a 3 or C (see Norris's transcript, University Archives n.d.). Upon his return from a two-year stint abroad for further study, Richardson accepted the permanent faculty position vacated because of the unexpected death of his cousin.

Source: Leon J. Richardson. Interview notes by Franklin D. Walker, March 18, 1930, Franklin Dickerson Walker Papers, BANC MSS C-H 79, The Bancroft Library, University of California, Berkeley.

In the year 1891–2 my cousin, George M. Richardson,[81] was teaching Latin in U.C. and I acted as his assistant. His frequent absences gave me opportunities to take over his classes and thus I had Frank Norris as a student. He would always sit in the front row and spend the time during class in drawing pictures in his Horace. Each ode he illustrated, having sometimes 3 or 4 pictures to the page. The pictures were well drawn and illustrative of the text. I regret that I did not offer him $10 for it as it would have been an invaluable memory.

He was an average student in Latin, doing about C work. Horace seemed to be his favorite Latin writer and his ideas he assimilated quickly with real critical ability. He was not so quick with the language work and displayed an individuality in his attitude towards study which marked him at the time.

The university was so small at the time that everyone was acquainted and faculty & students became close friends. He remained a casual friend throughout his four years.

He did a great deal of writing during his senior year—mostly waste-basket material. He often discussed his literary tastes with Miss Ariana Moore who is now in Carpinteria.

At one period during his college career he was much interested in writing poetry and wrote *Yvernelle.* His uncle read it and admired it, sending it to Lippincott's for publication, paying for same and the illustrations.[82] Later (senior year or 1st after) Norris was much disturbed because of its publication and was heard to say that he wished he could get hold of all the copies & burn them.

His somewhat foreign air added to his reserve while among the students. He was not a great mixer but made close friends and was reputed to be a man of high literary and artistic taste. It was known that he had a serious interest in literature, was doing some experimental writing, and took a strongly individual interest in books. Close friend of Benjamin Weed—opposite type to Brick Morse.[83]

He had a strikingly sallow complexion, almost diseased in appearance. His hair was dark, with sideburns and mustache, and except for the sallowness, he was a good looking man. When he returned from Harvard he was not looking well.

I do not remember much about the junior farce.

Benjamin Weed was interested in producing a Greek play in the amphitheatre which he discovered.

21 / Maurice V. Samuels

A member of Norris's class at Berkeley, Maurice Victor Samuels (1873–1945) was one of his few friends not in Phi Gamma Delta. As recalled by Charles Norris, Samuels, Norris, and Myron Wolf were together so much as freshmen on campus that their classmates dubbed them the Three Guardsmen, an allusion to Dumas's *The Three Musketeers*. Samuels, a member of the university's newest fraternity, Sigma Nu, was also on the staff of the 1894 *Blue and Gold* and joined the Philosophical Union, which may have led to his membership along with Norris in the Society for the Study of Ethics and Religion as a senior. Originally a lawyer, he practiced in San Francisco for a few years (1895–1902) before turning to drama, writing plays and screenplays.

Source: Maurice V. Samuels to Franklin D. Walker, letter, May 20, 1930, Franklin Dickerson Walker Papers, BANC MSS C-H 79, The Bancroft Library, University of California, Berkeley.

My dear Mr. Walker,

I am very glad to learn that you are writing a biography of my old friend Frank Norris and only regret that vivid as are my recollections of Frank himself the particular questions you ask regarding the publication, *Smiles* and the Society for the Study of Ethics and Religion fail to evoke definite memories beyond the fact that I think I had to get out the last few issues of a humorous paper that died in its early youth and no eulogy of which ever came to my attention.[84] As far as the Society is concerned I seem to hear its name for the first time despite your discovery of my name on its list. I very gravely doubt that Frank ever took any live interest in anything of that sort. Perhaps we just joined out of politeness. Maybe we thought it would be a good thing for our respective fraternities if our names figured so respectably. Ralph Hathorn, his frat brother, might know, however.

In our Freshman year Frank Norris, Myron Wolf,[85] who was Insurance Commissioner at the time of the Fire and easily one of the finest men I have ever known and I were inseparable friends. On the Campus they called us The Three Guardsmen. As Frank was every inch Athos and Myron had the warm heart and portly figure of Porthos it must have been left to me to suggest Aramis in some way. Frank at that time had but recently returned from Paris where he had spent some years studying Art in the Latin Quarter. He was very reserved, cared little for the crowd, loved poetry and romance, had just published an edition de luxe of a Medieval poem *Yvernelle* and thought and expressed himself frequently to me at least in terms of an aristocrat of the period of the French Revolution—it was not a pose—despising the "canaille" and invariably confusing Socialism with Anarchy—he "wanted to see 'em all drowned on one raft," despite my frequent endeavors to make a case for modern Socialism toward which I was then inclined. How this contrasts with the splendid and very real sympathy and understanding of the hearts and hopes of the common people evidenced by his fine novels of but a few years later! I have often thought of the rapidity of his evolution once he had come into direct contact with Life.

I recall distinctly the pleasure he took in showing me the first installment of "Moran of the Lady Letty," a novelette published serially in *The Wave*, a "society" paper of the time published in San Francisco. I know how I envied him the ability to write a story never dreaming at that time that somehow influenced by what he had done I myself would one day turn from the practice of the Law—from childhood it was understood in my home that I was to be a lawyer—to writing for the stage for the remainder of my days. For accuracy's sake, however, I admit that although I have no present idea what it was about except that it burlesqued the Faculty I did submit something when, in our Junior year I think it was proposed to stage something but so did Frank who was already known among the boys to be a real author—vide *The Wave*—and it was his play—something too as I remember it of a college thing—No. On second thought I've a notion it was a real play—even possibly a "society drama"—that was so incomparably better than mine that after seeing it I waste-basketed my own and have always since said and believed that I wrote my first play in 1902.

He and I spent our first college vacation together at Coronado Beach. Frank made me his Father Confessor and being a little younger I joyed in listening to his wildly enthusiastic eulogies of a certain girl only to realize time and again that each description was of a new one. He idealized one and all of them and I distinctly recall that he never once suggested that he had made a conquest. When in later years I wrote a play, *Elaine*,[86] I think I put something of Frank Norris into my Lancelot.

Subsequently we joined different fraternities and while we remained the best of friends we saw much less of one another. I met him on his return from South Africa where he had gone I think as a special correspondent during the Boer War and met a man who could write the great epic of Grain, who could picture the dentist's office on Larkin Street and the gripping drama in Death Valley but never again the romanticist who had brought to the Campus and to me perhaps its only example of a man who all but lived in an earlier century or rather in a blend of several with little or none of the prosaic one that afflicts us.[87]

I might mention that he loved a horse and on one instance at Coronado his ability to all but read the mind of one of them saved me from an accident. Apart from that the incident is of no interest.

May I suggest that you locate a copy of his first publication, *Yvernelle*, and draw your own deductions from it. For some reason it does not seem to be referred to when his works are discussed. I rather fancy that it represented a period in his life of which little is known. But contrastually at least it seems to me to be of rare interest and I only wish I could remember after all this time just what the story was about. I know it seemed to me to be a wonderful thing at the time, a thing of beauty, poetic, idyllic.

O'Hara Cosgrave used to visit his home in those days. He is now connected with one of the magazines in New York I think. He could help you out, I am sure.

Probably you already know how much Frank owed to his gifted and sympathetic mother, herself a profound Browning student. I never knew his father who I understood was the head of a jewelry firm in Chicago.

Perhaps I should add an incident that remains fresh in my memory. In our day it was a custom in the English Department of the University of California to write a "theme" a month. Subjects were assigned to us. This didn't prevent Frank from writing just as he pleased. I recall his exasperation when one he had written and in which he had great faith was held up as an example of *what not to do*. He had devoted pages I seem to remember to a description of the moon at the start. That same month I got away with murder. Not liking any of the subjects assigned and having chosen Mazzini,[88] in order to avoid research work I started with the dramatization of an incident and filled up with pseudo-psychology and it just happened that the English "Instructor" as he was called [. . .] was keen about the stage. The result was that I got the praise and Frank the roast and the absurdity of it impressed me not less than it did Frank at the time and I was his consoler for the injustice done. If I could have gotten values out of the moon the way Frank did I should have then and there devoted myself to literature instead of waiting seven years in the dry practice of the little Law I ever learned.

Years later, over a Picon punch at the much lamented "Mint" on Montgomery Street[89]—my memory couldn't play me a trick on that name, could it?—Frank's critic with whom I had contracted a fine after-graduation friendship expressed a belief that the incident I hinted at was just a bit of college legend, and as he had directed my wandering footsteps to the Mint I failed to remind him that I was in a position to know the facts of the case. Perhaps a little later I wasn't, for being customarily a bit abstemious—a fortunate thing now that we are in the throes of the Noble Experiment[90]—the splendid traditionary hospitality of California evoked confused images and my host stood out among them as one of the first discoverers of the genius of Norris.

Some time when you find yourself risking closer acquaintanceship with the actualities of much maligned Hollywood I hope you will find time to spend an evening with me and perhaps some data that you have already obtained will remind me of other phases of Frank's unique personality that may be of possible use to you in writing the biography of one of California's most gifted and lovable sons.

Will you pardon the chaotic character of my reply to your enquiries? Your letter which lay for some time at my club is being answered at a time when I am in the midst of a screen story and were I to rewrite this I should have to cause further delay or else fail to deliver something promised for tomorrow to a collaborator.

If at any time you desire to enquire about any other matter connected with your present work please do not hesitate to do so. I regret that I haven't a line of personal correspondence with Frank to send to you. Cosgrave may be more fortunate and I think you would do well to get in touch with him. I think he edited *The Wave* at the time *Moran of the Lady Letty* was printed.

Sincerely yours,
Maurice V. Samuels

Myron Wolf also died many years ago, surviving Frank by quite a few, however. We began the practice of Law about the same time. He was the practical one of the trio in college days. A man of a very fine sense of honor and responsibility, he performed a great service for San Francisco at the time of the Fire. Although his strict duty as Insurance Commissioner did not involve his going so far by any means and silence would have meant making powerful friends for him he nobly and bravely took it upon himself to advise property owners in San Francisco not to yield to the claim of the Insurance Companies that losses should be adjusted on the basis that at least twenty five percent of losses should be attributed to earthquake to start in with. As a result with a three hundred million loss I think fully seventy five millions additional were saved to stricken San Francisco. You can readily see what disinterestedness his conduct manifested.

We are all three in the class of '94.

If you will send me a list of the names you find in your copy of *Smiles* it may start a line of thought that will yield the name of the man who instigated *Smiles*. It was neither Frank nor I—I feel certain of that—it might have been Frank Todd later of the *Argonaut* and a good man to consult. He could easily have been guilty of a thing like that—Of one thing more I am pretty certain—that neither Frank nor I wrote much of its actual contents and I can't visualize him helping to get it out. It wasn't the sort of thing Frank liked.

M. V. S.

22 / Edward A. Selfridge Jr.

Both Edward Augustus Selfridge Jr. (1872–1936) and Norris pledged Phi Gamma Delta Fraternity at the end of their freshman year in college. Selfridge, who began his association with the military as a student at the university, eventually being promoted to cadet lieutenant colonel, was also a member of the Banjo Club and Skull and Keys, acting in the latter society's production of *Minstrels*, for which Norris wrote the lyrics. Upon his graduation in 1894, Selfridge continued his education at Columbia Law School, electing to remain in New York for many years thereafter, which was fortunate for Norris as Selfridge details in his letter to Walker. Before the Spanish-American War ended, Selfridge was promoted to captain of his unit; he later worked in the United States Department of Commerce as a lumber specialist.

Source: Edward A. Selfridge to Franklin D. Walker, letter, June 18, 1930, Franklin Dickerson Walker Papers, BANC MSS C-H 79, The Bancroft Library, University of California, Berkeley.

Dear Mr. Walker,

This will acknowledge receipt of your letter of May 11 which has remained unanswered owing to an operation which I underwent on May 16th.

Frank Norris was a classmate of mine & also a fraternity brother but I did not know him until my sophomore year when he joined the Fijis, & we soon became very dear friends. His outstanding characteristic in college was his violent objection to all forms of physical exercise & he was in constant hot water on account of it, with both the physical culture department under Magee, & the military department under Randolph,[91] the latter of whom he dubbed "Red Paint" on account of his artillery stripes. He hated mathematics but loved history & literature, but notwithstanding his good work in the former under Bacon, Bacon told me that he did not think that Norris would ever amount to much as a writer! Norris's roommate for almost the entire time in college was Seymour Waterhouse, now living in San Jose & who was dubbed "Doodle" by him. If you have never heard of Denny Haggerty, some of the older members of the faculty, such as Haskell & Leuschner,[92] & possibly Senger, if he is still alive, can tell you about him. At any rate he kept a restaurant & beer joint right under the nose of Sather Gate & the Fijis, Chi Phis & Zetes were very regular customers.[93] As you know, Norris at that time was more of an artist than a writer & for a long time, in fact till Haggerty's burned down, there was one back room, the walls of which were adorned with Norris's sketches mostly in the nude, of which Haggerty was very proud & would never allow them to be removed. After Norris's death, I met Haggerty on Market St., for the first time since leaving college, & he grabbed me by the shoulders with both hands & wept like a child, heartbroken & sad. It was becoming so conspicuous that I asked him for the sake of old times to step into a nearby saloon & have a drink, which we did, but he would not let me pay for it, saying in his famous brogue, "Mister Selfridge, no friend of Mr. Norris & no Fiji, Chi Phi or Zete can ever pay for a drink of mine!"

Norris had very difficult sledding when he was in New York early in 1898 & he was very hard up financially—he lived in a cheap small back bedroom somewhere in the 30s on the East side as I recall & took his meals outside[94]—he was so hard up in fact that I not only gladly loaned him some money at various times but often took him out to dinner & gave him a square meal, all of which was a great pleasure to me on account of our unbroken friendship. Beyond the fact that he was with McClure's I know nothing about his position with that firm; his disposition was very reserved bordering almost on shyness & he made new friends very slowly—in fact I think that Fred. A. Juilliard, U.C. '91, who was living in New York, and I were about the only intimates he had. He spoke very little of his affairs or of his writings & nothing of his ambitions beyond hoping to make good someday.

When the Spanish war broke out I was a first lieutenant in the 71st N.Y. Infantry & just before we left for Cuba Norris came out to Hempstead, L.I., where we were camped to say good bye to me, telling me at the same time that he hoped to get there as a correspondent; so I was not surprised to see him turn up one day shortly before the battle of San Juan. Jim Archibald was with him & they were a sorry looking couple—I know Norris never knew how to rough it & if Jim Archibald did, his appearance was decidedly against him—neither had any kind of equipment & apparently they had not been near soap & water or a razor for some time. They had no rations & were ravenously hungry, so I not only invited them to share my next meal with me, but gave them hardtack, bacon & coffee to take with them. As I now recall, I saw them several times later before the surrender, but Norris never mentioned any of his writings or his experience. I saw nothing of him during the fighting, & learned later from him that he was at El Caney. Whether he & Archibald were together the entire time he was in Cuba I don't know. Gen. Rethers,[95] now retired & living in Washington was a '93 Fiji, & was a first lieutenant in the 9th U.S. Infantry in Cuba. He knew Norris in Berkeley, but I don't know whether they met in Cuba or not. I see him quite often & will gladly ask him to write you if he knows anything of interest.

Miss Eleanor Davenport who lives on Jackson St., near Fillmore, in San Francisco, (see telephone directory for correct address) was a great friend of Norris & of his mother during his college career & I am sure she also will be glad to assist you.

Such in brief & in the rough are my recollections after a lapse of over thirty years, but, meager as they are, I hope they will assist you in your work.

Yours truly,
E. A. Selfridge

23 / Frank M. Todd

Probably Norris's most articulate classmate was Frank Morton Todd (1871–1940). Although not members of the same fraternity—like Hull McClaughry and Stanly Easton, Todd was in Delta Kappa Epsilon—they shared interests at Berkeley, for Todd was editor-in-chief of the 1894 *Blue and Gold* for which Norris served as an artist, both were founding members of Skull and Keys, both had an association with *The Berkeleyan* during its first year, and both took an active role in preparations for their class's Junior Day exercises. Following Todd's graduation in political science in 1894, he took a law degree at Harvard, where he and Norris continued their friendship, as they also did upon their return to San Francisco the next year. Soon, both became reporters, but where Norris turned to fiction, Todd opted for journalism, working for a succession of newspapers and periodicals, including the *Merchants' Association Review* as editor, the *Argonaut* as managing editor, the *Chicago Daily Journal* as chief editorial writer, and in the same position for the San Francisco *Bulletin*, from which he retired in 1926.

Source: Frank Morton Todd. "Reminiscences of Frank Norris," March 1908, holograph, Frank Norris Collection, BANC MSS C-H 80, The Bancroft Library, University of California, Berkeley.

[. . .] Frank Norris entered the U.C. in 1890 as a member of the class of '94. He was unknown even to the members of his own class, and attracted little attention until preparations were under way for the celebration of Bourdon Burial, an elaborate ceremony formerly held by the Freshmen at the close of their first year, when the most difficult work in mathematics and English was supposed to have been completed. Bourdon was a mathematician and Minto the author of a book on English Literature.[96] Frank's success in English and his failure in mathematics made his selection as Damnator of Bourdon peculiarly appropriate, and he was grateful for an opportunity to consign Bourdon and his followers to the lower regions. In their efforts to break up the Freshman celebration, the Sophomores, natural enemies of the Freshmen in all things, went so far as to kidnap the Freshman speakers, Norris along with the others. After several days his classmates located him in a house where the Sophomores held him prisoner, and he was rescued. As a precaution against further interference he was secretly conveyed to the chapter house of Phi Gamma Delta, one of the best known of the Greek letter societies in college, at that time located on Dana St. within half a block of the University grounds. During the week he was in hiding there our friendship began and ripened into a delightful intimacy which continued until his death in October 1902. Among the pleasant recollections of that early friendship are the late suppers we enjoyed at Denny Haggerty's, whither we used to betake ourselves, first making sure that no lurking Sophomores were about.

On the night of June 9th, 1891, Frank rode triumphant in the Bourdon procession, and as the coffin was consigned to the flames, delivered his maledictions loud and deep on the inventor of mathematics and on all of his disciples. Many an over-ripe egg did the Sophomores hurl that night in their efforts to bring their enemies low. On the next [day], June 10th, Frank was initiated into the fraternity of Phi Gamma Delta and became one of its most enthusiastic members. His room in the chapter house was a wonderful den filled with queer things he had picked up in France—a steel helmet with linked mail, foils and masks, sketches and caricatures, the bones of a hand hanging in a manacle, a skull from whose toothless jaws a stuffed snake crawled, a scorched manuscript page of *Mignon* from the burned Opéra-Comique in Paris.[97]—Many a pleasant evening we spent in Frank's room, smoking, singing, and telling stories. After our recitations for the next day were prepared, and sometimes before, a cry of "burn gang" would be raised, and we would go hammering at Frank's door, which he would open from where he sat, by means of an ingenious arrangement of pulleys and cords. Then out would come the battered and abused old banjo from which he would produce a series of frightful discords, which we accepted as music. Occasionally he sang us French songs which he assured us had really been set to tuneful airs, but that he had forgotten them. His recollection of airs was exceedingly faint, and we never received any positive proof in the matter.

Frank's room-mate was Seymour Waterhouse, of Waterhouse and Lester,[98] the owner of the Big Dipper Mine mentioned in *McTeague*, in which Frank describes himself as "a tall, lean young man, with a thick head of hair surprisingly gray" (383). Waterhouse is the young man with the salient jaw. He was always "Doodle" Waterhouse to us. His persistence in smoking a vile collection of vegetation which he called cigars led to the establishment of a smoking room at the rear of the house where he smoked and studied in peace and which we dubbed the "Snap Back" room.[99]

Frank's experience with pets ranged through various breeds of dogs to monkeys. The mention of Charlie Ding, the monkey, always starts a story of his escapades, whenever the old guard comes together. My introduction to Charlie Ding occurred one morning when I went in to Frank's room to call him. The room was a sight to behold. Under the bed was a large gray cat, and on top of the head board sat Charlie Ding attending to several long scratches on his face, and looking quite forlorn. Frank had found a safe retreat under the bed clothes and was sound asleep. He often affirmed that his trials with Charlie Ding, and later on with Binkie, his dog, helped to sprinkle his hair with gray.

Frank was a fair student of the things he liked. What he did *not* like he would not or could not study. Mathematics was the bane of his life and after repeated trials and failures he finally gave up trying, and so failed to graduate from college. If I remember correctly he never succeeded in removing his entrance conditions in Algebra and Geometry.

An odd thing about him when one looks back on all that he accomplished is the fact that he seemed to have plenty of leisure, and that though he wrote a good deal, and was selling much of his work, one seldom heard him speak of it except in response to friendly enquiry. He always had time to join in with the college life around him.

On pleasant evenings we used to gather on the front porch and steps and listen to the music of his orchestra. His old banjo, occasionally wanting a string, was the leading instrument in his musical collection. A tin flute, and a couple of terra cotta wind instruments (ocarinas) very much the size and shape of a large sweet potato with a knob in it, completed the quartet. The noise this wonderful quartet produced was weird but not enchanting. In spite of adverse criticism and occasional outbreaks of violence on our part the quartet continued in existence, and occasionally we deluded ourselves with the hope that it would produce a tune.

The military department at the U.C. was an eternal abomination to Frank, I suppose because it required him to attend regularly and to carry a musket, which he always insisted was the heaviest gun in the battalion; and so he felt that he was evening up old scores somewhat by neglecting to explain for several weeks his absences from drill, caused by a sprained ankle he got one night, when, with both hands full of chickens, he jumped down from a fence which separated a neighboring chicken yard from the outside world. His failure to offer any excuse for his absences brought forth a notification that he was suspended for a period of one month, and that he could not come within the University grounds. He tacked the notice on the back of the door in his room, and beneath it wrote *Hinc Illae Lacyrmae* (hence these tears).[100] Later on when his ankle improved so that he could get about he used to go out to the edge of the grounds and sit on the old brick bridge to watch the football practice. And he was so interested in the game that we could not help but feel sorry for him when we had to leave him at the bridge on our way to the campus.

During our college days and for some years afterward, there was located on the South East corner of Telegraph Avenue and Allston Way in Berkeley, a resort known as Denny Haggerty's, where the finest of steaks were served, and other things were to be had by the initiated, for the one-mile liquor law and the morals of the students were not so carefully looked after then as they are in these days. The place was well known and was well patronized by the students of the '90's and earlier. We used to meet in one of the back rooms and have our steaks and beer, quite often the beer without the steaks. We did very little harm, but we did have a mighty good time. The walls were covered as high as one could reach with the names of students, and sketches and caricatures of college from the top of the table or a chair, on those old walls, deserved all the praise we gave them.

In his Junior year Frank became a member of Skull and Keys society, much of whose ritual he revised and improved. He wrote *Our Boys*,[101] the Skull and Keys annual play, and acted the leading part. The following year he took the part of Cheviot Hill in W. S. Gilbert's *Engaged*.

The Dispensator on class day 1893, R. L. Hathorn, presented a pig to the Dekes, a college fraternity which had managed to distribute most of the class honors that year among its own members.[102] The presentation took place, but the pig had mysteriously disappeared. As a matter of fact it had been killed a couple of days before in the back yard of the Phi Gamma Delta chapter house, after an elaborate and amusing ceremony prepared by Norris. The pig was roasted and served whole at a big dinner on class day night. Since then Pig dinner has been an annual event with Phi Gamma Delta chapters in Berkeley, and the alumni from far and near gather to do honor to Sir Pig. The idea spread to the eastern chapters of the order, and now the Norris dinner as they term it is held annually by them all. On last Saturday night, March 21, the chapter in Berkeley held its Pig Dinner with its silent toast to the memory of Frank Norris.

On his return from Harvard in 1895 we organized the Thirteen Club, composed of 12 of the alumni of the Berkeley chapter, and one member from the Stanford chapter. Dinners were held several times during the year. The Cliff House, Frank's, the Old Poodle Dog, Luna's, the restaurant mentioned in *Blix*,[103] were our gathering places. These dinners brought forth stories from Frank and from others, that would have delighted a much larger audience than our baker's dozen.

On the night he left for South Africa in the interest of the S.F. *Chronicle* I accompanied him across the Bay and left him at 16th St., Oakland. He exacted a solemn promise from me that I would write him an account of the Stanford-California football game immediately after the last whistle blew. He reached South Africa just in time to get mixed up in the Jameson raid, was arrested and finally ordered to leave the country. My letter was months on his trail, and did not overtake him until he returned to San Francisco. Mention of that letter in after years would put him in good humor immediately. He always insisted that it must have been written under the most trying circumstances.

Frank was at the surrender of Santiago during the Spanish American War. In a frame in our library now we have a piece of the Spanish flag that spread over the city. His friends here were always with him. His answer to our invitation to a football game & dinner on Thanksgiving Eve, 1900, was the pathetic "Exile's Toast."

Nothing showed better the manfulness of his spirit and the greatness of his heart than his chivalrous defense of Dr. Lawlor of the Glen Ellen Home for Feeble Minded Children.[104] Dr. Lawlor was at that time Supt. of the home and had been attacked by the public press and accused of negligence of duty. To defend Lawlor it was necessary not only to oppose a mad flood of popular prejudice, but to assail almost the entire daily press of San Francisco; and from a man whose bread depended on his fame, that called for courage. He did it in no compromising half-hearted way.

The San Francisco *Argonaut* gave him space, and he gave the offending editors such a castigating as they had not read for many a year and one they never dared openly resent. It was a brave and generous act. It put upon him the mark of nobility, the unmistakable stamp of the "gentleman unafraid."[105] It showed that besides being a great artist, he was a great citizen. Be Lawlor innocent or guilty, to Norris, who went to Glen Ellen and investigated the superintendent of the home, he was a blameless man, whose reputation was being slaughtered in the shambles of politics, and single handed he went to his aid.

In 1902 Frank was back again in San Francisco and he had the simple human weakness to say that he was back because he was homesick, liked the city better than any place in the world, and wanted to be with the fellows he used to know. He bought a small place near Gilroy, spending every cent he had in the world, which was characteristic of him. He could not keep away from the chapter house in Berkeley and was over every few days. Everything about the place interested him, and he delighted and amused us all with stories and anecdotes picked up in his wanderings. The Saturday before his death he and his wife attended the California-Stanford freshman football game on the campus, and afterward had dinner with us at the club-house.

Frank had no satellites. He was above it. He was thoroughly a part of his crowd and never tried to be a larger part than the other fellow. He was as simple and natural in his manner as a child. He was very human, and had his weaknesses and we loved him for them.

And speaking of his plans for the future, he told me a few weeks before his death, that he felt completely "written out," that he was going to take a long rest and then by slow stages journey westward to Southern France gathering material for "The Wolf," the last of the trilogy, *The Octopus, The Pit* and "The Wolf."

Norris had just begun to grow. The sap was still rising in him.

It was yet spring time in his brave heart, and morning in the day of his achievement. He died in the city he loved best of all cities, the city where his happiest years were spent, where he met and won his wife. He was not only a genius; he was a genius who was brave, just, clean, and actively righteous. What such a man could have done for humanity, had Fate given him 32 more years, it is bewildering to try to imagine.

24 / Seymour Waterhouse

Norris's first roommate in the Fiji house at Berkeley was Seymour Waterhouse (1871–1949). Waterhouse, a serious student, graciously performed the role of straight man to Norris's more exuberant japes, in the process acquiring a variety of nicknames, two of which Norris himself originated, "Doodle" (see Selfridge, chapter 22, this volume), which Waterhouse in turn bestowed on his daughter, Dorothy L. Thompson (1903–?), and "Strainer." A third was "Watson," as well as the middle initial "W," both of which Waterhouse himself created (Crisler 1986, 211). Unlike other members of Phi Gamma Delta, Waterhouse participated in almost no other aspect of campus life, another difference between himself and Norris. Even so, the two remained in contact with each other long after their university days. Probably during his senior year Norris drew a pencil sketch of his roommate, which he inscribed "à mon ami 'Strainer.'" While writing *McTeague* he visited Waterhouse twice at the Big Dipper Mine, which his father owned and which Norris incorporated into the novel; during his first visit there in September 1896, he drew a portrait of Waterhouse's wife-to-be, Annie Cadwalader (1875–1961), dated September 9, 1896, and three years later he drew another to accompany his note to her and Waterhouse, congratulating both on their forthcoming nuptials to occur in April 1899 (Crisler 1986, 212, 63). Finally, he inscribed copies of *McTeague* and *The Octopus* to Waterhouse (ibid., 214, 221). Nor was their friendship one sided: the Waterhouses visited the Norrises in their home in Roselle, New Jersey, during the Christmas season of 1900 (ibid., 63, n. 3).

Source: Seymour Waterhouse. Interview notes by Franklin D. Walker, June 5, 1930, Franklin Dickerson Walker Papers, BANC MSS C-H 79, The Bancroft Library, University of California, Berkeley.

He showed me a number of photos, papers, etc., which he loaned to me. Note one of Marsh, Hathorn, Waterhouse, and Frank. Transit photos. Has other photos including one of room in Fiji house and one of Frank in Uitlander outfit,[106] which he will send when he finds time. Letters burned in S.F. fire.

He came up to the Big Dipper mine soon after he returned from South Africa and he was probably recuperating from his illness. Was wearing Uitlander outfit. George Blood and Ralph Hathorn were up there at the time.

Waterhouse was running the mine all of the time he was in college and for this Frank admired him particularly.

South Africa. Frank spoke about having letter of introduction to John Hays Hammond[107] and being invited to dinner. No dress clothes, so Hammond wore his business suit to make him comfortable. He had no use for the Boers.

Late in 1897 he came up to write *McTeague*; two or possibly three months. Before the snow came, but it was getting cool; note collars in picture. He met him at Colfax and they rode out on horses on the trail. He was always making notes; he wrote most of *McTeague* there—had part in ms.—but left with some undone as he read a later part of it to him at another time. He didn't think much of it as a story as it was lugubrious. Tried to advise him to revise his work a little more carefully but Frank maintained that that tended to kill the freshness of it. He is quite sure that Frank was not working on any novel at the University; they were rooming together.

Frank gathered in a good many copies of *Yvernelle* and burned them up. Tried to get his but he would not give it to him.

Doesn't remember his saying much about Cuba but remembers that Selfridge spoke of having seen him there.

Waterhouse was married in April 1899 and he and his wife called on Frank and Jeannette in Roselle. Remembers the heavy curtains which seemed to him to be gloomy. He was reading mss. and traveled back and forth to N.Y. a good deal. They walked down to the drug store with Frank in his shirtsleeves.

He didn't see him much after he left in 1897.

At Big Dipper Frank might have been observing carefully but it was not apparent. Made notes. Didn't want him to tear down the shack to make improvements. Waterhouse was carrying gun as there was a dispute with the neighboring mine and the Cornishmen had been taking shots at him. One through saddle and one through hat. Frank had him pull out his revolver for the picture.

College. He loved Frank very dearly; a wonderful friend. They were not at all alike; he didn't take Frank's writing very seriously. They never made fun of him because he was too dignified. He liked Le Conte greatly. Was in love with a college girl but can't remember her name. He was a fine poker player and they spent much time playing penny ante. A good bluffer. No puritanical strain in him.

In making his will his father left him one dollar. Not bitter about it.

He wasn't such a good fisherman in college; too much waiting. Suffered much from indigestion of the stomach at that time. A moderate eater. Very polite. Taught him much.

He liked a ne'er-do-well named Eugley who didn't turn out to amount to much.[108]

Resentful toward military. Suspended. Refused to go on the grounds with Waterhouse. Typical.

Mrs. Norris gave a reception after the printing and success of *The Octopus*. Frank and Jeannette were there. Very grand.

25 / Benjamin Weed

With a common interest in literature generally and drama in particular, Benjamin Weed (1869–1941) and Norris could easily have been natural college comrades. Yet such was not the case. Although Weed was not one of Norris's intimates, both served as class officers during their junior year, Weed as president and Norris as historian, both worked with *The Berkeleyan*—Weed was its first editor and Norris drew its second cover—both were members of Skull and Keys, and both were on the staff of the 1894 *Blue and Gold*, Weed as assistant editor and Norris as artist. Thus Weed's memories of Norris's involvement in college dramatics is important, though his own essay, "The Genesis of the Greek Theater," a kind of introduction to the student plays collected in *California Play and Pageant* (1913), which included Norris's own effort, "Two Pair," belies his hazy recollection in his interview with Walker that Norris possibly had "some connection" with "Vehmegericht," the first play performed where the Greek Theatre at Berkeley now stands, a spot Weed himself selected for the play's performance.

Source. Benjamin Weed. Interview notes by Franklin D. Walker, March 21, 1930, Franklin Dickerson Walker Papers, BANC MSS C-H 79, The Bancroft Library, University of California, Berkeley.

Weed's memories of his college days were not very vivid and, although Norris remained in his mind as a person, he could add few details to the picture.

Of professors of the time Gayley was most interesting in his reading of poetry, Lange a good scholar,[109] Bradley of the old school. "Uncle Joe" Le Conte was the favorite and the most influential man on the campus. His two courses were "Geology" and "Reproduction."

There was little literary life on the campus and practically no discussion. Norris' interest in Zola must have been entirely personal.

Norris probably took military in senior year to make up for cuts.[110] It was looked upon as a bore as it is today.

His failure to graduate was reputed to be due to inadequacy in math. Harry Wright coached him.

Personal appearance. Slender, dark hair, slight mustache & side-burns, marked sallow complexion with pitted effect, immaculately dressed.

He was a good mixer, open & sincere, almost "gushy." Foreign air partly due to careful dress. Thoroughly at home in society. Remembers his saying that he preferred a well dressed woman to a beautiful one.

He was fond of dogs.

He always impressed one as being a man with a purpose, clear headed, and one who knew the world and had interest in literature as well as being able to write. *Yvernelle* was not read on the campus. Norris loaned him his copy.

Little sympathy for the *Occident*.[111]

Remembers little about Bourdon, *Smiles*, Junior Farce, "Vehmegericht."

Under the impression that Norris was connected with "Vehmegericht." Maida Castelhun would know.

Skull & Keys. Oedipus in Plumptre translation to be produced. Meeting with G. M. Richardson, Kellogg, Clapp, Loring. Thought Norris was to play Creon.[112] Fell through. Norris may have taken part in one of Skull & Keys plays.

Friends. Frank Todd
Gelett Burgess
Jessica Peixotto
"Dusty" Rhodes (hiking trips?)[113]
Dr. Houston
Harvey Corbett
Charles Keeler[114]
Ralph Hathorn (Michigan fishing trip—see cards)
Harry Wright
William Denman

He met Norris after return from S. Africa. They had been in the "Louvre."[115] Noticed his hair had become white.

He was not much interested in women in college days.

He possibly contributed to *The Wasp*.[116]

Morse Stephens gave a memorial dinner at which Todd & Weed spoke.[117] Held in Bohemian Club.

26 / Harry M. Wright

One of Norris's earliest friends, their friendship dating from their student days at San Francisco Boys' High School, was Harry Manville Wright (1872–1947). Wright, a member of Phi Gamma Delta, Skull and Keys, and the editorial board of *The Berkeleyan*, was a proverbial big man on campus: he attained the highest rank among student cadets, leading them as colonel; garnered his class's medal; delivered the major student address at commencement exercises; contributed pieces to various campus publications; and took the role of Mr. Fitzwoggins in Norris's "Two Pair," the Junior Day farce. With much in common, the two friends kept in sporadic touch following their time at Berkeley. Wright eventually entered Harvard Law School, from which he was graduated in 1900; during his two years there, he visited Norris in New York, and Norris wrote him several letters in which he kept his fraternity brother abreast of his novelistic progress with *Moran*, *McTeague*, and *The Octopus* (Crisler 1986, 49–50, 61, 74–75). Three decades later, on September 11, 1931, Wright, by then a respected judge in California, wrote Walker to clarify that Fijis aimed the famous "goop" episode not at Norris but at his former roommate Seymour Waterhouse—Norris's model for the testy Annixter in *The Octopus*—suggesting that even after thirty years Wright's memory of ancient college escapades was still remarkably fresh.

Source: Harry M. Wright, "In Memoriam—Frank Norris: 1870–1902," *University of California Chronicle* 5 (October 1902): 240–45.

It is hard to write of Frank Norris as of one whose work is done; the fact is hard to realise and harder to accept. It is proper, however, that in this journal should appear the tribute we give to the dead, for he was not only a distinguished but a very loyal and enthusiastic son of this University. His work in American letters is for more competent hands than mine to write of. To me he was always a very dear college friend and it is out of the intimacy of those years together that I can speak, with knowledge, of the man he was outside of his books.

Norris was twenty years old when he entered the freshman class of the University in 1890. He was born in Chicago and with the exception of two years abroad, he had lived for most of his life in San Francisco. His earliest bent was toward art. He spent a few years at the Mark Hopkins Institute, if I mistake not, and then went to Paris to study in Julian's *atelier.* He learned a great deal about French literature while in Paris, and was unconsciously influenced a good deal by the French view of life—especially the love of beauty and of the pleasant side of existence. He threw himself with zest into the study of mediaeval French armor, costume and architecture. There is a story of his in the *Overland Monthly,* somewhere in the files of '95 or '96, which shows the result of this boyish enthusiasm. But he never became an artist, possibly because he did not persevere long enough to reach proficiency. Quite frequently he used to illustrate his own earlier stories; the *Blue and Gold* of the different years of his college life and later the *Overland Monthly* show some of his work.[118] It was not very good; his figures were apt to be wooden and the whole effect rather amateurish. His purely decorative work was more successful, though often imitative. I speak of this period of his life simply to suggest the influence which this artist life may have had in the development of his genius.

When Norris entered college I doubt if he had any friends here at all—the years of art study had broken off the friendships of the preparatory school. I remember him as a tall thin man, very dark, with hair just beginning to show the gray that was afterward so characteristic, his fashion of wearing a small moustache and side-whiskers giving him a rather foreign appearance that only wore away with longer acquaintance. He was slow in making friends at this time, strangely enough, for he was one of the most attractive men I ever met. When in the latter part of the second term he was named as one of the Bourdon speakers, there was some criticism of the freshman president for putting in an unknown man. Norris never had an opportunity to justify his selection; the sophomore class abducted him three days before the celebration and kept him in Oakland till it was finished.[119] Soon afterward he was asked to join the Phi Gamma Delta fraternity, and no man has ever shown so ready an appreciation of this offer of friendship from his fellows or given in return such wealth of comradeship.

Of Norris's work as a student there is little to be written, of his student life a great deal. Some college president has said that a good part of education is in rubbing against the walls of a great university. Frank Norris's university education was mostly of this kind. He hated study of the methodical sort and employed every means to avoid it. It may be a disappointment to classical scholars who have noted the effectiveness with which in *The Octopus* he uses the device so familiar in Homer and Virgil of reiteration of descriptive phrases, to learn that he knew no Greek and had his friends help him with his Latin which he hated heartily. He always passed by a scratch. It is just to say that his preparation had been poor. He liked history and I believe did good work in English literature. Minto and the prose composition of the freshman course in English were an abomination to him. In French he must have taken every course that the University offered, partly because he liked the literature and the genial professor who taught it,[120] but not a little because preparation of recitations was to him unnecessary. He took no philosophy or science, except the two courses of Professor Joseph Le Conte and those only for love of the man. Mathematics was his *bête noire.* As every examination approached he employed a competent tutor with a view of clearing away his entrance mathematics, but failed time after time. He never attained regular standing and never graduated. I remember once finding him in his room working hard and in great distress of mind, in preparation for an examination in algebra. His rather heroic method was to learn by heart the various demonstrations of the text; he simply refused altogether to exert his mind to reason it out.

In everything that went to make up student life outside of class-rooms, he found a keen delight. To him who was always seeking for real life, this and not study was the real life *par excellence* of the college period, which he would not live again; and so he lived it with all his might. He was always ready for any college prank or celebration and never missed a rush or a football game. Indeed he was an enthusiastic spectator of a game on the campus only a week before his death. His greatest joy in college, however, was in the club life of his fraternity. He was an ideal club man; he had the social gift beyond any man I have known. And all the time he was storing up material for his later work. The character of Annixter in *The Octopus* in the early part of its development is one of his club friends to the life, and many of the incidents in his books actually happened within the walls of the fraternity house.

With all his distaste for the grind of hard study, however, he was anything but an idler. He read a great deal. It was then, I think, that the influence of Zola began to exert itself. He read much, always of course in the original, and was an enthusiastic admirer of the French realist, refusing even to consider apology necessary for his frequent grossness. It is only in his later work, however, that Zola's influence can be seen. Norris scribbled quite a bit while in college for the college papers, and occasionally for the *Argonaut.* I doubt if he wrote anything of particular merit at that time—it was a time of whimsies when he would write his name with a "y," and of very evident imitation of Richard Harding Davis[121] and of Kipling, in the order named. Exception should be made of his Junior Day farce, which showed effective handling of humorous situations, and especially of *Yvernelle*, his first ambitious work. *Yvernelle* was a long poem of mediaeval love and chivalry in the style of Walter Scott, which was brought out in holiday form by Lippincott in 1892. It was the work, I think, of his freshman and sophomore years. To his friends it always seemed a great book, but it is a fact nevertheless that it had only a passing interest for the literary world, a circumstance which, let us hope, merely points to the obsolescence of its literary form.

I cannot now remember whether Norris had fully made up his mind to follow literature until after he left Berkeley in 1894. The succeeding year at Harvard, however, was given to earnest work with this purpose directly in view. He often spoke of the value of that year in teaching him the technique of his art.

What follows of his career is more or less matter of common knowledge. He went to South Africa in 1895 as a correspondent. After his return to San Francisco in '96 he began a literary apprenticeship of two years on *The Wave*, a San Francisco weekly that has since suspended publication. He wrote many short stories, some of remarkable power. *Blix* and *A Man's Woman* are of this period. *Moran of the Lady Letty*, a vigorous sea-story, attracted the attention of certain New York publishers and through them Norris was sent to Cuba as a correspondent during the operations around Santiago. Then began a connection with the New York house that was but recently terminated. Hitherto he had only been learning his art and trying his powers, "flying kites," as he expressed it.[122] *McTeague*, which appeared in March, 1899, was his first work of note and established his reputation at once as a novelist of the first rank. Its fidelity to detail and tremendous force are reproduced in *The Octopus*, his last published work, which shows, however, a greater refinement of style and an absence of the grossness often present in the earlier work.

A word with regard to his methods of work may be of interest. He was always gathering material and jotting down ideas in a little note book. In working up a theme, he made it a rule to get his impressions at first hand. In preparation for *The Octopus* he spent several weeks on Gaston Ashe's ranch in Monterey county.[123] He interviewed C. P. Huntington,[124] and the pen-picture of Shelgrim is the result. When his material was gathered, he worked continuously till his task was done. It was as if he were under the whip. An incident of a week I spent with him in New York in the holiday season of 1899 will illustrate this. We had spent the evening at the theatre and had supper afterwards and then a long chat till after midnight in his big bare room on Washington Square. About two I retired, but Norris, to my surprise, sat down at his table and wrote for another hour on *McTeague*, which was then literally seething in his brain. He said he had to get his ideas on paper.

I have made no effort to give a critical estimate of Frank Norris's work—that is for other pens. The purpose of this hurriedly prepared article has been to tell some things that only personal acquaintance would reveal. It is impossible to give more than a faint idea of the personality of the man as his friends knew him. A surpassing personal charm, a ready wit, and a capacity for finding the joy of life—all these were his in full measure. He was always the same to his friends;

he never used people as a means of advancing himself, and he never truckled or toadied to the powerful. He was simple and unaffected and always sincere to his friends and enemies alike, a strong friend and an open enemy. His death removes from American letters the most promising personality of recent years, and from among those who loved him a true friend and an "acquaintance tried."

Source: Harry M. Wright. Interview notes by Franklin D. Walker, April 7, 1930, Franklin Dickerson Walker Papers, BANC MSS C-H 79, The Bancroft Library, University of California, Berkeley.

Wright was a good friend of Norris during the major part of his life and in addition is gifted with an excellent memory and conservative outlook on things. He attended S.F. High School; was in Norris's class and fraternity; taught school in Lowell high school, S.F., for three years after graduating, having Charles in class who even then was imitating his brother; was thus in S.F. during *Wave* period; went to Harvard to law school in fall of '97; went down to visit Norris near Christmas of '98; returned to S.F. in '99 and thinks he remembers seeing him later. (Also North to Nome in gold-rush.)[125]

Did not pledge Norris to fraternity till spring of year because they thought he was a Jew. Norris was as pleased as a child to join. Moved into fraternity house on Dana where he lived in room right front upstairs; decorated with medieval casque, skeleton hand, woman's bust.

He was indisposed toward any violent exercise and not overly strong. Remembers him in black tights in the gym; not much muscle on parallel bars, looked like a great spider. Slight. Disliked military. Only sport was fencing and he was pretty good at it. Wright had learned at Olympic Club;[126] Norris used French guard, could always ping Wright. Disliked hiking—had turned down one summer invitation with Wright.

He was not in S.F. high school in '89. (Norris.)

He was not too inclined to work on studies and found the chief value in college in the extra-curricular life; pranks, binges, etc. Of special interest was his connection with Bourdon. It was found out by the Sophomores that he had been elected to one of speaking positions. They kidnapped him a couple of days before the event, keeping him in a barn in Oakland. The night of the Bourdon the frosh had rigged up a movable catafalque which they dragged out and burned—hence succeeded. Norris turned up the last moment but was of course unable to speak. He always entered into pranks with full zest.

In studies, he took the ones that were easiest, English and French, the latter because he knew the language. Wright took no French. Norris would have liked to graduate but did not wish to apply himself to things he did not like, especially mathematics. Impression was that each year he boned to pass entrance exams. Would see him trying to learn the formulae—remonstrated—tried to show that it could be done by reasoning but Norris did not feel that way about it. Wright did not know of the Leuschner coaching. Norris liked Paget very much. Interest in Zola earlier. Le Conte a greater personality than teacher and evolution a fairly fixed thing with the undergrads at time. Norris was a good orthodox Episcopalian—one thing one did not question. Influence of mother. He was much amused in Le Conte's course in reproduction and gleefully repeated the story of the spider with the seminal fluid on its feelers. "Madam, it is for the good of the race." (In high voice.) Don't remember the ethical society.[127] Wright was not in the house during the last two years.

R. H. Davis makes a great hit with "Gallegher"[128]—something new; about journalism in journalistic style. Norris constantly interested in Zola. Wright did not like grossness. That was what he was known for. Norris always repeated that Zola dealt with reality.

Norris chased around a good deal, drank, but never in the presence of ladies (gentlemen did not do so in those days), was in no sense a Puritan. Had had his affairs and always rather liked flashy women—his wife was rather inclined to be flashy. Norris always dressed extremely carefully and expected that of others; he was quite well-off at this time.

Bouguereau had been one of his instructors in Paris. He brought home some of the studies. Never seemed to get his figures in proportion but did well at designing, background, etc.

Vacations. Thinks he went up with Waterhouse to the Big Dipper mine and that Houston went along. Waterhouse is the prototype of Annixter. Rather gruff. Norris called him "Strainer" and "Doodle." He studies law by sticking the cases up around the room. One night some of the fellows put some sticky stuff in his bed and he got mad and left. Remember him driving away with a cigar in mouth—cursing them roundly. Came back later. Norris liked him. Houston was Norris's special protégé; not too much money but dressed as neatly as he could with what he had; Norris called him "Bertie."

Burgess came down to the house frequently with Norris. Norris called the white sauce on the pudding, Goop. Thinks that Burgess got the name there.

Norris married Nettie Black. Wright remembers meeting her at Norris's house in S.F. Not much impressed; did not think she came from a good family. Never did like her very much.

Norris's house was on Sacramento, near Franklin. Later owned by F. A. Hyde, who got in trouble for realty ventures.[129] Mrs. Norris a very fine, white-haired woman. He never did meet the father, who was away in Chicago most of the time (Norris and Alister, wholesale jewelers). Finally the elder Norris went off with a woman around the world. Later sued Mrs. Norris for divorce—on what grounds he does not remember. Frank was much incensed and refused to take more money from his father. Hence, when he was struggling along in S.F. and N.Y. he frequently was out the seat of the trousers. Mother suffered a good deal.

N.Y. Thinks Norris went to work reading for *McClure's* at $35 a month. Fred Juilliard ('91) knew him there. Invited Wright down to dinner from Harvard—note letter of Jeannette for time and place. Wright stayed with Norris in cheap room at 61 Washington Sq. S. (opposite the swell side). Front bedroom, double bed. Wright went to sleep, woke about two to see Norris writing—just some things he wanted to get down. Selfridge also in N.Y. and friend of Wright.

Yvernelle popular with Wright. Did not remember when written. Mrs. Norris had told him that Miss Lippincott knew Norris—met him in Paris—smitten but Frank did not react—persuaded dad to publish poem.[130]

Norris did not always get details right. He asked Wright for technical advice about injunction in *Octopus* and then got it wrong.

Remembers an excellent after-dinner speech on "Nothing at all."

Norris's death. He and his wife had taken an apartment in one of the new apartment houses; Van Ness and Sutter. His wife had just been operated on for appendicitis by Dr. Rosenstirn.[131] When wife told him pains after party were appendicitis he laughed and said that he did not have it just because she had. He laughed at operation—too late.

Mother. Doggett, New England. Prominent in Century Club and other social groups. Beautiful and white-haired. Charming manners. Doesn't remember that she acted. Came to him for legal advice. Houston's mother was one of her best friends.[132]

Frank said nothing about Cuba when he was in N.Y.

Friends Houston, Gibbons,[133] Ernest Peixotto, Burgess.

See letters.

3. Norris playing the lead role in Thomas Robertson's *Caste* in San Francisco, March 1, 1897. Courtesy of The Bancroft Library, University of California, Berkeley.

3
Apprenticeship
San Francisco and South Africa, 1895–98

Seven contributors afford insights into Norris's relatively brief literary apprenticeship during which he doggedly pursued his craft as a correspondent for the *San Francisco Chronicle*, writer and assistant editor for *The Wave* in San Francisco, and novelist whose *Moran of the Lady Letty* first appeared serially in the same weekly magazine. Most important among these contributions is, naturally, that by Jeannette Norris, consisting of notes Franklin D. Walker took during four interviews he conducted with her in May 1930. Remarkable for the comprehensive breadth of her memory, which details Norris's personality, work habits, and ideas during this period as well as after they married, they also describe the quotidian life of a writer in training, as do the recollections of Norris's boss at *The Wave*, John O'Hara Cosgrave. Simultaneously, more bohemian friends—Bruce Porter and Porter Garnett—emphasize a side of Norris's personality not seen in earlier reminiscences, that of the thoughtful observer and painstaking writer who above all desired to perfect his chosen occupation. Bailey Millard and Will Irwin shed light as well upon the novelist in the making they knew in San Francisco. The last piece in this section, Walker's notes from his interview with Bertha Rickoff, is notable as the single uncharitable commentary contributed by those who knew Norris. A confidante of Norris's mother, Rickoff jealously spurned Jeannette, blithely took credit for teaching Norris writing fundamentals, ironically deprecated the result, and unkindly disparaged his grasp of basic social expectations.

27 / John O. Cosgrave

Norris first met John O'Hara Cosgrave (1866–1947) at the end of 1891 when he began submitting some of his earliest work to *The Wave*, then owned and edited by Cosgrave, who had previously been on the staff of the *Alta Californian* under the flamboyant and outspoken John Powell Irish (1843–1923) and later a reporter for the San Francisco *Call*. Their early association soon blossomed into full friendship when, in the summer after Norris's return from South Africa, Cosgrave hired Norris as "subeditor" for his weekly. Cosgrave, a native New Zealander who had emigrated from Australia in 1885, did his best to showcase *Wave* writers, in particular in November 1897, calling attention to Norris, whose work with its "strong masculine flavor" S. S. McClure might want to consider for his magazine (C[osgrave] 1897); though not precisely a prophecy, Cosgrave's suggestion must have afforded him great satisfaction when McClure's partner, John S. Phillips, offered Norris employment with their firm less than three months later. Then in November 1900, Norris, now in a position to return the favor bestowed on him by his former boss, suggested that Cosgrave seek employment with Doubleday, Page & Co. Cosgrave did so and landed the editorship of the fledgling *Everybody's Magazine*, one in a stable of periodicals the publishing house oversaw (Crisler 1986, 125–27). Both of them now in New York, their friendship flourished, and *Everybody's* eventually published five of Norris's stories as well as a piece of investigative journalism.

Source: John O. Cosgrave to Jeannette Williamson Norris, letter [October 1902], Frank Norris Collection, BANC MSS C-H 80, The Bancroft Library, University of California, Berkeley.

Dear Mrs. Frank,

That Saturday morning I came to the office feeling in such a condition of blues that I stopped several times, en route & took myself to task.[1] What the matter was I could not think. Everything was going swimmingly, & the sky was blue. Yet I felt something was terribly wrong, that I had done something which would have a bad effect.

In the afternoon I heard. The elevator boy told me. I'm not sentimental, but I've not felt so since my mother died.[2]

You know how much I thought of Frank, how fond I was of him & how proud that I'd had a big hand in shaping the man who was the biggest force in American letters.

Entirely apart there were our years together—& they were hard years for me, I know that Frank knew me & no one except you, knew him half as well as I, & how much there was to care for & love. There's nothing any better in the male kind. Mrs. Frank, I've known no cleaner, whiter soul. They don't happen.

You & he have had a big spell of real happiness, such happiness as comes to the lap of few humans. You fitted him. He had some spells of real joy, & you gave them to him as he gave them to you. To see you together did everyone good: it was so obvious that you were all the world to one another. Frank hasn't lived in vain—& you haven't. Remember that. Don't live in vain.

It's hard to write to you. It brings home so keenly the fact that there won't be any more Frank for either of us. It's so hard to give one's highest regard, & as one goes along one doesn't love. I like lots of people very much, but there'll be with no one else the years of struggle, of makeshift, of fight that knit hands of friendship & weave them strong. Frank had his faults, but they were almost as lovable as his virtues & he was just as good & straight & sincere & true & brave as a man can be.

There's little I can do Mrs. Frank, but there's nothing you can't ask me. The D. P. people are going to make a great success of *The Pit*, if it can be made, & they say it's the best Frank has done. Certain people have written me letters about Frank. I'll send them to you, after a while.

Always your friend
J. O'H. Cosgrave

Source: John O. Cosgrave to Franklin D. Walker, letter, June 5, 1930, Franklin Dickerson Walker Papers, BANC MSS C-H 79, The Bancroft Library, University of California, Berkeley.

Dear Mr. Walker,

It is rather a larger order and more than I've time or mind to meet. I'm writing a philosophy of my own. It takes every available moment. I have no secretary so there's no one to dictate to & I don't dictate or talk easily, anyway. To answer your questions I should have to do a lot of explaining. Just when Frank came to *The Wave* I don't remember. He left it to go to New York having been sent for by Sam McClure. This was after the beginnings of *Moran of the Lady Letty.* Frank was my editorial assistant, did paragraphs, articles, editorials—anything required to fill out. I can't be sure about Justin Sturgis—whether that was one of our pen names or one that he invented for himself.[3] Probably he used several writing names. *McTeague* was written before he joined us, but published afterwards, I think. That was a development from his Harvard days. I imagine he joined with me after his return from South Africa—tho' I can't be sure. He may have broken off to go there & returned afterwards. If I remember aright he had an attack of fever there & returned the worse for wear. I gave Frank nothing—but the opportunity to practice his talent. Criticism of course. Suggestions—offering opportunities suitable to his capacity—that's all any editor can offer a writer—I must not forget sympathy & appreciation, which he had from me in full measure.

It was a subjective talent & a subjective personality. He never saw things with his eyes. He had no faculty of physical attention but after having been to a place, exposed to its stimuli he could describe it—on paper with complete verisimilitude. I used to say that his pores served as his visual organs. If he thought over a subject he wrote dully. It was not a good mind. When we needed an editorial to fill a gap—I'd ask if he had a subject. Perhaps one would occur to him. I'd say, "Now don't think—write." I have no letters of his, unfortunately. Yes, I saw him regularly until he left for California the last time. I was with Doubleday Page, editing *Everybody's Magazine.*

J. O'H. Cosgrave

I'm going abroad July 3, to be about 3 months. If you care to write me again thereafter I'll tell you more. You might also tell me something about yourself—what have you done in the writing way?

28 / Porter Garnett

Under normal circumstances Norris and Kennedy Porter Garnett (1871–1951) might have been poised to become great friends rather than merely acquaintances who moved in similar circles and thus had other friends in common. For as an artist, writer, fine printer, librarian, illustrator, and bookbinder, Garnett clearly embraced many pursuits that had also appealed to a young Norris. But by the time their paths began crossing fairly frequently Norris had moved beyond the interests that had initially attracted him to Les Jeunes, the iconoclastic and bohemian group that Garnett, Bruce Porter, Gelett Burgess, Ernest Peixotto, Willis Polk, and various others had formed in 1895 to publish their signature journal, *The Lark*. Thus when *The Lark* died and Burgess and Garnett turned to even more outlandish productions such as *Phyllida: or, the Milkmaid*, only two issues of which appeared, and *Le Petit Journal des Refusées*, appearing only once, Norris, riding the crest of his journalistic success with *The Wave*, had already moved to New York as a serious writer. Garnett ultimately rejoined the establishment as a distinguished typographer, calligrapher, and graphic artist, but by then Norris had been dead for many years.

Source: Porter Garnett to Franklin D. Walker, letter, March 26, 1931, Franklin Dickerson Walker Papers, BANC MSS C-H 79, The Bancroft Library, University of California, Berkeley.

My dear Mr. Walker:

I am afraid that such memories of Frank Norris as I have are so slender and so diminished by the passage of time that they can furnish no worthy contribution to a biography. If anything I recall of him seems to you worth using, I hope you will preface it with this (or some other) deprecatory statement regarding its significance or value. I feel my inadequacy the more because I know that the persons whom you mention in your letter have far richer memories of him than I have.

Since I am more interested in people for what they are rather than for what they do, I did not and do not think of Frank Norris as a literary man, but rather as a companionable person, gentle, humorous and alert, with whom conversation occasionally turned on literary matters. I recall his saying once (a little naïvely perhaps), at the time when Zola was beginning to influence his approach to writing, "The important thing in writing is *not* to be literary."

Such, shall I say, "sophistical" declarations have since then become commonplace among both amateur and professional free spirits, but Frank Norris was not one of these and we must accept his utterance as sincere. Revolutionary and near-revolutionary ideas in the 90's were usually sincere. They were not, moreover, ready-made ideas such as are to-day caught on the rebound and juggled (often very cleverly) by the members of that Cult of Defiance which so divertingly combines "sophistication" (without understanding the meaning of the word) and naïveté.

In the statement I have quoted Norris was, I think, voicing his repudiation of those early and decidedly "literary" efforts of his such as *Yvernelle*. That "First Period" of his represented a phase through which all young writers of his time had to pass. It was before the day of the disillusioned adolescent whose resolute realism Norris in a way foreshadowed.

I remember his interest in Theodore Dreiser's *Sister Carrie*, of which he had somehow acquired a copy of the suppressed and now extremely rare first edition. He gave it to me shortly before his death, and it remained in my possession (unread) until it was burned, with the rest of my books, in the San Francisco fire of 1906. Had I it now I should gladly part with it (still unread and for a consideration) to any first-edition fanatic.

What I shared with Frank Norris during our rather brief acquaintanceship was not so much an interest in literature as an interest in the raw material of literature—a life. I did not read his books when they were published and have not to this day read one of them. But from what I have been told about *Blix*, I am inclined to believe that it reflects certain phases of life in old San Francisco that we observed in one another's company.

Norris in common with some of the rest of us (Gelett Burgess, Bruce Porter) enjoyed an occasional evening spent in the then unexploited Latin quarter. I remember such evenings in a certain Mexican bodega on a back alley, where red wine was served in tin pint-measures for ten cents. We did not go there as slummers (slumming was then unknown) but for a table, some chairs, something to drink, and the enjoyment of that all but vanished pastime, conversation. I remember also our visits to more than one "*bocce*" court, dimly lighted stretches of packed earth hidden in the interior of a block of ramshackle wooden houses, where, when not occupied by clamorous Italians, we would try our novice hands at this Mediterranean version of the ancient game of bowls.

All of this, as you see, adds little or nothing to the picture of Norris.

There may be, however, some slight biographical interest in a discovery I made on one of these occasions, namely that Norris (at that time at least, it must have been 1897) was surprisingly undeveloped muscularly. His experiences in the Far North would seem to belie this statement and there would really be no reason for mentioning it but for the fact that the softness of his biceps was so extraordinary that the impression made upon me by this chance discovery, amounting to astonishment, has ever since been fixed in my mind.[4]

Norris was idolized by his mother, a circumstance which he doubtless found easier to accept than the lionizing to which he was at one time subjected. I recall in this connection his telling one of his experiences with great unction. He was, it seems, entertained by a group of ladies, one of whom, a Mrs. G—, prominent in the Browning Club, addressing him fervently with clasped hands, said, "Oh, Mr. Norris, *when* did you first *know* that you had this *wonderful* power?"[5]

Frank Norris died, as everyone knows, after an operation for appendicitis. A conversation we had shortly before he was stricken reveals an interesting aspect of his case. We were sitting one day in the "Owl's Nest" (a bay window overlooking Post Street and Grant Avenue) in the old Bohemian Club.[6] His wife had recently been operated on for appendicitis and was recovering. The disease was at that time less familiar and less understood than it is now. Norris expressed the conviction that the reason death so often resulted from appendicitis was because the patient so frequently wished the operation deferred after the physician had pronounced the case operable. "If," he said, "the operation is performed immediately upon the case being pronounced operable there is almost no danger of a fatal result." It was only a few days after this that Norris himself was stricken. The attending physician wished to operate, but Norris resisted and wished the operation deferred. The delay, which, only a few days before, he had so earnestly inveighed against, resulted in his death.

You may not have been apprised of the fact that *The Hamadryads*, the Bohemian Club Grove play of 1904, by Will Irwin, was dedicated "To the Memory of Frank Norris, verray parfit gentil knyght of letters."[7] I am not absolutely sure of the form of what is, as I think you will agree, a most fitting tribute.

Faithfully yours,
Porter Garnett

29 / Will Irwin

While William Henry Irwin (1873–1948) and Norris met only once and thus could hardly be termed friends or perhaps even acquaintances, Irwin, by his own admission in a brief note to Jeannette when Norris died, felt great admiration for Norris as both writer and man. Irwin had good reason to admire Norris, for his first employment after he left Stanford in 1898 was on *The Wave* where he took the position of subeditor, the same post Norris had vacated over a year earlier; like Norris again, he had left college without a degree, expelled for high jinks. Over the next few years, Irwin's life continued to mimic his predecessor's as in succession he became a special correspondent for the *San Francisco Chronicle*, as had Norris before joining *The Wave* staff, a reporter for the New York *Sun* (1904–6)—Norris wrote articles for a number of newspapers in New York, Brooklyn, Chicago, and Boston—managing editor of *McClure's* (1906–7), where Norris worked when he first moved to New York, and finally a freelance writer, the direction Norris certainly had taken with his short stories and articles.

Source: Will Irwin, "Introduction," *The Third Circle* (New York: John Lane, 1909), 7–11.

It used to be my duty, as sub editor of the old San Francisco *Wave*, to "put the paper to bed." We were printing a Seattle edition in those days of the Alaskan gold rush; and the last form had to be locked up on Tuesday night, that we might reach the news stands by Friday. Working short-handed, as all small weeklies do, we were everlastingly late with copy or illustrations or advertisements; and the Tuesday usually stretched itself out into Wednesday. Most often, indeed, the foreman and I pounded the last quoin into place at four or five o'clock Wednesday morning and went home with the milk-wagons—to rise at noon and start next week's paper going.

For Yelton,[8] most patient and cheerful of foremen, those Tuesday night sessions meant steady work. I, for my part, had only to confer with him now and then on a "Caption" or to run over a late proof. In the heavy intervals of waiting, I killed time and gained instruction by reading the back files of *The Wave*, and especially that part of the files which preserved the early, 'prentice work of Frank Norris.

He was a hero to us all in those days, as he will ever remain a heroic memory—that unique product of our Western soil, killed, for some hidden purpose of the gods, before the time of full blossom. He had gone East but a year since to publish the earliest in his succession of rugged, virile novels—*Moran of the Lady Letty*, *McTeague*, *Blix*, *A Man's Woman*, *The Octopus*, and *The Pit*. The East was just beginning to learn that he was great; we had known it long before. With a special interest, then, did I, his humble cub successor as sub-editor and sole staff writer, follow that 'prentice work of his from the period of his first brief sketches, through the period of rough, brilliant short stories hewed out of our life in the Port of Adventures, to the period of that first serial which brought him into his own.

It was a surpassing study of the novelist in the making. J. O'Hara Cosgrave, owner, editor and burden-bearer of *The Wave*, was in his editing more an artist than a man of business. He loved "good stuff"; he could not bear to delete a distinctive piece of work just because the populace would not understand. Norris, then, had a free hand. Whatever his thought of that day, whatever he had seen with the eye of his flash or the eye of his imagination,[9] he might write and print. You began to feel him in the files of the year 1897, by certain distinctive sketches and fragments. You traced his writing week by week until the sketches became "Little Stories of the Pavement."[10] Then longer stories, one every week, even such stories as "The Third Circle," "Miracle Joyeux," and "The House with the Blinds"; then, finally, a novel, written *feuilleton* fashion week by week—*Moran of the Lady Letty*. A curious circumstance attended the publication of *Moran* in *The Wave*. I discovered it myself during those Tuesday night sessions over the files; and it illustrates how this work was done. He began it in the last weeks of 1897, turning it out and sending it straight to the printer as part of his daily stint. The *Maine* was blown up February 14, 1898. In the later chapters of *Moran*, he introduced the destruction of the *Maine* as an incident! It was this serial, brought to the attention of *McClure's Magazine*, which finally drew Frank Norris East.

"The studio sketches of a great novelist," Gelett Burgess has called these ventures and fragments.[11] Burgess and I, when *The Wave* finally died of too much merit, stole into the building by night and took away one set of old files. A harmless theft of sentiment, we told ourselves; for by moral right they belonged to us, the sole survivors in San Francisco of those who had helped make *The Wave*. And, indeed, by this theft we saved them from the great fire of 1906. When we had them safe at home, we spent a night running over them, marveling again at those rough creations of blood and nerve which Norris had made out of that city which was the first love of his wakened intelligence, and in which, so woefully soon afterward, he died.

I think that I remember them all, even now; not one but a name or a phrase would bring back to mind. Most vividly, perhaps, remains a little column of four sketches called "Fragments."[12] One was a scene behind the barricades during the Commune—a gay *flâneur* of a soldier playing on a looted piano until a bullet caught him in the midst of a note. Another pictured an empty hotel room after the guest had left. Only that; but I always remember it when I first enter my room in a hotel. A third was the nucleus for the description of the "Dental Parlors" in *McTeague*. A fourth, the most daring of all, showed a sodden workman coming home from his place of great machines. A fresh violet lay on the pavement. He, the primal brute in harness, picked it up. Dimly, the aesthetic sense woke in him. It gave him pleasure, a pleasure which called for some tribute. He put it between his great jaws and crushed it—the only way he knew. [. . .]

30 / Bailey Millard

In his extensive memoir Frank Bailey Millard (1859–1941) neglects to mention the first interaction he and Norris had, when in January 1897 Norris responded to Millard, then "Literary Editor" of the San Francisco *Examiner*, who had written a three-part series discussing possible candidates for the honor of the "great American novel." In his response Norris suggests two possibilities, *Ben-Hur* (1880) by the popular historical novelist Lew Wallace (1827–1905), if one were thinking of the "best novel yet produced by an American author," or Howells's *The Rise of Silas Lapham* (1885), if one meant "the best interpretation of American life" (Millard 1897). Millard, who claimed discovery of Edwin Markham with the publication of "The Man with the Hoe," was a journalist and later a historian of the Bay Area. While other sources do not independently verify the intimate friendship he insists he and Norris enjoyed, he certainly kept track of Norris's career, wrote appreciatively about it, and joined in the public lamentation following his early death.

Source: Bailey Millard, "Frank Norris," *Phi Gamma Delta Quarterly* 41 (January 1903): 293–300.

[. . .] The Norris painted by some of his critics and biographers is not a man to inspire deep sentiment, but his portrait often has been loosely drawn, and from fancy, not from life. Let me tell you of the Norris that I knew.

Tall, straight, clean-limbed, with a fine, smooth, likeable face, big, brown, frank eyes, with an easily kindled smile lurking in them, and—at only twenty-five—the freely frosted hair of a man of fifty. The gray of the hair gave a strangely romantic interest to the boyish face, and in a roomful of average men the eye of the visitor—and particularly the feminine eye—invariably would be drawn to Norris. A gentle habit of speech, an easy manner, and an elusive and at times barely palpable foreign air were coupled with a charm of presence such as I have seen in few men. Yet he could be outspoken enough, as he was not without some of the male vices you are always likely to find in a catholic man, and never in a prig. In other words, he did not pose, nor preach, and was never afraid to say or do the thing that would not look well in his biography. He was a man's man and a woman's man, and what better word shall I say of him?

The young writer went east in 1897, or thereabouts, and was for some years reader for a New York publishing house. From New York came *Blix* and *A Man's Woman*, both of which novels Norris' literary friends opened with large expectations, which, unhappily, were in each case deferred. He married the beautiful young woman on whom he had modeled the character of Blix, and after that there was quite a book-publishing pause.

In September, 1898, I went to New York to do newspaper work, but remained only about two months, during which brief period I saw Norris several times and remember one happy afternoon with him, when we talked and talked, and then went to dinner at Keens chophouse, a favorite resort of Bohemian New Yorkers.[13] Norris told me of his plans. He was unsatisfied. The manuscript reading for the publishing house was irksome to him and fettered him. What he longed to do was to go back to California and work up a series of novels of the life there. And yet his daily task as the reader of unpublished fiction was not without lights as well as shades. He told me how he lately had been reading a long story written by a man who must have had wheels of very rapid revolution. There were over forty chapters of the story, and an absolutely novel situation in each chapter.

"It's all intended to be serious," said Frank, "but imagine! He has a little locomotive running about the yard after him, and he feeds it coal out of his hand."

When I shook hands with him on leaving New York he was sad of face as he said, "Can't you take me with you? I'm dying to go back to California and write my great novel."

If ever you meet a Californian exile in New York you will find him possessed of one big, burning, yearning idea, and that is to get back to the Sierran land so loved of Zeus as soon as circumstances will permit. In that Babylon of Manhattan isle no true Californian ever finds what he calls home, and whenever he watches the westering sun sinking through the red haze uplifted by the Paterson smokestacks his heart goes with it.

Frank Norris loved California. He wanted to roam its jovian plains and mountains, and he wanted to draw upon a large canvas a great story of them and their people.

When I had bidden him goodbye in New York that day he had told me he could not leave the city, yet I was not surprised when, a few months after my return to San Francisco, my office door opened one day and in sprang Frank, his eyes aglow.

"I've come back," he said, "and I'm going to get busy on that novel. Only it isn't to be one book. It's to be three—'A Trilogy of the Wheat.' The first book is to tell the story of the railroad, bringing in the old Mussel Slough tragedy, and connecting it up with the big grainfields of the San Joaquin valley. Nobody has done it, and it's great stuff. You can help me with the railroad story, and you can start me out on the wheatfield end of it, too. Who is there that can tell me all about grain-growing down that way, and who knows how the railroad has robbed the farmers?"

"I know your man," I replied. "He has lived down there, is a keen observer, and knows the ranch life. His name is Morrison Pixley,[14] and he would be a good character to put into your book. Original as they make them."

A few days later we had Frank over to our house in the Marin hills, near to where Pixley lived, and after luncheon at our table Norris and Pixley had a great talk. Frank was full of questions, and Pixley had an answer for every one of them.

I could see by Frank's animated and sometimes excited way that he was getting what he wanted, and while Pixley told him the whole story of Mussel Slough, where the embattled farmers were shot down by railroad hirelings, I could see the dark eyes of the novelist gleam. Of course, Frank had to go down into the San Joaquin country and interview a good many ranchers, but it was Pixley who started him off and who told him just where to go.

Before leaving for New York, where he returned to write the first book of his trilogy, which he already had decided to call *The Octopus*, he left some short stories with me to be published in our Sunday paper. One of these, I remember, was a tale about a young fellow who proposed to a girl in a novel way. He could see her only in the presence of others, so he wrote, "I love you" on the palm of his hand, went to meet her and, though company was in the room, managed to display his fervid words before her eyes, with the usual happy result.[15]

Norris worked like a maniac upon *The Octopus*. Puffing his perpetual pipe, he would write for hours on end, turning out as much as six thousand words a day, a literary performance that was enough to kill a much stronger man.

One day Frank Norris came back from New York looking rather pale and thin, but with eyes that burned like coals.

"I have finished *The Octopus*," he announced, "and I've put you into it. Your part is the editor who discovers the poet and prints his great epic with a sound of trumpets that brings him immediate fame. Of course, I am paraphrasing what you did with Edwin Markham and his 'Man with the Hoe.'"[16]

I thanked him and told him I would not rest until I had read about Markham and myself in *The Octopus*.

The book, when it came out, was applauded by the critics. It made a wonderful appeal. In his story of the wheat Norris struck a note that vibrated far.

He typified California after the most vital, the most searching, the most earth-gripping of European literary models—models in which everyone must recognize the saliency, the movement, the color, the virility of human life.

Norris was not vain. He did not court publicity. He was indifferent to the little "ad." While he was in San Francisco, resting up from the terrific toil of *The Octopus*, he happened to be in a public hall and to witness a little "gun play" in which he enacted a part that was altogether to his credit—that is, he helped to suppress the gun-player.[17] The local newspapers made a lot of the story, extolling Norris, and the New York dailies were clamoring for particulars. A telegram came from the *Sun* requesting an interview with Norris on the affair. The correspondent handed me the message, and wanted to know if I would telephone to Norris and arrange for the interview. I called him up at his hotel and read him the telegram over the wire. Instantly he blazed forth like the back draught of a furnace:

"Tell the *Sun* to go to hell, with my compliments."

"But you will miss a lot of New York publicity," I suggested. "Then I will miss it," was his reply.

And the dismayed correspondent actually wired Norris' fiery message across the continent to his paper. It was the disdainful fling of an author who held himself above free advertising. The *Sun* critic had treated him badly,[18] but it was an opportunity for publicity that few writers would have felt that they could afford to forego, especially in a case like his, for he had four novels on sale at the time. Perhaps it was all right, from his point of view, which was that of the artist; but think how his publishers would have gnashed their teeth had they known of it!

After a brief rest the author, then only about thirty, went back to his desk and with wonderful facility, turned out the second book of his trilogy, *The Pit*, from material gleaned by close research in the wheat marts of Chicago.

The Pit, though inferior to *The Octopus*, upon which Norris' fame always largely must rest, was a strong novel, and had wide acceptance. But after its completion Norris felt that his powers were failing.

It made me sad to see him on his return to San Francisco after the publication of this, his last, novel. Yet his dauntless spirit spoke forth in words of merry jest when he told me that he had come back to California to stay.

"I'm going to be a farmer," he said. "I've bought a place in the hills down near Gilroy. I'm going to live in a cabin there and raise fruit and write novels."

That cabin in the hills—how often I think of it! It always seems to me to have been filled full of literary promises. It stands there now. It may be occupied, but to me it is empty. Norris never wrote there. He might be writing there now, but Death spoke up suddenly and insistently, saying the one word, "No!"

Never a strong man physically, Frank had been laboring far beyond the limits of the endurance of the ordinary literary man. His digestion was badly impaired, and his heart had become weak. It seemed that in writing the finishing chapters of *The Pit* he had been running a race with death. But he did not know it, and it was not in him to capitulate even after the completion of the second book of his "Trilogy of the Wheat." When he had talked with me about his third and final book I had advised him to take a good, long rest before he should begin work upon it, and he had promised to do so.

I had wanted him to meet Herbert Bashford, an old friend of mine, then editor of the *Literary West* and now a playwright and literary editor of the *Bulletin*.[19] Norris had invited the two of us to meet him on a certain day at the Hotel Pleasanton,[20] and both Bashford and I had looked forward to the meeting with much pleased expectancy. But on the day of the proposed visit we were told over the telephone that Norris had been taken suddenly ill of appendicitis the night before, and that he had been sent to the hospital to undergo an operation. Within a day or two later I was informed that he had passed away. All that was left for me to do was to write a eulogy for my friend,[21] which I did with an aching heart. Soon after his death I had a long talk with his sweet-faced mother—a woman who came as near to my ideal of a lady as I ever have seen. She was calm as she talked with me, but I know what was beneath her calmness.

There was the more pity in the death of this brilliant young writer at the age of thirty-two because of the sad fact that his work had not satisfied him, as it would have satisfied a less ambitious writer. His was the artistic conscience of a man to whom intellectual and spiritual growth was the essential fact of life and work. Like all those who have in them the making of great artists, he cared nothing for the gauds and baubles of life; but only for the realization of his dreams of literary art.

All this is not to say that he did not succeed, though not in the large measure that would have been his had he lived. But the color of the soil was in his pages, and the blood and bones and viscera of humanity as he found it—the wholesome and the unwholesome, the pleasant and the repellant—painted with a painstaking brush. His creations, even though sometimes imperfectly individualized, were far better than the work of many others who made use of their own insufficient literary forms and set forth their own trivial estimates of life with their own weaknesses of presentation.

What Norris had written up to within a short time of his death, at the still unripe age of two-and-thirty, had been from the point of view of the earnest literary student, the Bohemian, and the young man of the world. It was often morbid and nearly always material, with little of the spirituality that one finds in such great artists as Hardy[22] and Eliot. It came from the young man enthusiastically devoted to his Zola and his Kipling, the young man who loved the stirring sight of the flying wedge, the breathless bucking of the center, the burly midwaist tackle, and the heavy fall, the young man who loved the gleam of guns, the infantry tramp, the crash of conflict, the sweat of the fight.

And undeniably the infantry tramp was heard in his work, as well as the surging bugle note of the strenuous realist. It is the swing of that infantry tramp and the insistent blast of that bugle that carry the Norris fiction over the great marshes of prolixity, through the mires of sodden brutality encountered in his pages. Many another writer with his obvious faults never could have won; but his sweeping scheme, his grip of character and his genuine humanity won for him where a less vigorous and less sympathetic fictionist would have failed.

Norris was gradually creeping away from the Zola influence, though he still believed that life was more than literature. He had written some essays in which he had maintained the idea of life as opposed to books. As an essayist he wielded a stout pen, and in each paper he could be relied upon to force his point of view throughout.

All his life he had been a city man, of city habits and of city thought, but as he attained intellectual stature there came the inevitable yearning for Nature. With his power of observation, his keen appreciation of life, what would Nature not have done for him? What artistic growth might he not have reached? What soul-growth awaited him there in the hills by that log cabin, where, listening close, he might have heard "the beating of the hearts of trees" and been led to "think the thoughts that lilies speak in white."[23] Yes, great is the log cabin idea in the literary life, and I am glad that it came to Norris, even though too late. Years of life may be passed by the artist in that artificial state which we call civilization, and for a long time he may contemplate with approval the march of that malady which manifests itself to us as "progress"; but dissent, followed by open revolt, will come in time. He will see, as Norris saw, that a protracted period of literary effort in a great urban center, full of urban ideas, must work an atrophy of the intellectual sympathies and appreciations, and thus enfeeble the creative faculty. As a vital and necessary part of his spiritual and artistic growth he must at the last come to see, as Norris saw, that one must step from the deoxygenated atmosphere and heat of rooms out into the open; that to renew the creative current and keep it at high voltage one must remain for long seasons in close connection with Nature's great storage batteries.

Our young artist was denied the life that gives—the life he had come to long for—and all that it would have meant to him; but at the end he might have said with Browning:

What I aspired to be,
And was not, comforts me.[24]

Then, too, there remains the volume of good work achieved which will not soon be forgotten. But, above all, there remains the characteristic influence, the strong example of rigorous and unstinted endeavor which must be a tonic to the minds of writers, young and old. That influence was wide, and to those of us who knew the man familiarly it was helpful and inspired us all.

31 / Jeannette Norris

As members of San Francisco society's upper crust, Norris and his future wife, Jeannette Williamson Black (1878–1952), should have had ample opportunity to meet each other long before they did in the fall of 1896, though an eight-year difference in their ages easily accounts for this. What Jeannette characterizes as "a mild flirtation," the lighthearted courtship Norris chronicles in the autobiographical *Blix*, occupied the ensuing year until her departure for her mother's alma mater, the Monticello Ladies' Seminary in Godfrey, Illinois, in September 1897. Norris visited her there before he took a position in New York with S. S. McClure's. According to Jeannette, a mastoid infection prevented her from taking a second year at the seminary. But she and Norris were by then already engaged in a lively correspondence, augmented both by Norris's return to California in August 1898 to convalesce from his Spanish-American War experience and then the next spring by his visit to undertake research for *The Octopus*. With Gertrude as escort, Jeannette later traveled across the continent to New York, where she and Norris married on February 12, 1900, at St. George's Episcopal Church. Jeannette eventually married twice more, first to Frank Carlton Preston (1884–1951), a cattle rancher in Applegate, Oregon, whom she divorced, and then, after her interviews with Walker, to Charles Newbold Black (1867–1935), president of the United Railroad Company, headquartered in San Francisco.

Source: Jeannette Williamson Norris. Interview notes by Franklin D. Walker, May 8, 1930, Franklin Dickerson Walker Papers, BANC MSS C-H 79, The Bancroft Library, University of California, Berkeley.

Mrs. Preston was very cordial and said that she would help out all she could. She said that Thomas Beer and Van Wyck Brooks had both been interested in the subject, but that they had not gone forward with it.[25] She corresponded regularly with Frank from their engagement in 1899 to marriage in 1900, receiving letters as often as one a day. On marrying, they decided to burn them and did so in one grand fire. Had kept them in pillow-case.

Frank was always very reserved with strangers and hated any kind of a scene or any kind of posing. Particularly disliked the small literary poser and tended to remain by himself in N.Y., choosing his friends carefully. He was particularly fond of Hamlin Garland and James A. Herne and his daughters.[26] Bohemianism was to him an anathema; he spoke of it as "drinking beer out of tea-cups." He remained fond of Ernest Peixotto, Gelett Burgess, and Bruce Porter, specially the last. The studio on South Washington Square which they rented after first marrying had been the Peixotto apartment. Mrs. Joseph Strong, now Mrs. Salisbury Field of Hollywood, daughter of Mrs. Osbourne, was also a very close friend, together with her son, Austin Strong, who wrote *Seventh Heaven*. They all lived in New York in those days; also Lloyd Osbourne, who was a casual friend and is now at Cap d'Antibes, near Nice.[27] These friends were all out at Gilroy when they came west. The group saw the new century in together. Mrs. Juliet Wilbor Tompkins Pottle did not know Frank well and Mrs. Preston resents her note on Frank in the *Collected Works*.[28] Says it tends to make him flamboyant.

Life in New York. Publication of *Blix* had made it possible for them to marry. Frank went to Doubleday and asked for his royalties in monthly installments—amounted to about $125 (including salary). Mrs. Norris brought Jeannette to N.Y. where they were married. Lived in an apartment in N.Y. at first but found it little to their taste. In October, 1900, they decided to get out into the country; got on train deciding to live wherever they landed. Roselle, N.J., was the spot chosen. They chose a most inadequate frame house, knowing little of the eastern climate. When winter came on Frank would go down and stoke the furnace only to stand over the grate the next morning with the announcement "There is only a little cold air coming up." They grew tired of the place and in the spring of 1901, when *The Octopus* was finished, they went to Chicago to work on *The Pit*.

In Chicago. In Chicago they were received well as the literary group there were most ambitious. The Chatfield-Taylors were the centre of the circle. They tried to go each day to the library to read through old newspapers but found social engagements too pressing. Finally at the end of the first month they bid every one farewell, saying that they were going west. They moved their hotel and spent a month in hiding.[29] When they would run across friends, they would say they had just stopped for a few hours on their way through. Thus they got a good deal of work done.

They then came west for two months and returned to New York. It was during Frank's vacation and they went up to a place which they rented at Greenwood Lake,[30] where Frank could fish; a sport of which he was inordinately fond. There they remained until the end of their vacation in October.

While writing *The Pit* they lived in an apartment out near 145th Street.[31] *The*

Pit was finished in June. The baby was born that winter. They went down to live during July with the Hernes in Southampton, where the baby was christened.[32] Jeannette prevailed on Frank to write a little squib in the baby book at this time.

They then came west and rented a house owned by his mother on Broderick and Sacramento.[33] There was a good deal of trouble in getting a nurse for the baby. Up to this time Frank had taken the baby as a joke and somewhat of an encumbrance. One day they took one of their old walks through the Presidio; one of the old steam trolleys whistled while Frank was carrying the child, whereupon it jumped in his arms, cuddling up next to his shoulder. ("By Jove, the child has brains!") They later went down to stay with the Stevensons and became enthusiastic about the cabin at Gilroy. Were planning at this time a trip around the world. Frank was very enthusiastic about "The Wolf." Planned to have wheat flow through the streets like blood.

Blix. Blix is in the main autobiographical, with a tendency to caricature his own traits. The house on the top of Washington St. hill was fictitious, as well as Blix's family. Jeannette was living with her mother and father at Octavia and Geary; "Papum" some character he knew; no Snooky or Howard. She did have a younger sister whom Frank would amuse. The sister came in one day telling how a boy was torturing a cat, Frank sympathized with her and then turned completely around and suggested they go out and torture it, intriguing her with his dramatic method. She has since become a nun. Her father had been a '49er. The sewer pipe was true. Also the part about her singing.[34]

Frank was living with his mother and Charles in their house at 1822 Sacramento. At the time the story starts they had been acquainted for some months, having met at a dance in the fall of 1896—a sub-debutante affair. They had carried on a mild flirtation until the summer of 1897, when the events of the book took place. Frank was working on *The Wave*; probably $100 a month is correct. He seemed to enjoy his work there but was developing a more serious interest in writing novels. Thinks that his parents' discouragement of "Robert d'Artois" was responsible for him losing heat in writing for a long time.

At this period he was quite mad about Kipling and read all of his stories to her. This was before the Kipling vogue. Frank always had an individual taste and even while traveling with his mother through the art galleries of Europe would insist on his own likes and dislikes in spite of the double stars of Baedeker.[35] Was also interested in Zola—is sure this interest began while at the University, not in Paris. He always appreciated Zola as a romanticist; probably first read him as a risky writer. He used to sign the books which he gave her, "the boy 'Zola.'"[36] Was particularly fond of *L'Assommoir*.

In his caricaturing himself, he loved to play with the gambling idea; he was really not particularly inclined to gambling. He also made fun of his dressing, although he was usually quite tasteful about it. Once, on his last trip to California he dressed for a party in a red and white striped shirt, telling her (his mother) it would please the crowd, and putting her in tears.

At the end of the summer she went East to the Monticello Seminary in St. Louis and there went to a boarding school. No planning to be a doctor. In the spring of 1898 Frank came through St. Louis to see her and there he received the letter from *McClure's*.

All the detail about the whale-back story was true.[37] Also the Luna Restaurant stunt, except for the red headed man. They returned there later and Frank autographed Dick's, the one-eyed waiter's, copy.[38] They did not see the couple after the restaurant incident. The encyclopedia incident was made up.

Captain Hodgson could blow smoke through his ears and was a little deaf. He was unmarried.

Frank did not like Armes; wrote a limerick on board once. He did remember and speak of Professor Le Conte.

In *The Wave* days, his best friends were Bert Houston (who was always the original for the *Overland Monthly* pictures), Jimmy Corbett, Bruce Porter, Gelett Burgess, Willis Polk, Jimmy Swinnerton, and Cosgrave. Also Fred Greenwood,[39] and Seymour Waterhouse. He admired *The Lark*, but did not contribute to it.

In morals, he had a very high ideal of the way to treat women and always stuck to it. He liked good wine, and they always had it on the table. He did not drink too much because it made him sick.

The picture of his action with the ptomaine was typical.[40] He was not overcareful of his health and always suffered from the fever; had another attack in Cuba and had to return to California. When she was ill with appendicitis, the case was none too serious and he used to bring raffia to the hospital for her to use so that she could make baskets; banned because of too many germs. He did not take his own attack seriously.

He did not drop his work on *The Wave*, but kept at it till *Moran* was written.

His relationship was fine with Charles, who idolized him. They were very close friends.

Blix was not her nickname; Buck, among others.

They made the fishing trip to San Andreas Lake. Also all of the hikes. Material compressed.

He was not a particularly poor young man at this time, as he had a home with his mother and his *Wave* salary. He was very hard up in East; had eschewed his father's allowance. Wrote he had enough for board, room, and seven stamps a week. She tried to teach him to count change. Once he came home exultant that he had done so and returned extra dollar, when of course he was wrong. She used to read some of the mss. for him at their home.

Harvard. He always said he disliked it there because of the lonesomeness. His feeling similar to those of Flandrau in *Harvard Episodes*.[41] He had a good friend there from California who went into the auto business.[42] Bring list of names. She has some of themes with Gates' comments upon them.

Isaac Marcosson was the first critic to give *McTeague* a decent write-up; in the Louisville paper.[43] Most of the early criticism was adverse; one started—"Wipe out this breed of Norrises." They often imagined what Marcosson would be like. Finally, when he came to N.Y., they found him to be a young and little Jew, but very likeable. Probably some correspondence. Has seen him frequently since then.

Another friend was Hubert Henry Davies, a young Englishman with some money, who used to be at the house frequently. He used to read the mss. for pleasure and to while away time. Went back to England, wrote *Cousin Kate* and other successes; killed self during war.[44]

John Harrold, another friend, now deceased.[45]

James Archibald. With him in Cuba. Disliked him very much. The greatest liar that ever lived. Arrogant and hard to get along with. Frank had one of few horses in Cuba; loaned it to Archibald to interview general, Archibald referred to him as his orderly. Archibald to dinner once after Boer War; said he was intimate friend of Roberts; Frank scoffed and Archibald produced letter.[46] Doesn't know what became of him. Doesn't remember Frank's publishing at time; feels that he was annoyed about it.

Frank ran into Stephen Crane. Didn't like him in Cuba because he drank too much and made a fool of himself. Did like his writing.[47]

Theodore Dreiser. Frank used to bring home Doubleday mss. in the afternoon, and she would read some. One day ran across *Sister Carrie*. Sat up all night to read it. Page also liked it.[48] Went down to Dreiser and signed contract. Doubleday came home and wife didn't like it because it wasn't pure. So finally Doubleday, Page published it without advertising; Dreiser insisted on contract. No effect until Heinemann republished it in London where it made a great impression.

Only once does she remember when Frank wrote definitely for money. They had lost $100 bill—a great loss to them in those days. He went up & wrote account of Coal Strike—not very well done.[49] Always regretted it.

People kept writing about stock market after *Pit*; Frank paid no attention to market after writing. Just part of book.

Often became too enthusiastic about dramatic pictures. She never approved of flash backs on banquet scene in *Octopus*—pure melodrama.[50]

They talked all of work over together.

Source: Jeannette Williamson Norris. Interview notes by Franklin D. Walker, May 14, 1930, Franklin Dickerson Walker Papers, BANC MSS C-H 79, The Bancroft Library, University of California, Berkeley.

Doesn't remember name of man who knew Frank at Harvard. Went into automobile agency for Pierce-Arrow afterwards.[51] Ask Charles Norris.

Jeannette's family. Her father was a north Irish protestant, born in Rathmullan, son of a clergyman. Came west in early days and mined in Virginia City; made and lost money, but cleaned enough up so that he could retire in San Francisco. Was a semi-invalid. His name was Robert Black.

Her mother was Carolina Virginia Williamson. Her parents died while she was yet a child, and she was adopted by an Englishman named Morris. Educated at Mills Seminary and Monticello, St. Louis.[52] Met Robert Black in the West.

Jeannette was born in San Francisco in 1878. There was a younger sister who later became a nun.

Manuscripts, etc., at time of death. What there was has been scattered. Frank kept no letters. Household goods had been packed in N.Y. Much of mss. were turned over to Doubleday, Page and C. N.[53] She received a number of letters from friends at the time of his death, which she has in Medford.[54] Jeannette, Jr., made a scrap book, which she would be glad to show me. Ordway 0294.[55] There was a list of things which Frank had made to be done, just before he became ill. One item was to see Doubleday, Page "and eat crow." Among other things that she turned over to Charles Norris was an illustration of a Zulu war dance made in South Africa.[56]

Mrs. Norris. Appeared very distinguished, with dark eyes and white hair, rather tall. She started the Browning society for which she was the reader. A woman of great talent, with a fine sense of the dramatic, she could interpret Browning in an unparalleled manner—had never heard a better reader, even among the professionals. She had a very wide interest in poetry and was specially fond of Shakespeare. She used to read to Billy, who could remember much of it. She was very devoted to Frank; proud of his works and only criticized parts which were contrary to her Victorian code. Used to read a great deal to Frank, Charles, and Lester in the evenings. Fond of Dickens. Must have made a great impression on Frank's mind. Is sure that he inherited his flair for the dramatic from her. She was always a high church Episcopalian, although she attended the Presbyterian in deference to Mr. Norris.[57]

Mr. Norris was a business man, not inclined to encourage Frank's tastes. His mother was responsible for the art work in Paris. At time of separation of his parents Frank was quite immature and did not react deeply. He matured slowly. He was inclined to feel resentful, and took his mother's side until a little older, when it wore off a bit. He got out of touch with his father, who remarried; felt the second woman was responsible for divorce. Gave up allowance. Father left all his money to his second wife.

Just as *Blix* testifies, Frank began to develop a sense of responsibility when he fell in love, and matured rapidly. Really lent purpose to his life. A broad and deep sympathy began to develop; his attitude was that of "Salt and Sincerity."[58] Was inclined to be conservative, but Jeannette feels that might have changed. For his ideas when in New York see Mrs. Field, who knew him well.

He was not particularly interested in formal psychology but was always fascinated by the way the mind seemed to work. No matter how deeply he felt, he could always feel a little something in him seeing the dramatic side.

He read very little during their married life, tending to drive shy of fiction. Liked books of exploration, etc. Favorites, Nansen's *Farthest North*. Also, *The Voyage of the Jeannette*. (De Long.) Of other books, his favorite of Stevenson was *The Wrecker*.[59] He read more French than English fiction. Zola, Goncourt brothers. Specially fond of Flaubert's *Madame Bovary* and *Salammbô*. Read *Madame Bovary* over several times; greatly admired style. Also fond of *Lettres de Femmes*. Hugo. Maupassant (less). He was very interested in style; valued Zola for his construction. In English fond of Howells, Henry James, especially *The Turn of the Screw*. Discovered Conrad as a reader for Doubleday. Crazy about him. Didn't care for Meredith—refused to try him; made fun of her for her interest in him.[60] He read little during these later years because he believed one should observe life.

He was very fond of Mrs. Stevenson, whom he met in N.Y. and who encouraged him a great deal. After Frank's death, Jeannette spent some time with Mrs. Norris, then went east with Mrs. Stevenson. Mrs. Field came back from Italy and they lived together for years. Mrs. Stevenson died ten years ago.

Miss Carleton, niece of Mrs. Norris, married a navy man and is now deceased.

San Diego. Mrs. Norris used to spend summers at Coronado hotel taking her boys with her.

Paris. Thinks it was three years. Greatly interested in armor; haunted the galleries. Didn't do the things he was supposed to do. Learned Old French in order to learn about armor. Used to make fun of illustrators who were incorrect. He really was not greatly interested in art; loved it for the dramatic.

Religion. Remained an Episcopalian, although he was decidedly not orthodox and disliked particularly the high church. He loved to go to the Catholic church for the beauty of the services. Rainsford in N.Y. fascinated him because of his dramatic activities and energy. He went to talk to the boys' club, which Rainsford started, going about once a week. Intrigued by his work. Was responsible for Doubleday, Page publishing a volume of his sermons and felt them trite when they got into cold print.[61] His attitude was ethical and aesthetic.

They went to church once in Roselle—high church—no good. Decided not to go again. His nature was really very spiritual. Was beginning to have ideas on raising children; should say *no* very infrequently because otherwise big *no* means nothing. Imagine man in this situation. Jeannette had been a Presbyterian but had joined Episcopalian church and had been married there for Mrs. Norris's sake.[62] Mrs. Norris not in favor of her marriage; had higher social and literary ambitions for Frank. Got to like each other later.

Belmont School. Frank attended it as charter member—forgets the name of it; named after a man, famous athlete. A fellow member was Dr. Philip King Brown of San Francisco. See him.

Sports. Never inclined to take active part in them, except fishing. A good fisher; he had a strong love for the out-of-doors. Not particularly fond of long walks. They used to take some in S.F. and Roselle. They went in strong for ping-pong when it first came out.

Book-binding. He had dropped his interest in drawing, but later became interested in individual book-binding. Decided to bind all of his paper-backed Zolas. Bought leather, endpapers, gold fabric for tooling. Once they discovered evil smell and found he had left egg in drawer which he had planned to use.

Vandover and the Brute. He didn't say much about it, used to refer to it as having good stuff in it and possibly could be rewritten some day. Wrote it either at Harvard or University of California she thinks. He let her read it once. He never did any retouching of it.

McTeague. Does not know when he began it. Had it written before they met? Turned in some part of it as an assignment at Harvard. The murder might have taken place in the Lester Norris kindergarten, started by his mother.[63] Doesn't know. Remembers his writing about *McTeague* while at Big Dipper Mine just after she went east. Thinks most of it was written there. Doesn't know its history from then until time it was published. He considered it his best book.

Blix. Liked Gibson and *Soldiers of Fortune*.[64] Description of Blix about right. Hair was much lighter in those days. She maintains eyes were not small. Dog-collar right. He wrote *Blix* in N.Y. during winter after he had come home with the Cuban fever. Did not tell her about it—only hinted. Said he had never had so much fun in writing any book. They decided to announce their engagement when it came out. She was rather startled.

Life between their courtship and marriage. The events of *Blix* took place in summer of 1897. She went east to St. Louis. He went down to Big Dipper mine. In Feb. he came through St. Louis on way to New Orleans to write up Mardi Gras. While in St. Louis he received letter from *McClure's* and decided to go on to N.Y. In May-July in Cuba. Fever. Returned to N.Y., could not shake off fever.

Decided to come west to recuperate. Having attacks every few days. In West August and September; together. Talk over *Man's Woman*. (He always had ideas for books a long time before he wrote them; seethed in mind.) Instead of going back to St. Louis she became ill with mastoid infection. It seemed at this time that he was not to have enough money for them to marry. He returned to N.Y. that winter; wrote *Man's Woman* and *Blix*, published *McTeague*. Came west in summer to work on *Octopus*. They decided she should become trained nurse. He believed in a career for women. Did not put it into effect, because Frank made arrangements to receive royalties by the month and so they were married. She was to have studied at Children's Hospital.[65]

A Man's Woman. Had got technical advice from Dr. Houston at time when he was in West. One reason why the book was not so good was that he had lost his enthusiasm for it. The ideas rather cramped the characters; let idea conflict with same. Always having trouble with this. (Mrs. Norris advised *Zelda Marsh*.[66]) Book partly a result of enthusiasm for arctic explorations.

Moran of the Lady Letty. Written episode to episode. Liked it. "I'm reading a jolly good book by Frank Norris." Always looked upon it as a good yarn.

The Pit. When in Chicago had an awful time trying to learn manipulation of stocks. Mr. George Moulson, cotton-broker, used to come over to help him. He would listen for evening and after Moulson left would ask her to explain it. Couldn't make head or tail of bull and bear. Invented radiator game.

October, 1898. Jeannette did not return to school this year because of illness. Very ill about middle of October; Frank in N.Y. a couple of weeks by that time.

Source: Jeannette Williamson Norris. Interview notes by Franklin D. Walker, May 16, 1930, Franklin Dickerson Walker Papers, BANC MSS C-H 79, The Bancroft Library, University of California, Berkeley.

Although *The Wrecker* was his favorite Stevenson, he liked *Travels with a Donkey* and *Ebb-Tide*.[67]

Vandover. Many of the characteristics of his father in the governor. Also in Jadwin of *The Pit*, whom some people thought was Leiter.[68] *Vandover* was probably a dramatization of his reaction towards college sin. He enjoyed the idea that such might happen to him if he did not follow better nature. Once told her when she admitted cribbing in college at 17 that she would never feel that serious about life again. His pleasure-loving qualities were uppermost in college and they were directly opposed to attitude of mother who was quite Puritanical. She used to rebuke him about little things with, "go on as you are going on now, young man, and nobody knows where you will end up." He probably felt reaction on passing from California to Harvard, more serious sin, and dramatized on it. He liked rich things to eat. No strong weakness for drink as it made him sleepy or sick. His gambling might have been more real as it had the strong appeal of the dramatic. He used to tell her that he liked to get away from the gambling crowd, and they would play poker, but rarely for money. His mother probably found his light-heartedness and absent-mindedness distressing. He continued to grow out of this as he grew older. His father's point of view was that of a business man; Frank fools around too much.

Harvard. He felt Harvard was effete and lonesome. Agreed with Flandrau in his description of the freshman who died without anyone knowing it.

Chicago. Used to talk about it when he was there writing *The Pit*. He would talk about the great humiliation at being torn away from his gang to be sent to dancing school in a Velvet Suit (black). He hated dancing school. He would screw his face up to annoy the girls so that they wouldn't dance with him; once he took three kittens to the school with him and they ruined the velvet suit. The gang was made up of rough necks and used to play hounds and hares by the week; his favorite was "Peely" MacKay. He enjoyed *Stalky and Son* when it came out.[69]

Wave. Cosgrave may have fired him but she doesn't remember it.

Attitude in writing. His humor was something intimate so rarely appeared in his writings. His straight-forwardness and brusqueness was affected; he aimed for it. Cf. Stevenson, who said that he never would have written his books if he could have lived them. So Frank admired athletes and business men partly because he was not one of them. He had great scorn for the small literary person, as Mrs. Pottle. Note his essay on Accuracy and Truth.[70] He may have inherited some of this from his father, a self-made business man.

Life a dramatic story. One weekend they went up to a place in Connecticut, and had to entertain themselves on the journey. Frank decided to make up a story for the occasion, with themselves as characters and they got so interested in it that they nearly missed their stop. Stokes the publisher and his wife were in the party and they admitted that they had eavesdropped all the way up and wanted the story finished at the party.[71]

Mother had the purpose of a Mary Anderson in going on the stage and was never affected by the Bohemian set.[72]

He practically educated her and her taste was so much like his that she (Jeannette) could get a perspective on his work and criticize it from his own angle.

Her mother's name was Carolina Virginia Williamson.

W. D. Howells. He used to dine with him frequently on Sunday evenings and was much impressed by his cordiality and informality in carpet slippers before the fire. He seems to have been in Europe much soon after their marriage. Their life was more or less of a closed corporation after that. Met Mark Twain with Howells at a dinner with Doubleday. Frank had liked *Joan of Arc.*[73]

Roselle. Few people came to see them there, but Mrs. Pottle occasionally as well as her former husband Gilbert Pottle, who is now in Hollywood. Use to say of Tompkins sisters that they vibrated rapidly in a small arc. See story about man who was ruined by writing one story.[74]

McClure. Probably the one who recognized him. He liked him but found him very visionary and romantic. Jeannette Gilder told them that she once called on McClure to find him with the kitchen apron on so decided that he was not good business head and failed to invest in magazine.[75] When the firm broke up Frank probably went with Doubleday, because they later made the royalty arrangement which made their marriage possible. Steadier. Gave him about $30.00 a week; instead of paying it every six months. Also, he earned about $12.00 a month reading. This was what he was getting when he first came to N.Y. This reading was sporadic, as he sometimes took off time for vacation. At first after their marriage he would go up to office in the afternoons. Later took the stuff home and she helped him. Stopped reading before writing *The Pit.*

Short Stories. In these days he did not like to write the short story and would but rarely do it in order to get enough money to keep going. He wanted to get her a Xmas present and wrote a story to sell; fearing it would not, wrote another, and still another. Finally sold all three and then had to spend all of the money on her present, putting the last fifty dollars in a purse for her. He was particularly fond of "Miracle Joyeux" with the illustrations of Christ without a beard.[76]

Doubleday. Closer friend than McClure. Also of wife.[77] Loyal to him when offered more money for *The Pit.*

Henry Lanier, son of Sidney Lanier,[78] in the firm and he was also fond of him. Page was a good friend and probably more compatible about literature than any of the others. She has a nice letter from him. Doesn't remember much about Phillips. He was with *McClure's.*

Jeannette Gilder was sole editor of *The Critic* and the man of her family. She persuaded Frank to write the "Salt and Sincerity" articles. He had been much impressed by La Rochefoucauld (they had been collecting books, Sappho, Racine, etc.).[79] Remembers once when he was writing article he took one point of view; the gentleman from Porlock arrived,[80] and when he finished the article he took the other side. They had to toss up to see which one to print.

Ida Tarbell, a good friend. Ray Stannard Baker, an acquaintance, but Frank didn't like muck-raking.[81]

Liked Bierce very much. Also much impressed by Robert Chambers' "The Yellow Tiger."[82]

The Pit. Frank didn't know much about business. They rigged up an arrangement with the grate for heat so that a windmill on a string would go up and down with the heat. Each would bet, one being the bear, the other the bull. Thus they learned. (Charles says Moulson rigged this up for them.)

Townsend he knew but not well.[83] Doesn't remember Garnett. Must [have] known Arthur Goodrich before she came.

Rainsford was a great influence on him. He went down to the boys' club before their marriage. He had wanted him to marry them, but he was out of the city. They were married at St. George's.

Hamlin Garland. When living out near 145th Street, working on *The Pit*, Mrs. Katherine Herne, wife of the man who wrote *Shore Acres*, brought her daughter Julie Herne to see them; Julie wanted to dramatize *The Pit*. Nothing came of it, but they became good friends; also second daughter, Chrystal Herne, now famous actress. Through them they met Garland, whom Frank admired very much. Garland always said he liked his looks.

Appearance. He had dark olive skin and large brown eyes. His hair was quite gray. Height 5' 11". A little heavier than I am. Towards end he was getting a little bulge and was quite proud of it. Very distinguished looking; people recognized him easily on the streets.

Gaston Ashe. Didn't know him before he wrote *The Octopus*. Thinks that his ranch was in the San Joaquin.

Source: Jeannette Williamson Norris. Interview notes by Franklin D. Walker, May 22, 1930, Franklin Dickerson Walker Papers, BANC MSS C-H 79, The Bancroft Library, University of California, Berkeley.

Hernes. The widow of James A. Herne, the man who wrote *Way Down East*.[84] Knew her and her two daughters, Julie and Chrystal. Chrystal is now a famous actress and has married Pollard, editor of N.Y. *World*.[85]

Paris. He didn't talk much about it. Thinks incident used in story about being shut up in a coat of mail is partly true. Very fond of museums. Believes he traveled in Italy with his mother.

South Africa.[86] Very fond of Hammond and wife. Mrs. Hammond looked after him when he was ill with the fever. Liked her and Miss Betty Hammond.[87] Returned with a snakelike bracelet tattooed on one arm and fraternity insignia on other. Done by a Chinaman in South Africa. Mother was horrified.

The Wave. Doesn't remember his being fired after she knew him. Frank very fond of Cosgrave. Used to say to Frank, "Don't agree with me or I may be wrong." He was sardonic and critical. Is sure that he went up to Colfax after she left as she received letters from him.

The Lark. Enjoyed it very much and used to bring up the copies and read them to her.

Women were quite crazy about him. One, Miss Burton, who played in *Caste* later died.[88] He must have had some flirtations. Quite fond of society up till the time he met her. German sort of a dignified Paul Jones. His attitude towards society changed after meeting her. She was much younger than his group.

She went away for two weeks in July up to Mill Valley and he came up to tell her that friendship was not enough.

Was working on *Moran* all of that spring and summer. Used to go out to see Capt. Jack. Once went dynamiting fish in the life-boat. Hodgson was a great story teller and would act his stories out as he went along. They had discovered him together.

Believes that he worked on "The Drowned Who Do Not Die" during that summer. Too ill on return from Cuba.

St. Louis. He probably received a telegram there although she doesn't remember. He did not go back to S.F. before going on to N.Y.

New York. He stayed in a boarding house opposite Waldorf. Board $50 on a $48 salary. Does not think he read at this time; not until the Doubleday, Page company was formed and they decided to marry.

Blix. He was in S.F. when it was published and took great pride in showing it to his mother, to whom it was dedicated. They read it together as it came out in installments.[89]

Cuba. She had not left school when he started; would read his letters to her literary society. He went down to Tampa and spent some time there before sailing. Saw a carload of boxes unloaded which proved to be coffins. Archibald went on the *Gussie* and returned to Tampa to strut around. Saw a good deal of Archibald. Bright but shifty. Remembers once at mess he came in just after officer had made a slurring remark about him. "Good evening gentlemen, and Lieut. So and So." He irritated him very much but had an attractive side; would pick up refugees on his horse. Frank very glad to get a horse. Stephen Crane was on the *Three Friends*. Didn't like him. Also met R. H. Davis and was a little disappointed with his boyhood hero. Years after Jeannette had dinner with Davis and he remembered Frank. Believes that Frank was at San Juan hill and wrote an account of it. Had tremendous enthusiasm for Roosevelt.[90]

Fever. Came down with it in Cuba. Returned to N.Y. but had miserable time with it. Finally had to come west for mother to take care of him. Looked terrible. Ran high fever every afternoon. Stayed with mother in an apartment on Washington near Jones.[91] They read a good deal together. Mother read *McTeague* to them. Went fishing a few times. Down to see Hodgson to talk about Arctic; he had been on rescue ship for the *Jeannette*. Much interested in Nansen. With

Houston on medical terms. *Blix* must have been practically finished. He did not work on two books at once.

Return to New York. Soon after his return Jeannette went up to see some friends, attacked in ear with mastoid infection. Returned to S.F. Afraid she was going to lose hearing. Wrote Frank that he had better break off engagement. He wrote west that he would come out if she continued to make a fool of herself. (October.) He was not well that winter and that probably influenced *A Man's Woman*. Much of "Comida!" had appeared in her letters.[92]

West to write *Octopus*. She thinks that he was out here for about three months. They spent a good deal of time together. He looked through material on Mussel Slough in Mechanics' Library.[93] Kept very full notes. Went to the Ashe ranch; she believes it was in Tulare county. Bruce Porter was Vanamee. Dyke? He interviewed Collis P. Huntington in the East. They grew to be good friends. After *Octopus* was published they had dinner at the Huntington house. Also good friend of Mrs. Archer Huntington with whom they stayed in N.Y.[94] Did not know Markham, but believes he used "The Man with a Hoe." He had luncheons with president and vice-president of Southern Pacific in S.F. Possibly Waterhouse helped. He was just gathering material. He favored the long novel; admired Zola's construction.

Zola. He read intensively rather than extensively. Note chapter on run-away train at end of one of his novels. Monomanias.[95]

Ashe. Mrs. Ashe divorced. Originally Dulce Bolado. Lives in Piedmont now. Mrs. Derrick. Influence.[96]

Return to N.Y. In October Jeannette applied to enter Children's Hospital. Frank wired from N.Y. that he was making arrangements with Doubleday. He was very disturbed about making decision with whom to stay when companies split. McClure was out of town. Had to deal with Phillips. He was staying again in room on Washington Square. Ate at Judson hotel.[97]

Marriage. [. . .] Washington Square. Colony there. Juliet Wilbor Tompkins at Judson. John Harrold in the Benedick, also on Square. Also Davies.

Marriage. Returned to apartment for the honeymoon. They sang with banjo. He let her sing. Said he would let her sing as often as he got married.

Bertha Rickoff a friend of his mother's whom he much disliked. Used to name his horse after her. She lives in Berkeley. Didn't approve of his engagement.

Roselle. After they had made a two weeks' trip to Greenwood Lake decided that they had to live in the country. Very quiet in Roselle. Frank went to town twice a week and brought out manuscripts. Davies used to come down on weekends; working on *Cousin Kate* but would read them one called "Aida of Wyoming." Mrs. Field and Austin Strong down for New Year's. Argument on the melodramatic portion of *Octopus*. Must have finished it about Xmas time.

Feb. To Chicago. Then west; back to N.Y. where they spent week in Doubleday house; then up to Greenwood lake for two months where Frank did no writing. Fished all the time. Went to N.Y. once a week.

Back to N.Y. Work on *Pit*. Moulson lived in N.Y. That winter Frank wrote the Christmas stories.[98] *Lord Jim* brought down in rough copy. Wild about it. Few books. *Virginian* he liked because coarse word could be used. *Gentleman from Indiana*. Stevenson. Garland. Crane. No O. Henry by then. Stanley Weyman.[99]

He was not writing short story. Probably those published were some he had on hand—remembers him writing "Dying Fires," "Three Crows" stories, "Peg-Leg."[100]

The Pit. It did not give scope for his abilities. Used to groan over it a good deal. Was glad to get it done. Would often tear portions up. Does not think Lanier influenced him.

Page edited *World's Work*.

Jeannette lost $100 bill. Wrote article on strike. Went up from Herne's. Did not like to do it.

Came west intending to go around the world. Stored furniture. Engaged passage to Australia for end of October. Bought bracelet for Jeannette on Aug. 12.

On way west read about the Lawlor case; went out immediately; tried to place article everywhere. Went down to Gilroy; enthusiastic and bought cabin where they could settle down on return from Europe. Wanted to know people. Liked Hardy. Lloyd, Mrs. Field, Mrs. Stevenson. Jeannette returned to be operated in Sept. Used to go over to see Charles at the college.[101]

Were going to sail and lay "Wolf" in Genoa. Leave baby with grandmothers. Frank had contracted for a series of articles.

32 / Bruce Porter

To term Bruce (Edmund Cushman) Porter (1865–1953) a Renaissance man hardly stretches the truth, for as a painter, stained glass artist, landscape architect and designer, art critic, writer, sculptor, muralist, decorator, and aesthete, he involved himself in much of the artistic life of San Francisco for several decades. Along with Norris, Gelett Burgess, and many of their friends and acquaintances, Porter was a member of the Bohemian Club, which may have been where he and Norris first met; they also knew each other through Les Jeunes and *The Lark*, which Porter and Burgess initially conceived. Then when Porter, having already allied himself with both the Art Nouveau and Arts and Crafts movements through his window designs for several churches in San Francisco and his early paintings, came to New York in 1899, Norris took up with him once again, since both for a time lived on Washington Square, Porter at the Benedick, number 80 on the east side, and Norris at number 61 on the south. Porter's penchant for mysticism—he espoused Swedenborgianism—influenced Norris, who drew upon his friend's personality and interests in creating Vanamee in *The Octopus*; not surprisingly, then, Porter's memoir of Norris treats his friend's temperament in considerably more detail than do those of many of his other friends.

Source: Bruce Porter to Franklin D. Walker, letter, June 4, 1930, Franklin Dickerson Walker Papers, BANC MSS C-H 79, The Bancroft Library, University of California, Berkeley.

My dear Mr. Walker,

Will you accept the excuse for the delay in answering your request, that your letter was mislaid, and I have no clue how to find you in Berkeley?

I have no letters from Frank. I think none passed between us (which in itself distinguishes our association in a period when everybody else communicated hourly).

I find it painful, this attempt to summon him out of those particular years.

One was living and producing at such speed that the *best*—what was of deep & lasting value, that should have registered in quietude—was registered confusedly, and was smeared over with unimportances.

That is why these notes are scant: you may use them or discard them, or incorporate them as a whole, as the contribution of a contemporary.

I do not like to remember into that confusion: and I do not like the manner of my writing. Words should build as honest stone is builded: and here is the staccato of the facile writing machine again (by the same old bad habit of speed).

I wish you pleasure & success in your interesting & touching labour. Norris should be so approached & remembered. He was a very dear, a very charming & very solitary human being.

Yours very truly,
Bruce Porter

Strange, that the quickest memory I have of Frank—(the picture summoned when I think of him)—is of a slouched figure in an Inverness cape, passing beneath a blown gas-light, in the winter dusk and in a down pour of rain. It was a momentary impression from a "dummy" seat on the Sacramento St. Cable, in the old San Francisco of the earliest '90s.—Some poignancy of drama in the figure of the unknown young man hit me: and the next day I painted the impression into a sombre little canvas and called it "Spring Floods."

He laughed dismissingly, at my impression & my title, when I told him, years later: and I smile now, as I recall his chagrin, when he learned that the picture had been destroyed.

Where, when & how I first met him I cannot remember: likely enough on a Sunday evening at the Cosgraves[102]—perhaps casually at the Bohemian Club (where neither of us properly fitted).

He was at work on Cosgrave's *Wave*: doing a variety of things in an extra inclusive journalistic job. But that job gave him the chance to do the thing he wanted to do.—a short story a week. But he gave the effect of being intensively "worn-out," tired out, "written out," according to his own declaration.

He came with increasing frequency to the studio, mornings, when there was the uninterrupted chance to talk of what he was doing, what he planned to do. Grimly fulfilling every demand of the job: his story for the week, came to be discussed, plotted, beaten out, for the inexorable hour of "going to press" in the studio and between us he'd present his plot and likely enough take mine but he only once accepted my development of it.

The story was of a tailor, squalid at a basement window, who looked up, year after year, into a poplar tree on the sidewalk above him: unconscious that his spiritual sustenance was drawn from the life of the tree: the tree is cut down: and the tailor turns insanely upon his wife and murders her.[103]

It proved to be not the best of his stories, and I learned then, that what I could best offer for his purposes, was the instigating flash and let him manage the illumination.

Burgess and I were fooling with *The Lark*.

Frank made no connection with that sprightly publication and came into no particular relation with the group that gathered about it.

But, when we had killed *The Lark* and Burgess had gone on to New York to harvest a surprised reputation, I read a letter of his success to Frank at luncheon. To my amazement that vivid face went ash-grey, and beating the table with clenched fists—"Damn him! Damn him! He's got it and it belongs to me!"

I knew then, why he could not "Lark" with literature: that there was in him, a fierce determination that was the measure of his gift, and that his defined, hard goal was never out of his vision.

We picked up the intimacy again in New York (in 1899, I think).

I had gone on there, for a term of work, in a studio in the Benedick, and found him established in a big room diagonally across on the south side of Washington Square.

In this proximity, he dropped in upon me at odd hours: mostly neighbouring midnight; when he saw my light turned on.

He, apparently, had no life outside his work and refused every social contact.

He had won a first place with the triumph of *McTeague* and there was eagerness on all sides—waiting to see and hail him.

But, ill, intense, he had promptly dedicated him self to a bigger work—He was brooding the complete Trilogy of "Wheat"—and was getting the warp of *The Octopus* on to the loom. He was bothered, tangled in loose threads.

He burst into my room one morning before five o'clock—flung him self at the foot of my bed. Exhausted & satisfied. He had made his leap an hour before,—had cleared his entanglements and had his story & his form, and couldn't contain himself at daylight.

From that moment he used me as a spring-board: He'd sit for hours listening to the compelled memories of a California he had missed. Then, suddenly, he'd pounce! Here was what he wanted!—Here was what he could use!

Scattered through *The Octopus* are actual names & the accompanying incidents he seized upon, out of my childhood memories.

"Blum" for instance was the true name of a Jewish store keeper, who became a grain dealer and manipulator & who was even then a living figure in his community—of importance. But no persuasion—no warning of a libel suit would make him resign "Blum." That name was "his" and he took it and left the trepidations to me.[104]

He was a "tiger" for names.—a tiger crouched to spring. While he waited for an incident that, as he put it, "belonged to him."

When you produced it, it set him on fire. He grasped the bone in his jaws, and retired with it into the lively solitude of his realistic imagination, built up the skeleton, clothed it with flesh, and the man walked, in that peculiar world of Frank's brain, as a reality.

Now here is the deeply interesting question regarding Norris and writers of his kind. From observation of his processes I believe that "Realists" of the order of Balzac[105]—Zola—Crane—Norris have the smallest possible dependence upon actuality.

All they require, is the instigation from reality: and the curtain rises upon the lighted stage within the brain—(a stage "set" complete)—and the characters begin their drama, with never a second reference to the actual, nor a single "prompting" from the world beyond the wings.

With Frank—I never heard him participate in or contribute to the analysis of any man or woman who was under discussion. What he seized upon, was some oddity of manner or habit or predicament—(a crisis in the human drama)—& that sufficed him.

The instances in his stories, where he attempted delineation of a man or woman whom he knew, and brought them, furnished with their own personalities, upon his prepared stage: they, in every instance I can recall, awkwardly balk the act in which they appear.

He twice "did" me: and after his second misrepresentation, offered me my copy of *The Pit* with his arm posed for defence of his laughing face.[106]

He had to wholly create his characters—on what ever rag or tag he had picked out of the life about him—more than the inevitable right *hint* embarrassed him—cumbered his imagining.

Well, he left New York too ill to do more than sit gaunt & shaken in the hansom that carried us to the station. Established in his section, he revived to a grin: "Bruce, see that?"—as he waved a little swagger stick between his hands—"I'm going to walk down Sutter St., swinging that!—and they'll say, '*That's Frank Norris*'!"

I never liked him better than at that moment, pitiable in his weakness, going "home" to his boyish reward, for the struggle and the travail—but with his goal attained.

It happened that I was never alone in his company again—until, again, on his hour of departure.

He came into the studio in San Francisco, haggard and despairing.

His wife was in hospital: had been operated upon—was out of danger, he told me—and we lunched together and then walked to the Hospital.

Outside the door, we stood for a moment:

"Bruce—I'm afraid!" I gave him the formal assurances: His wife had come through—Everything was well.

"Yes—but I'm *afraid*."

"Afraid of what, Frank?"

"I'm afraid of *Death*!" He turned and the door closed behind him; and I never saw him again.

33 / Bertha Rickoff

A self-styled journalist—on the 1920 census she listed her occupation as "writer" for a "magazine"—Bertha Monroe Rickoff (1862–?) proved more a nemesis for Norris and at least one of his fraternity brothers, Harry M. Wright, than a friend (see Crisler 1986, 75–76). Her claim of confidante to Gertrude may indeed have been true, however, for in her interview with Walker she manifests a knowledge of rather private details concerning the Norris family; even so, Walker opted to use almost nothing of what she told him and over forty years later discounted her reliability entirely: "She did not seem to be a very trustworthy witness" (Walker to W. John Bauer, September [17], 1972). That Gertrude plumped for her as a possible wife for Norris prior to his courtship of Jeannette does in fact seem suspect, since Rickoff was nearly a decade older than Norris. Thus the information Rickoff imparts perhaps derives from one who despite the passage of many years still harbored the grudge of a woman scorned: tellingly, hers is the only wholly negative portrayal of Norris left by those who knew him.

Source: Bertha Rickoff. Interview notes by Franklin D. Walker, May 29, 1930, Franklin Dickerson Walker Papers, BANC MSS C-H 79, The Bancroft Library, University of California, Berkeley.

Miss Rickoff said that she knew Frank from the time that he came back from South Africa till he went East. Saw him at other times when he came west. She is the one who wrote the answer to "Zola as Romantic Writer" for *The Wave*;[107] also referred to in Frank's letter to Harry and [by] Jeannette.[108] She says that she came of a very good family in the East, her father being president of National Education Association and put out the Applegate readers.[109] She knew many literary figures in the East and had written some for the *North American Review*.[110] When she came west she gave a paper before the Century Club on Zola and Hall Caine which appealed to Mrs. Norris and she took her up.[111] She then continued to give lectures in the bay region on current literature, stressing the realistic movement. Many were scandalized at her treatment of Zola and *Quo Vadis*.[112]

When she met them, Frank, Charles, and his mother were staying at the Pleasanton Hotel—they later moved back to the house on Sacramento Street. Frank was trying to console his mother for the divorce. His mother decided that Bertha was just the person of the proper literary background for Frank to marry and tried to encourage the match. Frank, however, struck her as a man of the world, quite fast, and she decided he was not for her. He was only interested in a woman in order to live with her. His attitude he had picked up when in Paris, according to his mother. There were several girls who were crazy about him and he used to go over and stay with one married woman in Sausalito.

Frank had no manners at all and would do what he felt like doing at any time. He would never engage in small talk. Once he picked up a macaroon from the floor at a fine dinner at her house and ate it. Like his mother, if he liked a person he would be kind, otherwise quite brutal. Charles was really hopeless, much more like his father. Frank would do the unexpected but was never crude. As far as she knew he never did an unkind act so he was always liked. She was simply not his kind, and although the mother encouraged the match for three years nothing came of it.

Frank was receiving money from his mother but was very bitter towards his father. Mrs. Norris had married while on the stage after being disappointed over another man. She never cared an awful lot for Mr. N. and was inclined to neglect him for the children and her nieces, whom she was putting into society on his money. He went around the world with a S.F. woman, and then the divorce followed, Mrs. N. getting the alimony. She was quite a free lance herself, although very orthodox and a strict church member. She loved life, however, and enjoyed specially the parts of Zola and Browning which were outspoken. She was quite a tartar and could express herself in very strong language when angry; as Frank put it, the cat would get under the bed. She always felt that the neuralgia was partly responsible for her husband's irregularity. Mrs. Norris had high social aspiration but was never quite successful because she was too brilliant. She was one of the founders of the Century Club and founded the Browning Club. She was by all odds the most brilliant woman in San Francisco. She read Browning in a way she had never heard duplicated. She was always a good sport.

Frank had gone to South Africa with his mother's consent, as she had paid half of the fare. She had been greatly upset by his failure to wire.

Jeannette. She was terribly common, and if she has improved it was due to Frank. Her mother was a singing teacher of no importance. Frank had to marry her; a shot-gun affair. He was very decent about it after he got her into trouble. The affair with the mastoid was merely a screen; Rosenstirn took care of it. Mrs. Norris had said to her that she knew what it was. Next morning, said she would tear her hair out if she said anything about it. Mrs. Norris did not approve at all of the marriage but it just had to be. When they were married in N.Y. they had a dinner for Howells and the rest and Jeannette looked very pretty but couldn't say a word, she was so dumb. Only the three at the wedding. Mrs. N. was always disappointed because Frank would not take to the social life, but he was very democratic and did not give a hang what social class people came from. She remembers once seeing Jeannette's picture in Frank's room and Mrs. N. spoke of her as "that hussy."

She found Cosgrave very charming. After Frank got him a job in N.Y. he said, "I pulled you out of the gutter, and now you have pulled me out."

Rainsford. She had been very much influenced by Rainsford and had been responsible for Frank meeting him. Frank wrote back a letter about it. Pierpont Morgan gave the money for the church which Rainsford preached in.[113] Greatly interested in social work.

She really taught him how to write. She persuaded him of the necessity of a soul in his work; of considering the necessity of humanity in everything he did. This was the social sense. Previously his work on *The Wave* was just hack work. Now he wrote *McTeague*; his mother had been reading Zola to him, whom she greatly admired. She told him he could not sell the book but he decided to try. She really had picked up the soul idea from Rainsford. She said that he must get something entirely original, something that would startle people. That was what Kipling had done.

His mother frequently came over to stay with her in Berkeley. Once she came over after Frank had been gambling all night and said that she was going to leave him for good. Such the dramatic. Frank came over after looking through all of the hotels; found her there. Next morning she (Bertha) told him that he needn't reform for his mother but he could go to hell if he had no more strength. This he took to heart, getting white. Thus her influence on him was mainly through skinning him. Mrs. N. was afraid of his gambling because she had a brother who had become a professional gambler.[114]

When Frank went to St. Louis he really ran away from his mother. Told her he was going to New Orleans. In reality he was going east in order to publish *McTeague*. He got some money from one of his frat brothers and went on to N.Y. where he got a job. There he had dinner with Howells who read *McTeague* and approved.

She bawled Frank out for Auguste scene in *McTeague*. English publishers took it out. He said he could not write love scenes; had never been in love; never stayed awake an half hour over a woman.

He thought that R. H. Davis was a snob when he met him.

William Keith who had a studio in S.F. was very fond of Frank.[115] Said he had fire in his eyes.

4. The professional writer in New York. This is one of several publicity photos Doubleday, Page & Co. made to advertise Norris's newly released novel, *The Octopus,* in April 1901. Courtesy of The Bancroft Library, University of California, Berkeley.

4
Professional Years
New York, Cuba, Chicago, and San Francisco, 1898–1902

When Norris left San Francisco in the late winter of 1898, ostensibly to report on Mardi Gras in New Orleans but, of more personal consequence, to visit Jeannette, then studying at Monticello Female Seminary in Godfrey, Illinois, he had little idea that his departure from his second home state would be permanent. Such proved the case, however, as an offer for full-time employment with S. S. McClure's firm reached him at a hotel in St. Louis. Assigned to duty as a correspondent for *McClure's Magazine* when the Spanish-American War began, Norris cultivated in earnest the persona of successful writer, and fellow authors James F. J. Archibald, Hamlin Garland, Arthur Goodrich, William Dean Howells, and Elizabeth Knight Tompkins and her sister Juliet had no trouble accepting him as such. Neither did his associates in the publishing industry, such as Frank Nelson Doubleday, Henry W. Lanier, and John S. Phillips, each of whom regarded Norris both as friend and employee. Young journalist Isaac F. Marcosson, one of the first to trumpet Norris's talents in a series of enthusiastic reviews appearing in the *Louisville Times*, left an incisive account of their association, and Julie Herne summarizes the friendship she and her family enjoyed with the Norrises. For their part, business journalists George D. Moulson and Edwin Lefevre good-naturedly attempted to assist Norris in comprehending the intricacies of the stock exchange during his research for *The Pit*, while Dulce B. Davis had earlier opened her home to him, encouraging liberal access to her ranch in California and her knowledge of the area's rich Spanish-Californio heritage when he was working on *The Octopus*. As rector of St. George's Episcopal Church, W. S. Rainsford welcomed Norris as both communicant and volunteer in educating young immigrants, and Grant Richards, publisher of Norris's novels in England, amusingly recounts not just Norris's own active literary production of six novels in five years but also Norris's selfless support of Theodore Dreiser's *Sister Carrie*, when his own firm, Doubleday, Page & Co., had all but withdrawn its backing of the controversial novel. Yes, these were heady years for Norris, and all too brief ones as well. Still, that he was able to live them fully, engaged in the writing he loved, is as much as anyone has a right to ask.

34 / James F. J. Archibald

Journalist James Francis Jewel Archibald (1871–1934) did not attend the University of California with Norris but had made his acquaintance by, at the latest, 1893 when he was with members of the Norris family in Chicago at the World's Columbian Exposition. While his relationship with Norris continued after 1898, its most important phase occurred when they traveled together in Cuba during the Spanish-American War—where Norris represented *McClure's Magazine* and "Jimmy" wrote for the San Francisco *Post, Scribner's Magazine,* and *Leslie's Weekly.*

Source: James F. J. Archibald to Franklin D. Walker, letter, October 9, 1930, Franklin Dickerson Walker Papers, BANC MSS C-H 79, The Bancroft Library, University of California, Berkeley.

My dear Mr. Walker:

It is with considerable satisfaction I hear you are working on a biography of Frank Norris. I doubt if there is any one who was closer to him or knew him better than I did. We were very close friends during his early days and campaigned the entire Spanish War together, starting from San Francisco with the First Infantry, on Shafter's Staff,[1] and returning to New York on an empty transport. We were the first persons to arrive at New York after the surrender of Santiago because of the fact that I had been given orders to go to Porto Rico on a transport, and while we were at sea the protocol was signed and the ship ordered to proceed to New York.[2] I have some photographs and considerable very vital matter regarding the man whom I consider the greatest young writer of our day, who without doubt would have been one of the foremost writers of the world had he lived.

Unfortunately I am contemplating a trip to Washington some time next week, although I may not go. I will know in a few days. I will be gone a matter of only a short time and will return to this address. You could wire me before the date you suggest and I will let you know, if I am here at that time. If not, I will be glad to see you at some time in the future.

Very sincerely yours,
Jas. F. J. Archibald

Source: James F. J. Archibald. Interview notes by Franklin D. Walker, October 18, 1930, Franklin Dickerson Walker Papers, BANC MSS C-H 79, The Bancroft Library, University of California, Berkeley.

Davis' manner was arrogant but he was not in reality so.[3] One of Arch's best friends. Arch got permission from Sampson to land on first day and Davis peeved.[4] S.: "Who the hell reads what you write?" Hence attack on him. Frank probably did not like Davis—not many did.

Arch left S.F. with First Regiment on the 20th of April—showed me the *Post* of that date—does not remember whether Frank joined him there or in Tampa. Could be found out from war department on pass.

Frank was representing *McClure's* but as far as he knows published nothing. Arch did not know of the articles in v. 10.[5] Probably this was due to presence of Stephen Bonsal and other experts.[6] Arch was writing for *Post*, *Scribner's* and *Leslie's*.

Frank was with Arch throughout campaign. Really attached to Fifth Army Corps but stuck with Arch because the latter was an aide-de-camp as well as a correspondent, giving him special privileges.

He did not go on *Gussie* expedition. Very restricted.[7]

Does not remember *Three Friends* trip.[8]

They sailed from Tampa on the *Segurança*, boarding June 8, sailing 8:53 June 14. (Note Arch uses *The Santiago Campaign*—C. D. Rhodes. Santiago society. He and Frank mentioned on p. 378. They called on July 14.)[9]

Does not remember anything much about Crane—he drank a good deal. "Shots in the Rain" best thing on campaign.[10]

Frank got a horse from one of the Cubans. Arch has picture of the two, horse, and guide. Also good drawing by Frank in Washington. Also Christy drawings of campaign, including one of knifed girl.[11]

They lived on meagre rations—hardtack, bacon, coffee, and sugar. Twice a week tomatoes. Anecdote of how they found a large potato. Feast planned. Frank keeps putting it off; finally admits he fed it to horse—was in saddle-bags. Horse really a company affair.

Arch invented a hammock and tent arrangement. They spent much of time sleeping together in it. Frank knew nothing about camping.

They slept in the church at El Caney.[12] Frank cut the head out of one of the religious paintings and nearly got in trouble about it but Arch fixed it up.

After surrender. They were assigned to McKibben's staff. He was in charge of Santiago, later relieved by Wood. They spent a week at the Palace Hotel, headquarters, and then moved into an abandoned restaurant. Electric lights. Hung up hammock. Proprietor appeared and they arranged to have him cook meals—opened up for business. Wood and Roosevelt used to come in and eat with them.[13] They had flour and bread and a good stock of wines.

Return. They found life in Santiago monotonous. *Iroquois* was sailing empty for Porto Rico. Arch and Frank get permission to go—only passengers. The war ended on the way there and they turned to N.Y. The first ones to return.[14] Greeted royally. Very sick on the way back—fever and let-down. A broker gave them his car for the day.

Asseraderos. Frank landed also on trip to Garcia.[15]

El Caney. After El Caney they marched all night back to San Juan. Alternated on pony. Hearst came along on a black horse; gave Arch his horse and walked back with them. A good fellow.[16]

Remington's only provisions was a bottle of whiskey which he shared liberally. Frank found kindred artist spirit.[17]

Cuban guide attached himself to them—a great help. Frank called him Bonito[18] because he was so ugly. Kept his rifle clean and never shot it.

Decorations in Cuba. Began collecting them after surrender. See letter. They played stud for them. Arch was unpopular with newspaper men because he dressed well and was cultured.[19]

After San Juan. Frank was under fire during entire campaign. Of the sixty correspondents most stayed out of danger. Only Crane, McIntosh, Remington, Davis, Christy, Bonsal, Whitney, Marshall, Creelman, etc., under fire.[20]

El Caney. Clara Barton in charge, Bangs support.[21] Clara real figure of campaign.

Notes—and sketches voluminous.

El Caney. Went out in churchyard to sleep. Frank finds he had his head on a leg.

Souvenirs. Included Mauser rifle and part of the flag which was flying over Santiago.

Santiago. Expenses high. Coffee and bifteck at Café de Vénus, $7.50. Arch's difficulties in rounding up the lawless soldiers.

Arch had known Frank well before. He was in love with Ida Carleton but not encouraged by Mrs. Norris. She a great formalist—strict as hell. Terrific temper. Frank bored by this society life—hence loved people like Blix.[22] Always perfect respect for father. Knew him in *Wave* days. He was far too reticent and nonaggressive about his writing. Arch on *Overland Monthly.*

35 / Raine Bennett

During his long life Raine E. Bennett (1891–1981) was a reporter, editor, playwright, poet, and radio journalist. Born in San Francisco to John E. Bennett (1863–?), an attorney, and his wife, Emma J. (1862–?), he founded the Western Arts Association there, worked for the *San Francisco Chronicle*, and edited *Bohemian Magazine*, before eventually moving to New York, where he continued his journalistic career. The incident he recalls involving Norris, Lloyd Osbourne, and his own father occurred in the early fall of 1902, when Norris and Jeannette had returned to San Francisco to tidy their affairs and place their daughter with her grandmothers before embarking on their proposed voyage to research the third novel in the Trilogy of the Wheat.

Source: Raine Bennett, "The Norris Who Made Life Real," *Westways* 26 (December 1934): 17.

Vague, vague is the memory of a morning in Berkeley when my father led me, eagerly, to the postoffice—that haven of hope for all writers. We stood in line while those before us, one by one, enquired and departed. In due course father was about to ask the clerk for his own mail when a large, blustering fellow strode in from the street, swinging a cane, shoved my parent aside, poked his great head into the cage, and bawled:

"Any letter for Lloyd Osbourne?" I recall the momentary confusion, the glare of resentment—the unfairness (as it was afterwards explained) of a man who would not stand his turn in line, and, that is all.

The incident is trivial, were it not for the fact that Lloyd Osbourne was the son of Mrs. Robert Louis Stevenson. Having received his mail, he stalked away with a quieter companion. Father and I returned home, where, in commenting upon the incident to my mother, he remarked:

"The more mannerly fellow with Osbourne was Frank Norris, who has just published *The Octopus*."

"What is an octopus?" I pleaded, waving my spoon at the table.

"An octopus, little boy," replied my father, "is a black-hearted monster that breeds Lloyd Osbournes."

Mother tells me this momentous event took place while we resided in Berkeley, between 1900–1902.

Those two young men are (to my recollection) only long, twin shadows moving toward the light of Shattuck Avenue. [. . .]

When Frank Norris attended the University of California he spent much of his leisure in association with Myron Wolf and Maurice V. Samuels. They were known on the campus as "The Three Guardsmen." It was my privilege, while living at The Lambs in New York,[23] to meet and engage in long Sunday afternoon chats with Maurice Samuels. Being expatriates from California, we had many views in common. [. . .]

On another occasion—one late evening, in the same place—I sat out the hours with Charles Norris and Dan Totheroh,[24] over mugs of beer. Frank Norris was not the topic of our conversation, but the comment was passed and affirmed that Frank never dreamed of writing for sales. But his uncouth, overworked characters had the grip to survive. [. . .]

36 / Dulce Bolado Davis

Having acquired by 1867 nearly 100,000 acres of Quien Sabe and Santa Ana, adjoining land-grant ranchos in San Benito County, California, Joaquin Bolado (1822–1894) lost little time in creating Santa Anita Ranch out of them, which his only daughter, Julia Dulce Bolado Ashe Davis (1873–1952), inherited. Beautiful, elegant, intelligent, gracious, Dulce, then married to Gaston M. Ashe, whom she later divorced, entertained Norris at her ranch near Tres Piños during his research for *The Octopus*, regaling him with tales of her proud family, which had by then lived in California for five generations, and stories of social and ranching life in the surrounding area. Finding a kindred spirit in Dulce who had artistic aspirations that her brief study in 1900 at the California School of Design in San Francisco would fan, Norris, ever attuned to realistic detail, transferred to the novel much of what she told him, appropriated the name Quien Sabe as part of the book's setting, and adopted some of Dulce's own personality for the character of Annie Derrick. In 1912 Dulce married Francis Hewitt Davis (1867–1947).

Source: Dulce Bolado Davis to Franklin D. Walker, letter, June 12, 1931, Franklin Dickerson Walker Papers, BANC MSS C-H 79, The Bancroft Library, University of California, Berkeley.

Dear Sir—

In reply to your letter of June 4th, [I] would say that I believe I can give you in writing the details of Frank Norris's visit to the Santa Anita Rancho—if you can supply the dates.—My very good friends, Mr. and Mrs. Ernest Peixotto, sent him to me with a letter of introduction, and requesting me to invite him down during the harvest season;—as he had been detailed by Scribner's (I believe) to write an "Epic of the Wheat"—which I believe he did in two volumes or rather in two stories, the first being *The Octopus*, the second *The Pit*.—He remained at our ranch a month and most of *The Octopus*, I think, was written during that time. He was at that time engaged to the lovely girl he subsequently married—(he wrote a book of their courtship called *Blix*). It was my duty as hostess to see that he received his mail daily;—it was a hot dusty summer, before the days of automobiles, and I took many a tiresome ride to the then distant town of Tres Piños to see his pleasure when his mail arrived.—He was always looking for "stories" from every one with whom he talked and said that "Only the elect had muses." Also "that if a Book had entrails it did not have to have style"—with which, I violently disagreed, being a great lover of Pater and Browning.[25]—Later his brilliant Mother, who was one of the first promoters of the Browning Society of San Francisco, invited me to become a member; this was long after Frank's death,—there was a great bond of understanding, admiration and devotion between Mother and son.—Frank was a great lover of Zola and the realistic school, he seems to me, as I remember him, now, as very mature and experienced for his years. I never saw him after his visit, but my friendship with his Mother always kept his memory fresh in my mind.—While he was here we had a dance in our huge old barn, which my father built and has since burnt down.—When he sent me a copy of *The Octopus* I found it replete with the stories of early California anecdotes of my family which I had recounted to him.—

I trust this covers all you wished to know.

Very truly yours,
Dulce Bolado Davis.

Source: Dulce Bolado Davis. Interview notes by Franklin D. Walker, undated, Franklin Dickerson Walker Papers, BANC MSS C-H 79, The Bancroft Library, University of California, Berkeley.

Very attractive

Visited at Santa Anita ranch, Aug 22, '31. Said she was only 20 when Frank came to ranch.[26] Peixotto sent him down—he a likeable Jew.[27] The Alvarado story she told him. Alvarado was her grandmother's brother.[28] Sure that Frank did not meet Sewall. He was charming; seemed to her an old young man. Lines in face. Very anxious to hear from Jeannette. Wrote in evenings. Didn't go in much for riding etc. Harvest, barn dances, (Ferry). See Morse Seed farm.[29] Doesn't remember serving girl. Frank never made up stories—put everything she told him into *Octopus*. Did not write. Thinks he was there about six weeks.

Mrs. Norris didn't take proper care of Billy.

37 / Frank N. Doubleday

Frank Nelson Doubleday (1862–1934) ended his relationship with the book and magazine publishing firm of Charles Scribner's Sons in 1897 to cofound with S. S. McClure the Doubleday & McClure Co. By late 1899, however, they had dissolved their partnership, and Doubleday formed a new company with former *Atlantic Monthly* and Houghton, Mifflin editor, Walter Hines Page. Norris too ended his relationship with McClure that year, to serve as a manuscript reader with Doubleday, Page & Co. and to publish his novels with that firm. Doubleday and Norris enjoyed an amicable relationship, though his response to Walker's query posed three decades later illuminates only one minor aspect of it. As with Theodore Dreiser's *Sister Carrie*, which allegedly offended Doubleday's wife and thus his firm's suppression of its sale, so with *McTeague*. Doubleday here denies the rumor that she was responsible for the bowdlerization of the pants-wetting scene in the original printed version of *McTeague*.

Source: Frank N. Doubleday to Franklin D. Walker, letter, May 4, 1931, Franklin Dickerson Walker Papers, BANC MSS C-H 79, The Bancroft Library, University of California, Berkeley.

My dear Mr. Walker:

I have read your letter of April 16th with care and attention.

Personally, I had little or nothing to do with matters concerning *McTeague*, but I know that Mrs. Doubleday was not in the habit of passing on such matters for the publishing concern. Some one who has it in for me is always starting this story anew. Mrs. Doubleday died twelve years ago[30] and the subject is very painful, and I wish it might be dropped. I am positive that she had nothing to do with any changes which may have been made and about which I know nothing.[31]

The same thing is true of *Sister Carrie*. I don't think that Mrs. Doubleday ever saw the book; at all events, I know that she expressed no opinion which affected the treatment of it by the publishing house.

Very truly yours,
F. N. Doubleday

38 / Hamlin Garland

Hamlin Hannibal Garland (1860–1940) was a novelist, short story writer, and literary critic. In the late nineteenth century he was a high-profile representative of the Realistic school of American authors and an advocate of Local Color writing dedicated to the truthful (rather than sentimental) depiction of regional life. In both his novel *Rose of Dutcher's Coolly* (1895) and collection of stories titled *Main-Travelled Roads* (1891) he expanded the limits of what was acceptable in high-culture works of art, anticipating the violations of Victorian standards for which Norris was becoming known when the two men met in 1900.

Source: Hamlin Garland. Memorandum on recto of front endpaper of Norris's *Blix*, undated, PML 75123, The Pierpont Morgan Library, New York, New York.

One day I went into the office of Doubleday, Page and Co. I saw Frank Norris sitting at a desk bent over some MS. I knew him but slightly, had met him once or twice, but I had just read *McTeague* and was powerfully moved by it. This must have been about New Year's, 1900. As I was about to pass Norris I stopped and shook hands and asked him for an autograph in *Blix*. There was only this "sample copy" in the house and so he wrenched it from the shelf and put his name on it. This was the beginning of our more intimate friendship.

Source: Hamlin Garland. Excerpts from unpublished diary, Papers of Hamlin Garland, mssGD 1–1158, The Huntington Library, San Marino, California.

20 January 1900.

At the home of Juliet Wilbor Tompkins we met Mr. Frank Norris for the first time. We had a joyful evening except that Zulime[32] unthinkingly touched on the justice of the Boer War—This brought out the Butcher in Seton-Thompson who blazed with imperialism for a minute or two. I smiled through it all but let him know that my sympathies were with the Boers.[33]

We were greatly taken with Norris who is very handsome—almost the handsomest American author. A clean-cut, alert, and manly type. We drew closer together by reason of this evening. He was admirable at all points and held his own with Thompson with unfailing good nature. He had been in Africa and knew what he was talking about.

15 December 1901.

Dined with the Hernes[34] and met Frank Norris and his wife—Norris—a stunning fellow—an author who does not disappoint me as a man. He is perilously handsome—tall and straight with keen brown eyes and a beautifully modeled face. His face is that of a boy altho his hair is white. I have hardly known a handsomer writer. He looks as a poet should look.

We had a very pleasant chat and really got at each other. He seems confident of his future and well he may.—I know no one for whom I can predict a finer career. His wife seems very bright also. We are likely to see a good deal of them during our stay—for they seem "our kind," and should prove most delightful neighbors.

20 December 1901.

We dined with the Norrises. A group of western adventurers, all of us.[35] Norris grows in interest and charm. A fine fellow. He told us a little of his grand scheme for a trilogy on wheat—the second number to deal with Chicago and the wheat pit.—I bantered him a little on his debt to Zola in *The Octopus* which he calls "The Squid" at times.—

17 January 1902.

Frank Norris came down to lunch with me at the club. Met the *Century* editors and Cosgrave of the Wanamaker *Everybody's*.[36] In the evening dined with the Norrises, a very quiet family dinner. Zulime begins to think that the social pace is wearing. Norris pleased me more than ever—there was something fine and sweet and boyish about him and his gay wife and bright home made a most delightful impression on us both.—He was full of big plans for future books. He is in a full tide of his powers and so handsome and confident that there can be no question of his success. His wife had given him a very handsome desk for a Christmas present and he was filled with pride and joy in it.

5 March 1902.

We had much pleasure in helping Jeannette Norris celebrate Frank's birthday. Jeannette filled us with wonder—three weeks ago she gave birth to a little Jeannette and here she sat gay and blooming at the head of her own table. Such maternity seems rational as a part of human life. Frank was very happy over his new desk and his new daughter. Life is coming to harvest with him. He deserves all that enriches him.

25 October 1902.

Frank Norris died today. The beautiful, valiant happy youth is gone. His taking off in the full flush of his joyous success—in the glow of his domestic happiness and pride of his paternity is cruel. Nothing of late has so stirred me and grieved me. It seems that some criminal neglect must have manifested itself, some physician must have blundered—I want to accuse someone—responsible and say—"See what irreparable injury you have done to American Literature!"[37]

39 / Arthur Goodrich

Arthur Frederick Goodrich (1878–1941), an honor graduate of Columbia University in 1899, would later become a successful novelist and playwright. He made Norris's acquaintance at the turn of the century as a colleague at Doubleday, Page & Co. Goodrich was an editor in its book department as well as a staff member of the monthly magazine *The World's Work.*

Source: Arthur Goodrich, "Frank Norris: The Estimate and Tribute of an Associate," *Boston Evening Transcript*, October 29, 1902, 14.

It is hard to realize that Frank Norris is dead. He seemed always to come out of the springtime, to carry with him the breath of eternal youth. He was just rounding out his career into that hard-earned great success and high usefulness which everyone who knew him felt to be his. He was the most virile, the most creative, the most broadly imaginative of the younger writers who were to make the American literature of the next quarter century. Whatever else may be said of his writing, it was living, pulsing, human. The "pity of it" must be doubly felt in the sense of deep personal loss—for no one could know Norris without having a real affection for the man, as well as an admiration for his genius and his high ideals, and in a sense of the national loss to our literature. If we could but have the occult power of his own Vanamee![38]

Until six or seven years ago there was nothing in Frank Norris's life that was unusual or especially prophetic of the work he was to do. He had gone from Chicago to California when he was fourteen, and after three years there, he went abroad and studied art in Paris.[39] Then back in California, he spent his four years at the university. There he was, his old chum has told me, a healthy, full-blooded, college boy full of enthusiasm, popular necessarily and unconsciously, a leader of his fellows by mere charm of personality. His room was the gathering place for the crowd, and he alone could entertain them all with the spontaneous good humor and unconscious wit which always characterized him. He wrote a play that was memorable in college circles, and when it was published later in the college annual, he drew the illustrations for it.[40] And even in those days he saw beyond the little things and felt the broad swift current of great events. He was utterly lacking in the petty prejudices which are so common to a man's college days.

Having completed his course, he added another year at Harvard, graduating there in 1894.[41] It was at Cambridge, without question, that the Zolaesque realism, which was to mould so much of his first work, gripped him. He plotted *McTeague* as a class exercise during that year, and was told that it was too grim and horrible to make a piece of literature. When he went back to California, responsibilities came upon him, and he began to write as an assistant editor of the San Francisco *Wave*. He did this journalistic work with more or less success, but it was not the serious, larger task he was born to do. It was only the other day when he was laughing over one incident of his *Wave* experience, which seemed to him particularly like a stage-play situation. But it unquestionably gave him that close touch with San Francisco life which he wrought with such perfect detail into *McTeague*. He was working along with the book in his spare hours. [. . .]

One day after he became reader for the new Doubleday, Page & Co., Norris came to a member of the firm, almost trembling with enthusiasm.

"I've got a great idea," he said, and he told his plan of the "Epic of the Wheat," perhaps the largest constructive task any American novelist has ever given himself. As a result, *The Octopus*, the story of the wheat growers' struggle with the railroads, was published a year ago. It gripped the people instantly with vivid realism, its grasp of tremendous problems, its broad epic sweep, and the blood and iron if its men. The book is instinct with the terrible earnestness of the man grappling, Titan-like, with the great elementary forces. And it prepared the way for "The Pit," which is now appearing in the *Saturday Evening Post*, and which will be published in book form early in the year.

Two years ago Norris was married at old St. George's Church, New York, to Miss Jeannette Black of San Francisco. With their little girl they started West, planning to take a trip around the world, during which he was to gather material for "The Wolf," the last of the wheat trilogy. A few weeks ago he bought a ranch in California, where he planned to do the large work before him in the next few years.

If you have read any of Frank Norris' little essays on contemporary writing, you will remember his continued reiteration of "sincerity, sincerity, and again sincerity." There is one paragraph that he wrote a year ago that carried his whole artistic creed. It concludes:

> To make money is not the province of a novelist. If he be the right sort he has other responsibilities, heavy ones. He, of all men, cannot think only of himself and for himself. And when the last page is written and the ink crusts on the pen point and the hungry presses go clashing after another

> writer, the "new man" and the new fashions of the hour, he will think of the grim long grind of the years of his life that he has put behind him and of his work that he has built up, volume by volume, sincere work, telling the truth as he saw it, independent of fashion and the gallery gods, holding to these with gripped hands and shut teeth—he will think of all this then, and he will be able to say, "I never truckled, I never took off the hat to Fashion and held it out for pennies. By God, I told them the truth. They liked it or they didn't like it. What had that to do with me? I told them the truth; I knew it for the truth then, and I know it for the truth now." And that is his reward—the best that a man may know; the only one really worth the striving for.[42]

It is because he could say that and mean it, because much as he desired the power and usefulness popular success would bring him, yes, and the popular success for its own sake, he struggled along with his conscience clear, "painting the thing as he saw it," that Frank Norris was the great novelist he has shown himself to be in *The Pit*, that his work has shown that progressive growth, that his death is the severest single loss American literature could sustain. The man was absolutely in earnest. He wrote novels because he believed it was his work—the only work that for him was worth doing. He wrought his literature from life as it is, from men and women as they are, and he accepted his audience, small or large, with good grace, biding his time. He knew that he could write a popular novel with duels and a machine-made romance, but he rigidly held himself true to his artistic ideals. His work unfinished, scarcely begun as it is, is more creditable than all the so-called successes of temporary popularity rolled into one. [. . .]

If a difficulty arose he did not worry, and when it was solved, he was as glad as a child let loose to play. One day when he went fishing with a mutual friend, he became so excited that he impulsively declared he would have a cottage near the shore for his next summer's outing and fish all summer. No one ever heard an irritable word from Norris, and the only time I ever saw a crease in his brow was once when he was bemoaning his own lack of business ability and foresight. He was as modest and democratic as he was lacking in any self-consciousness. He was just a frank, forthright, earnest seeker after truth, his broad sympathies alert to say a kind word or to hear one, considerate in a most delicate way of people's feelings, always saying the pleasant thing, and always absolutely meaning it. "Wearing the white flower of a blameless life,"[43] gentle as a child, vigorous with healthy manliness, with high ideals and quiet humility, naïve in his simplicity, in everything he did he "meant intensely and meant good."[44] He had beauty in his heart and, believing something with all his might, he put it forth arrayed as he saw it, the lights and shadows falling upon it on his page as they fell upon it in his heart, and neither that beauty which he has left on printed page, nor that which his open heart showed to all who knew him, "shall pass away out of the world."[45]

Source: Arthur Goodrich to Franklin D. Walker, letter, March 4, 1931, Franklin Dickerson Walker Papers, BANC MSS C-H 79, The Bancroft Library, University of California, Berkeley.

My dear Professor Walker:

About Frank Norris's letters. I have quite a number among the things I have in storage, and I had hoped before this to have a chance to get at them. In fact, I had thought that I might have all of my things out of storage by this time and that his letters to me, therefore, such as I have, would be available. This hope has not come true as yet.

It happens, however that I have a couple of letters here in my apartment. One of them which has to do with his signature to an article in *World's Work* is, I think, perhaps worth your while. On the chance that it may be, I am enclosing a copy. The other letter has to do with payment for an article and its wording is characteristic enough so that it, too, may be interesting and amusing to you.[46]

My little article in the *Transcript*, written directly after Frank's death, sums up so completely my feeling about him that I doubt if I have much to add. I can remember so well the day we heard of his death. I got off by myself and tramped up Fourth Avenue and on into Madison, a good forty blocks all told, simply unable to believe that this thing could have happened. And, youngster that I was, hit harder than I ever had been by death before. I was in my early twenties then, very fortunate in breaking in at Doubleday's just as they were starting *World's Work*. It was a small house then and we youngsters had a rare opportunity. I was managing editor of the magazine under Walter Page six months after I entered the office.

Frank did an occasional article for us and my impression is that he did some manuscript reading as well—the selected manuscripts which the routine readers had passed upon favorably. He was in and out of the office almost daily and I occasionally saw him as well at his apartment down at Washington Square which was only a stone's throw from my own.

At that time, I remember, Ruth Frederic (Harold Frederic's daughter) had a desk near my own. John O'Hara Cosgrave came in shortly from the coast, at Frank's suggestion, to manage the editing of *Everybody's Magazine*. Henry Lanier (son of Sidney Lanier) was running the art end of both magazines and books. And pretty nearly all of the famous writers of the day, including Mark Twain, Hamilton Wright Mabie, Julian Ralph, Irving Bacheller, who had just had his big success with *Eben Holden*, Ellen Glasgow and many others came in at one time or another.[47] To all of us, I think, there was none quite like Frank. Certainly this was true as far as I was concerned. Whenever he stopped at my desk for a chat, it always gave a new lift to my day. There was a sort of tonic quality about him, quiet and simple though he was, that stirred and warmed you. Why he, who got such joy out of life and who had so much to give, should have been fated to pass out in his youth, is one of the many things I have never been able to understand.

I wish I had more for you. I hope you got in touch with Cosgrave and Lanier. Cosgrave particularly ought to be able to give you many interesting personal reminiscences.

All cordial good luck to you.

Sincerely yours,
Arthur Goodrich

P.S. Incidentally, if you haven't copies of the articles referred to in the two letters, copies of which I am enclosing, you ought to get hold of them. One, I remember, was a very clear-cut statement of his writing creed, which I can remember now made a great impression on me.

Lord, what a busy, delightful, intimate, homey little office that early Doubleday, Page, third-floor-at-34-Union-Square housed! Everybody working all hours for mighty little money and enjoying every minute of it. I somehow have the feeling that there never has been, in the publishing game, any place quite like it, before or since. It was such a live, human, flavorous place. And Frank was one of its richest flavors. I can see him now, as he would come blowing in, with his boyish face and his gray hair and his long confident stride and an air of quiet good cheer which never failed. And what a grand sense of humor he had! In fact, I am afraid anything that I had to contribute to a biography of Frank Norris would be too eulogistic for the present public's taste. My attitude about him, inside, was just about as near hero-worship as was possible in a recently-graduated-from-college, supercritical, pseudo cynical youngster of the period.

40 / Julie A. Herne

Julie Adrienne Herne (1881–1955) was the daughter of Realist playwright James A. Herne, whom Norris had interviewed when writing for *The Wave* in 1897. Julie, who in this 1952 letter revealed that Norris was the author of the unsigned piece, "Herne, the Unconventional," was herself a playwright and popular actress. The Norrises' friendship with Julie and her mother, Katherine, began in late 1901. Just before the Norrises returned to California in July 1902, they vacationed at the Herne estate on Long Island's Peconic Bay—Julie's mother serving then with George D. Moulson as a sponsor at the baptism of daughter Jeannette Norris.

Source: Julie A. Herne to James D. Hart, letter, September 30, 1952, James D. Hart Papers, BANC MSS 81/107c, The Bancroft Library, University of California, Berkeley.

Dear Dr. Hart:

I have your letter regarding the collection of Frank Norris's letters and manuscripts which the University is assembling. I think it is a wonderful idea to create this enduring memorial to him. I enclose herewith one of two letters which I received from him, and which I am happy to give to your collection.[48]

The other letter from Frank Norris I gave to my nephew, Montrose Moses, Jr.,[49] some years ago. I have written to him to ask if he wants to give it to the collection, or send it to you to have a photostat made of it. I asked him to write directly to you about it, but if you don't hear from him and wish to write him, his address is:—Dr. Montrose J. Moses Jr., Honey Lane, Brookhaven, Long Island, N.Y.

These are the only two letters I ever received from Frank Norris. He may have written to my mother, but if so, those letters were probably lost in the fire which destroyed our home in 1909, in which many valuable letters and papers and some of my father's original manuscripts were also lost. I have found no letters from Frank Norris among the few papers my mother left. I am sorry to say that we never owned a set of the Argonaut Manuscript edition of Norris's works.

I suppose you have already been in touch with Hamlin Garland's daughters.[50] Garland and Norris were good friends, and probably corresponded. I haven't heard from the girls for years, but I believe they still live in Hollywood.

The story of the two letters to me may be of interest. In the fall of 1901, a few months after my father's death, I read *The Octopus* which had recently been published, and thought it would make a great play. I wrote to Norris and he replied, in the letter I gave to Montrose. I wrote a second note, asking for an appointment to talk the matter over, and his reply is the letter I am enclosing.

The dramatization never materialized, but our meeting led to a memorable friendship. Frank and Jeannette (now Mrs. Black), lived within a few blocks of our home, and during that winter we saw them frequently.[51] They spent nearly all the following summer with us, and my mother was godmother to their little girl, Billy. Frank was writing *The Pit* when we met, and that summer I read the galleys aloud to him and Jeannette. He died that fall, just as they were about to take a trip around the world.

There is one statement about Frank Norris which I should like to see corrected, in the interest of accuracy and in justice to him. Dr. Edwards[52] wrote me some time ago that Lars Åhnebrink, in his book, *The Beginnings of Naturalism in American Fiction*,[53] refers to the "influence" of my mother on Norris's writing, and also finds "echoes of James A. Herne in the novels of Norris." (I am quoting from Dr. Edwards' letter—I haven't read the book, but hope to do so.)

Much as I would like to believe this, it simply is not so. We did not meet Norris until after my father's death. Frank told us that he knew my father's work only by reputation, and he expressed regret that he had never seen any of the Herne plays. He also told us that, as a young reporter on a San Francisco paper he had once interviewed my father, but that was their only meeting.[54]

In the spring of 1901, a few months before my father died, William Gillette sent him a copy of *McTeague*. It was one of the last books he ever read, and he admired it greatly and talked about it frequently; but I don't believe he ever realized it was the work of the young man who had interviewed him years before.

As for my mother's "influence"—Norris was very fond of her and she adored him, as we all did. But he never discussed his work with her or with any of us. When we met, he was already a mature artist, who was very sure of himself, knew just where he was going and what he wanted to do. Moreover, he was a very reserved and reticent person, and it was almost impossible to get him to talk about his work. Whatever "echoes" of Herne Åhnebrink found in Norris's work are due, I believe, simply to the fact that both men were realists and were following, each in his own way, the realistic trend of those times.

I did not intend to write such a long letter, but your letter brought back happy memories. In closing, may I say that I find your American *Oxford Companion*[55] invaluable? I browse in it constantly. I especially like what you have said about my father.

Sincerely yours,
Julie A. Herne

41 / William Dean Howells

Novelist and critic William Dean Howells (1837–1920), known in Norris's time as the most aggressive American advocate of Realism in literary art, befriended and counseled writers of his own generation, such as Mark Twain, and the next, such as Stephen Crane. Norris met with him often following his arrival in Manhattan in 1898—one of his visits to the Howells home proving a memorable occasion for daughter Mildred (1872–1966).[56] Howells enthusiastically reviewed both *Moran of the Lady Letty* and *McTeague* (the latter of which he first read in whole or in part when still in manuscript). Shortly after Norris's death, Howells composed "Frank Norris," a lengthy, evaluative description of his literary accomplishments. In its penultimate paragraph he included a brief, more personal encomium—to which he added in a subsequent letter to Norris's widow on December 14, 1902, "I am glad that my words about your husband gave you some pleasure. He lived long enough to prove himself a great man; and I loved him for his work and for himself. His loss is a grief to me which I cannot match with yours, but which is most genuine."

Source: William Dean Howells, "Frank Norris," *North American Review* 175 (December 1902): 778.

[. . .] Personally, the young novelist gave one the impression of strength and courage that would hold out to all lengths. Health was in him always as it never was in that other rare talent of ours with whom I associate him in my sense of the irretrievable, the irreparable. I never met him but he made me feel that he could do it, the thing he meant to do, and do it robustly and quietly, without the tremor of "those electrical nerves" which imparted itself from the presence of Stephen Crane. With him my last talk of the right way and the true way of doing things was saddened by the confession of his belief that we were soon to be overwhelmed by the rising tide of romanticism, whose crazy note he heard afar, and expected with the resignation which the sick experience with all things. But Norris heard nothing, or seemed to hear nothing but the full music of his own aspiration, the rich diapason of purposes securely shaping themselves in performance.

42 / Henry W. Lanier

Henry Wysham Lanier (1873–1948), son of poet Sidney Lanier, was one of the chief editors at Doubleday, Page & Co. whom Norris advised as a manuscript reader. Upon Norris's death, Lanier, on November 12, 1902, wrote to his widow that he hoped she would take comfort not only in her late husband's success as an artist but also in his having refused to follow the lead of others who pandered to fashion for the sake of popularity. Lanier wanted her to remember that, when resisting popular trends, Norris, to be true to his genius, "fought out his fight on the lines he laid down—*and won*. I cannot imagine a prouder thing to be able to say of a young man, a modern American novelist, than that he *could* have written cheap popular books but that he was too sincere an artist to do so."

Source: Henry W. Lanier to Franklin D. Walker, letter, April 30, 1931, Franklin Dickerson Walker Papers, BANC MSS C-H 79, The Bancroft Library, University of California, Berkeley.

Dear Mr. Walker,

I have your letter, and only wish I could be of more help than seems probable.

I didn't know Frank Norris *intimately* though we published his books, and he did for a time work directly in my department, reading mss.

As I understand it, Frank came East from California in response to an impulsive telegraphic offer from S. S. McClure, who had read something of his which aroused the quick McClure enthusiasm. (Probably *Moran of the Lady Letty*.)

McClure with his partner, John S. Phillips, ran *McClure's Magazine*. He, or the company, held a minority interest in the young book-publishing firm of Doubleday & McClure, founded and controlled by Frank N. Doubleday, who had left Scribner's to start his own business. I also left Scribner's and joined Doubleday as editor—I think early in 1898.

We were all so busy with the new venture that I knew little of the details on *McClure's* though we had a couple of box-stall offices on their floor in

25th Street; but I have been told by people on the magazine that Norris's association was not a success. McClure was a genius but erratic; Norris was probably not given a chance at the things he could do best; my impression is that his Cuban stuff and perhaps other assignments were not right for the magazine.

Certainly Frank himself became quite disturbed over the uncertain outlook, having come here in a blaze of excited hopefulness over the career which he felt had been suddenly offered him.

That year or early in 1899 a difference of opinion between Doubleday and McClure (over the relations between the two organizations) became so irreconcilable that, though there was no break in their personal friendship, Doubleday decided to sever the connection and start an entirely independent publishing firm. This he did taking Walter H. Page, myself, J. L. Thompson and S. A. Everitt under the name of Doubleday, Page & Co.[57]

In Norris's state of mind he was anxious to come with us, doubtless feeling that his future was as a writer of books rather than as a magazine reporter.

Accordingly we arranged to pay him a small salary for half his time, devoted to reading manuscripts, he being free to write the rest of the time, and it being loosely understood that we would publish anything he produced which we could make mutually profitable.

Naturally he wasn't a balanced reader for a young firm which must make money or go out of existence: he had no conception of the business side of publishing and no sympathy with the book which provides entertainment merely and makes a profit. But when one read his own ms. of *McTeague*—on great foolscap sheets, in fine handwriting, 600–800 words on a page—it was sufficiently clear that he was something much more important than a publisher's reader. And one of his last activities in the latter capacity was to recognize the verity and significance of Dreiser's *Sister Carrie*. (There was, as you probably know, a distressing mix-up on that novel—but there was never any question of our editorial recognition of the book's quality.)[58]

I rarely saw Frank outside of the office. But he did come up to my Greenwich, Connecticut, home over one week end, and I took him back to a little reservoir pond a few miles north and taught him to cast a frog for July black bass. After experiencing all the backlashing and casting away of baits and other troubles of the novice, he got fast to a three-pounder—and an angler was created there and then. Indeed, he got so enthusiastic that he found a tiny bungalow at Greenwood Lake, N.J., then quite primitive; and for at least one summer he worked rather harder at bass fishing than at writing.

I remember quite distantly the genesis of his Trilogy. He came in one morning at the 25th Street office ('99 that must have been—or the early part of 1900) with his eyes fairly bulging and unable to talk of anything but the Big Scheme which had taken possession of him.

"I've got a Great Idea!" he announced.

And he proceeded to outline the "Epic of the Wheat" as it had come to him the day before: *The Octopus*, picturing the earth's fertility and the crop; *The Pit*, with the life grain a football for speculators; "The Wolf," when the stream of food poured across the ocean to relieve a starving European people in an Italian famine.

It did sound big, and we left him free to work it out in his own way, not requiring any reading or office reports till he was ready.

Mr. Phillips of McClure's tells me he (Norris) had for years planned to use in some way the stories of the San Joaquin and the struggle between the ranchers and railroad which he had gotten before he came East; but evidently the idea had grown in his mind and had just taken its final form.

There was never the slightest pressure put on him by his publishers to force any particular kind of treatment. There was doubtless an unconscious inner pressure: he wanted terribly to be successful; and while I don't believe he would have consciously compromised on an artistic point, he saw quite clearly some of the qualities that made a novel popular and probably made an unconscious effort after them.

But beyond any question *The Octopus* is a better book than *The Pit* mainly because the material in that case had been thoroughly digested and assimilated; he understood and had a burning youthful sympathy for the ranchers, whom he considered oppressed by the Octopus;[59] and the stark bigness of the fecund earth had a peculiar appeal to him.

Whereas in *The Pit* he had to do first a reportorial job, talking to grain brokers, watching the swirling activity of the grain trading in Chicago—and desperately striving to understand a thousand things of which he knew nothing and with the basic forces of which he had little sympathy.

My own feeling is that he died too young to give more than an indication of what he might have become. He was highly immature mentally; unconsciously under the influence of Zola and the literal realists who so often confused strength with mere stench; and it has always seemed to me that with more knowledge of life, more perspective, more certainty of his own point of view he might have done something by which his actual books would have appeared mere growing pains.

I don't know if these fragmentary notes will be of service, but send them along as the best I can furnish.

Sincerely yours,
Henry W. Lanier.

43 / Edwin Lefevre

George Edwin Lefevre (1871–1943) was a journalist and stockbroker whose *Wall Street Stories*, published in 1901 by McClure, Phillips & Co., was a collection of stories treating market speculations of the kind that Norris dealt with in *The Pit*. As did fraternity brother George Gibbs and journalist G. D. Moulson, Lefevre tutored Norris on the intricacies of speculation in commodities. Arthur Bartlett Maurice (1873–1946), himself a journalist and editor of the *Bookman*, knew both Lefevre and Norris.

Source: Arthur Bartlett Maurice. *The New York of the Novelists* (New York: Dodd, Mead, 1917), 45–46.

[. . .] In connection with Mr. Lefevre's Wall Street experiences there is a graphic little story concerning him and the late Frank Norris. During Mr. Norris's last year in New York the two were close friends, and it was at one time agreed between them that Mr. Lefevre should revise the proofs of Mr. Norris's story, *The Pit*, in all the chapters relating to the wheat market, receiving due credit in the preface for his share of the work. As it turned out, they never succeeded in coming together for that purpose, and the plan was abandoned. But frequently, at Norris's request, Mr. Lefevre explained the intricacies of the stock markets, speculations, corners and the like; and one night he found himself launched upon an eloquent description of a panic. He described the pandemonium reigning on the floor of the Exchange, the groups of frenzied, yelling brokers, the haggard faces of men to whom the next change of a point or two meant ruin. And then he followed one man in particular through the events of the day, and pictured him groping his way blindly out from the gallery, a broken, ruined man. So far, Mr. Lefevre had told only what he had seen, all too often, with his own eyes. But at this point, carried away by his own story, he yielded to the temptation to fake a dramatic conclusion, and he told how the man was still striding restlessly, aimlessly along the corridor, when the elevator shot past and some one shouted "Down!" and the ruined man, his mind still bent upon the falling market, continued his nervous striding, gesticulating fiercely and repeating audibly, "Down! down! down!" "There you are!" interrupted Mr. Norris, springing up excitedly. "There you are! That is one of those things that no novelist could invent!" And yet, added Mr. Lefevre in telling the story, "it was the one bit of fake in my whole description." [. . .]

44 / Isaac F. Marcosson

Isaac Frederick Marcosson (1876–1961) was a journalist and editor whose most memorable accomplishment was the promotion of *The Jungle* by Upton Sinclair (1878–1968), the 1906 best seller published by Doubleday, Page & Co. In 1898 he was employed by the *Louisville Times*, for which he enthusiastically reviewed Norris's *Moran of the Lady Letty*. The result was both a lively correspondence between the two men and a subsequent string of appreciative estimates of Norris's development as an author.

Source: Isaac F. Marcosson, "Some Recollections of Frank Norris," *Louisville Times*, October 27, 1902, 4.

The untimely death of Frank Norris not only removed a vital force from the creation of American fiction, but it marked the passing of a character of appealing interest. To the reading world at large he had come to be known as a brilliant young author already past the threshold of success, but on that small circle whose privilege it was to know him well he exerted a rare and almost inspiring influence. In the light of the fate which felled him in the very flush of splendid young manhood, it is indeed difficult to believe that the almost resistless energy and contagious enthusiasm which were among his chief characteristics have ceased forever. Youth, hope, the tremendous possibilities of the future, seemed to be always about him. He believed in himself as few men did and what he accomplished in the comparatively few years of his activity justified that confidence.

Norris was essentially American. There are those who contend that with him there died the present prospect at least of the great American novel. It was Norris who comprehended its requirements more than any of his contemporaries, and to his friends he always maintained that some day he would "hit it right," as he expressed it. *The Octopus*, as it stands to-day, a tribute to his heroic imagination and ambition, comes nearer the mark than any book produced in years, and probably will stand for some time to come.

The people who met Norris the first time were always surprised. They could hardly realize that this beardless, boyish-looking man with the kindly eyes and the cheery manner was the creator of McTeague and the group of characters such as move in the drama of *The Octopus*. The only old feature was his hair. It was gray from his boyhood, but even that did not dim the picture of youth that he always presented. He was a bundle of energy. He thought, worked and talked fast. When he spoke of his plans his face always brightened; he seemed to be fairly illumined by the fire of his ambition.

Norris was a careful writer. When he settled in New York after he had been "discovered" by S. S. McClure he lived for a time in Washington Square in a flat where you could sit at the window and watch the children play under the big arch. Here he wrote *Blix* and *McTeague*, and it was here that he brought his bride, who was his good comrade and inspiration.[60] He often wrote as much as 3,000 words a day. He was longer in writing *The Octopus* than any other book. He always referred to it as "The Squid." Some idea of the original work may be obtained when it is stated that he cut over 50,000 words.

The idea of the wheat trilogy was born before his first book, *Moran of the Lady Letty*, was published.[61] He realized that it was a great thing, but he waited until his art as story-writer had been seasoned a little. Fortunately, *The Pit*, the second book of the group, is finished. He had started "The Wolf," which was to conclude the series, and had written to a few friends that he expected to take a trip to Europe on a wheat ship and get his material at first hand.

The scenes of "The Wolf" were all to be laid in Europe.

California was always the land of promise for Norris. It was he who created a new fiction for the region. In a letter written on New Year's day, 1899, when he had one little book to his credit, he said: "I have great faith in the possibilities of San Francisco and the Pacific coast as offering a field for fiction; not the fiction of Bret Harte,[62] however, for the country has long outgrown the 'red-shirt' period. The novel of California must be a novel of city life, and it is that novel I hope some day to write."[63] He saw the realization of his dream, for he gave San Francisco beautiful setting in *Blix*.

Norris always said that he couldn't help being a realist. He was a great student of Zola, and once, after the critics from one end of the country to the other had reviewed his work as "suggestive of the Zola influence," etc., he signed a letter to me as follows: "F. N., the boy Zola."

He was a charming letter writer. He fairly reeled off page after page of the most delightful comments on many, many subjects.

His literary creed is set forth in the following passage from a letter written in March, 1899, when he said: "what pleased me most in your review was the 'disdaining all pretensions to style.' It is precisely what I try most to avoid. I detest 'fine writing,' 'rhetoric,' 'elegant English'—tommyrot! Who cares for your style? Tell your yarn and let your style go to the devil. We don't want literature. We want life."

As I write there lies before me, written in Norris' little, cramped hand, his outline of *The Pit,* which he sent over a year ago, and in this he says of the wheat motive: "A great and resistless force, moving from West to East, from Producer to Consumer, benevolent and beneficent, so long as it is unhampered, but destroying all things and all individuals who attempt to check, control or divert it."

It is a tragic coincidence that the foremost exponents of realism in three great countries should die suddenly, almost within a month. In France Zola's great heart was stilled; in England, George Douglas Brown, the author *The House with the Green Shutters,*[64] was cut down just after he had tasted of the first fruits of success, and in our own land it is Frank Norris who is taken away.

There are so many circumstances which combine to make the death of Norris particularly sad. Attached to the tragedy of the ending of the young life, the infinite regret "that youth's sweet-scented manuscript should close,"[65] there is the death of high hopes, the shattering of a happy hearthstone and the unfinished work so brilliantly laid out.

California, which was the home of his adoption, and which he had made to live in the pages of his books, was the place where Norris always said he wanted to die. He dreamed of a great ranch with an adobe house, after the style of the old missions built by the gentle padres in the long years ago. Here he hoped to do his last work and end his days. And fate decreed that he should die in that gold land, but too soon.

45 / George D. Moulson

Cited by name on the acknowledgments page in *The Pit*, George DeWitt Moulson (1872–1968) was a business journalist in Manhattan who assisted Norris in ensuring the technical accuracy of the novel's depiction of the speculative activities at the Chicago Board of Trade. The depth of his continued personal relationship with Norris is measured by the fact that he was one of the two baptismal sponsors of Norris's daughter at the St. Andrew's Dune Church in Southampton, Long Island.

Source: George D. Moulson to Franklin D. Walker, letter, October 25, 1931, Franklin Dickerson Walker Papers, BANC MSS C-H 79, The Bancroft Library, University of California, Berkeley.

My dear Mr. Walker:—

Replying to yours of the 4th inst. regarding my recollections of Frank Norris and his method of working up technical details while he was writing *The Pit*, I am hazy about the dates but it was about a year before *The Pit* was published, while I was working on the New York *Evening Sun* that I met Norris who had come on from Chicago and wanted to know more about the wheat market. He was at that time a reader for Doubleday, Page, and had just started writing *The Pit*. As you know he had in mind a trilogy, starting with the growth of the wheat crop in America, its marketing and the speculative end as part of the distributive process and third, something that he planned to call "The Wolf," which would be concerned with famine conditions in Europe, resulting in part from speculative excesses in interrupting the normal flow of the substance of the staff of life from the great wheat producing areas of the United States before reaching the ultimate European consumer. He had seen wheat growing in California and the West, had visited Chicago and spent many days observing operations on the Chicago Board of Trade and then planned to go on a tramp ship around the Horn and visit European cities to see for himself, at first hand, foreign living conditions and what might take place should necessary food supplies fail to arrive as usual. At the time of our meeting, he felt rather uncertain regarding his complete mastery of the middleman's function, just what processes were involved in making a wheat "corner" and the specific conditions, climatic and otherwise, which would lead an operator to attempt an operation of that character.

Though he told me he had spent days watching brokers in the Chicago pit, he was a writer and understood very little about the speculative end of markets. Someone had directed him to the *Evening Sun* which had a daily story of the wheat and cotton markets and he was anxious to secure concrete assistance from someone who was familiar with the grain situation. I recall he came down to Wall Street, met me and asked if I would be willing to assist him by coming up to his apartment while he was writing this book which he intended to call *The Pit* dealing with a corner in wheat and help him get the details accurate. I said I'd be delighted to render any assistance in my power and the bargain was made. At that time, he was living on upper Broadway in the Washington Heights section of New York, with his wife and young child.

We started in. He had written the first few chapters of the book which we went over together and he consulted me on all the technical developments up to that point. We then rigged up a sort of thermometer arrangement on the steam heater, whereby the fluctuations, in cents, halves, quarters and eighths would be shown and we had the market fluctuating as it would during an active day in the pit. We spent considerable time over this, as well as developing the general wheat situation in this country, Argentine, Europe and Russia, going over in detail various possibilities which might unite to render a "corner" in the Chicago market possible.

He then wrote another chapter, telling me what he planned and just what would be involved in that stage of the market's progress. At the next meeting, this chapter would be gone over carefully and all the technical details straightened out. He was most anxious to have that end of the novel conform to facts, having at the same time a well thought out story development of which the speculative end was to be the background.

I recall after the lapse of thirty years or more, how vividly he portrayed the scenes, endowing my matter of fact, technical information with life and soul and how rapidly and fluidly the various chapters were composed during the intervals between our sessions. This went for several months. He revised each chapter after our evening talks, so that the progress was consistent and timed to coincide with the progress of the marketing season. His grasp of the whole subject was amazing, and no effort was spared on his part in securing such thorough familiarity with a broker's psychology as would make his characters true to life.

Along with the development of the story, he seemed most anxious to fit *The Pit* into this larger scheme of the trilogy. He never lost sight of the larger vision in all the painstaking attempts to compass the details of the story in hand. When the book was finished, I was deeply touched with the mention of my own name in the foreword which was a pure tribute of friendship since our whole arrangement had been on a business basis and quid pro quo. In giving me his photograph, he wrote on it "To the man who helped" and later, gave me his own personal copy of *Blix* with a whole hearted transcription.

I wish I could put in words adequate expression of the depth of affection and admiration inspired by our association. He was a rare soul, magnetic, generous and affectionate. His extreme modesty was delightful as it was unusual. It would be difficult to appraise the loss to American literature of his early death.

Sincerely yours—
George D. Moulson

46 / John S. Phillips

John Sanborn Phillips (1861–1949) cofounded *McClure's Magazine* with S. S. McClure in 1893. In early February 1898, Phillips offered Norris a position in New York City with the magazine and their syndicate that sold short stories to newspapers. Thus began their working relationship, which also included Norris's involvement in the operations of the book publishing firm of Doubleday & McClure Co. That relationship ceased at the end of 1899, when Norris chose to take a more promising position with the newly formed book publishing firm of Doubleday, Page & Co. Despite Norris's decision to ally himself with the new venture, Phillips seems to have harbored no ill will toward Norris: his wife, Jennie Beale Peterson Phillips (1867–?), years later, on November 23, 1952, told Hart, "I remember Frank Norris perfectly, his genial manner and what an interesting conversationalist he was."

Source: John S. Phillips to Franklin D. Walker, letter, April 18, 1932, Franklin Dickerson Walker Papers, BANC MSS C-H 79, The Bancroft Library, University of California, Berkeley.

My dear Mr. Walker:

I rec'd the pages from your book ms. & also a letter from Mr. Norris.[66]

Reading the scattered pages gives me little idea of the tone or trend of the biography. I fear I can be of little help.

I have made a few corrections in the copy—inessential no doubt. It would be necessary for me to write many pages about Frank Norris & his life here & the McClure office, the work he did there in the book dept (Doubleday & McClure Co.), the writing he did on books-to-be to give life & color to the period. This I cannot do. In those two years we brought out 3 books of his, *Moran*, *McTeague* & *Blix*. He was writing much of the time; merely seeing the books through the press is something of a job in itself. You say he finished *Moran* & wrote *Blix*.[67] I am not sure, but I have an idea that both were either finished or near completion when he reached New York. Certainly he handed in *McTeague* very early. After we had brought out this novel (held up by Doubleday's hesitancy because of the realistic contents) Frank gave me the ms. of "The Brute."[68] Not only Doubleday but most of us were doubtful about publication. I sent the ms. over to William Heinemann, the English publisher of *McTeague*. But even the continental-minded Heinemann, who recognized its remarkable qualities, would not risk publication. After Frank's death the ms. was found by Charles Norris, who apparently had never heard of it, & published it with D. P. & Co. some fifteen years ago. There had been such a change in the sensitiveness or tolerance of readers that it did not appear to shock readers, as we & Heinemann feared it might back in '99. It was late in '98 or perhaps in '99 that Frank gave me a big chunk of *The Octopus* to read. We talked of a "Trilogy of Wheat": (1) *Octopus* ("Squid"), (2) *Pit*, (3) "Bread" (labor, poverty, hunger).[69]

In the meantime we sent Frank with the distinguished illustrator & printer W. J. Glackens to Cuba.[70] Frank returned with plenty of notes & some interesting loot; Glackens with a rich lot of sketches. But the interest in that war died a natural death in a comparatively short time, & there was little demand for the material.

You see Frank did after all a lot of work & had some interesting experiences in that year & those quarters. His concern was well founded in that period.

The separation of McClure & Doubleday, & the adherence of Frank to the latter, is an intricate story which I could not tell in brief space. After the separation arrangement was made, & we started the book publishing firm of McClure, Phillips & Co., I took my family to Italy on account of my health. It was during my absence that Frank made the connection with Doubleday.

I had no intention of writing so long a letter when I sat down at the desk. I doubt if there is anything of use to you.

Yours truly,
John S. Phillips

47 / W. S. Rainsford

William Stephen Rainsford (1850–1933) was the rector of New York City's St. George's Episcopal Church, where Norris was a parishioner and where he married in 1900. Typing the "social gospel" orientation in turn-of-the-century Christianity, Rainsford enlisted Norris's services as an instructor in the educational program for immigrant youth that he conducted. Norris was impressed by his sermons and was instrumental in their publication as *The Reasonableness of Faith* by Doubleday, Page & Co. in 1902.

Source: W. S. Rainsford, "Frank Norris," *World's Work* 5 (April 1903): 3276.

We need today men who can see, who, seeing things and men as they are, can still firmly believe—believe in the general soundness of life, the "worth-doing" of it all. And still more, we need men who can put down accurately what they see sanely. Such a student, believer, artist was Frank Norris.

He has left us in the very morning of his life. He has gone before he struck the stride of midday marching. The best he has given had promise of still better work. But he lived enough, and put enough life into his line, to give notice to all that he is of those who, even in youth, are content with nothing less than to see life sanely, and to see it whole.

The honesty, the bravery, the faith of the man, all live in his work. The pity of it, that time was given to him only to make a beginning. Frank Norris's work rings true—always true. There is not one unmanly or unhealthy note struck. He takes it for granted that ordinary people, if we could only really see them, are interesting enough to write about, yet he never knows a trace of the sordid.

It was my privilege to be counted among his friends for years. I seldom have met so lovable a man. He had unquestionably great dramatic power. He believed with all his soul in the future of democracy, and ever and always he tried to serve his brother men.

48 / Grant Richards

Franklin Thomas Grant Richards (1872–1948) established his eponymous publishing house in London in 1897, seeing into print the next year works of such major authors as George Bernard Shaw (1856–1950) and A. E. (Alfred Edward) Housman (1859–1936). He became Norris's English publisher in 1899, marketing *Moran of the Lady Letty* as *Shanghaied* and, at Norris's insistence, refraining from changing the titles of his books that followed. In May 1901 he visited New York City for the expressed purpose of arranging British publication of works by American authors. Norris took the opportunity to promote a then unsuccessful literary figure, Theodore Dreiser, whose *Sister Carrie* he had recommended for publication by Doubleday, Page & Co. in 1900.

Source: Grant Richards, *Author Hunting, by an Old Literary Sports Man* (New York: Coward-McCann, 1934), 169–74.

[. . .] The Doubleday, Page office was [. . .] at 34 Union Square. It was not long after the original Doubleday, McClure Company had split up, Doubleday going one way and McClure another. Arriving one morning at Union Square, I was at once hailed round to the Doubleday town residence in East 16th Street to one of those round-table luncheons where privileged visitors met not only members of the family but heads of the various departments of the firm: Walter Page, later, during the War, to be Ambassador to Great Britain, who had just started *The World's Work*, the first of the Doubleday magazines; Sam Everitt; H. W. Lanier, the son of the poet, Sidney Lanier; and others. Round the luncheon-table projects were threshed out and criticisms offered in the freest and frankest spirit. I could not at the time see quite the same thing succeeding in England. But we have improved since then.

One of my chief purposes in going to America was to secure, if I could, the English rights in the future books of Frank Norris, one of the earlier of the Doubleday discoveries, whose *Moran of the Lady Letty* I had purchased in London from Roberts[71] and had brought out under the name of *Shanghaied*. It was not easy; Norris had to be convinced that I was the man to handle his books. However,

I did convince him, and when everything had been arranged he lunched with me at the Waldorf-Astoria and talked about his ambitious and perhaps rather French-flavoured literary plans, "the many magnificent conceptions that lay about loose in his brain," as the *New Yorker*, who cannot be old enough to remember, calls them, and, more immediately, *The Octopus* and the other volumes of his wheat trilogy:

> "But, Grant Richards, I want to tell you something. You think I'm the man to go after—and you've got me. Well and good. I hope we shall both be satisfied. Listen! I can tell you of an author worth two of me. If you can get him—and you ought to be able to—you can go back to England satisfied with your trip."
>
> The ardour of the hunter blazed up in my veins. "Who is he? I'll go after him this very afternoon. But perhaps he's already fixed up."
>
> "No, I'm sure he isn't. He's a Doubleday author—but that doesn't mean that it's all plain sailing. No, indeed. His name's Dreiser—Theodore Dreiser. From Chicago. I read his novel in manuscript. Magnificent stuff. I'd give every-thing I have to be able to observe and write like that. *Sister Carrie* it's called."
>
> "Why didn't any of them mention it to me? I asked so particularly if they hadn't someone else they believed in."
>
> Norris smiled. "Yes, that's where the difficulty comes in. You see, my report on the book—I read manuscripts for them, you know—was so enthusiastic that I had him come through from Missouri and they signed an agreement right away. Most of the bunch read it and were as keen as I was. It was set up in type, printed off, ready to bind—"
>
> "Well, I'll go round and get a copy—"
>
> "Don't be in such a hurry—you won't easily get a copy there, anyway. You see, the Old Man's wife got hold of a set of proofs one day and read it and then—well, she kicked like hell. She wouldn't have her husband's name on the title-page of a book like that! Every puritan, old-fashioned, instinct she had was outraged. It was a shame. She's a very nice woman, but, my word, she doesn't believe in the modern spirit in fiction; I don't suppose she'll stand for my work long. She made 'Effendi' [F.N.D. = Frank Nelson Doubleday: the name 'Effendi' had been invented by Rudyard Kipling; in the original it meant one who had earned the right to command] read it and of course he caved in.[72] The book must be given back to Dreiser; the contract must be cancelled; the firm would cut its losses. Anything to prevent the Doubleday name appearing on its title-page!"
>
> "And what's happened?"

"Nothing settled yet. They think it is, but it isn't. Dreiser's heart-broken, of course; all hit up over his disappointment. But I've told him to sit tight—that is, to hold them to their agreement to publish. I'll get a copy of the book somehow and send it you. Mark my words, the name of Frank Norris isn't going to stand in American literature anything like as high as Dreiser's. I really don't know what the Doubleday people will do. I think if Dreiser refuses to budge they'll get over the lady's scruples—I hope so, anyway. It's a wonderful book" and Norris continued to urge it on me.[73] Then I read the copy he sent me, and I did think highly of it but, somehow, I couldn't see it in England and made no offer for it, and, worst of all, did not see Dreiser for some years. [. . .]

What I remember most vividly in that early Dreiser story is Frank Norris's generous enthusiasm for the book of his protégé, his insistence on its merit.[74] Praise from the man who was to write *The Octopus* was praise indeed. [. . .][75]

49 / Elizabeth Knight Tompkins

Sister of Juliet Wilbor Tompkins, Elizabeth Knight Tompkins (1865–1955) was also a novelist and playwright who departed San Francisco for New York City to advance her literary career. She too lived on Washington Square and remained a member of Norris's circle through 1902 when he and Jeannette left Manhattan for San Francisco on their way to research "The Wolf."

Source: Elizabeth Knight Tompkins to Jeannette Williamson Norris, letter, November 8, 1902, Frank Norris Collection, BANC MSS C-H 80, The Bancroft Library, University of California, Berkeley.

My dear Mrs. Norris,

I am thinking of you so constantly these days that it seems as if my thought must have reached you of its own motion. This blow that has befallen you is so needlessly hard, and in my eyes it is not softened by any of the fictions that people invent because they are not strong enough to face the awful sadness, the unprofitable cruelty of life as it is.

I have such a vivid remembrance of Frank that winter in New York when I first knew him. It was the winter before you were married,[76] and he was so preoccupied that he did not take the trouble to make connections with other women,—not that I think he and I could ever have been congenial,—for one thing, my mental detachment in regard to the life in which he took so keen an interest would have jarred upon him. Still, it was always a pleasure to me to be with him; his personality was always so extremely attractive to me that I liked him better than many men who would have liked me better.

Of course his air of distinction and great good looks made one ready to like him, and then, back of that, there was the pleasant surprise of finding qualities that one did not anticipate. A man so good to look upon generally feels that he has no further obligations, and perhaps he has done his share. Perhaps the sunniness, the kindliness, the simplicity of Frank's nature, the intensity of life in him, were more than one had a right to ask for,—not to speak of his mental alertness and the interest his literary promise aroused. I had a great curiosity to see what the man would accomplish who had written *McTeague* so young.

I have never lost anyone very dear to me by death and yet I have a keener realization of that sorrow than of some I have felt. I feel as if I knew all its phases, as if I had experienced every pang. I know so well what to miss anyone means that I recognize the hopelessness of saying anything that will really help. This letter is more to free my mind of a little of the burden of sympathy than for any other reason.

The little poem of Lowell's that was in all our readers is running in my head:

Console if you will, I can bear it;
'Tis a well-meant alms of breath;
But not all the preaching since Adam
Has made Death other than Death.[77]

I do know what I am writing when I say that your little daughter will help you through. My little nephew, my sister Bonnie's boy, is a daily joy to us. She lost her husband—as the result of an operation—when she had been married only two years, and now her life is in little John's.

I shall hear of you when I can through the friends we have in common.

Poor Juliet can write or think of nothing else but your sorrow. It has been a great shock to her. And yesterday a letter from Gilbert expressed his deep sympathy.[78]

Just this minute the postman brought the letter that always comes from Juliet on Saturday. In it, she says: "Be sure and tell me if you hear how Jeannette is. I can't get over it—it's the saddest thing I ever knew. We have talked about Frank so much this week. I am going to miss them very much out of my life here."

Sincerely, your friend,
Elizabeth Knight Tompkins

50 / Juliet Wilbor Tompkins

Like Norris, Juliet Wilbor Tompkins Pottle (1871–1956), novelist, playwright, and sister of Elizabeth Knight Tompkins, wrote for *The Wave*, and then relocated to Manhattan where she served as editor of the *Puritan*, a monthly magazine. They both lived on Washington Square, and Norris's *Blix* first appeared in the *Puritan* as a serial. The Norrises' relationship with both sisters remained vital as they moved to Roselle, New Jersey, and later back to Manhattan.

Source: Juliet Wilbor Tompkins, "Foreword," *The Argonaut Manuscript Limited Edition of Frank Norris's Works* (Garden City, NY: Doubleday, Doran, 1928), IX: vii–x.

I see Frank Norris in glimpses, as one sees the Sierra through the cracks of the snowsheds: a flash of living colour, and then the darkness of the twenty-five years in between. His romantic good looks—thick iron-grey hair with a young, brown face; the stare that had always a widening of astonishment in it; the rather swaggering clothes—his hat was a broad-brimmed Stetson, his coat had a line at the waist, and the stick in his hand was telling the world as he took the Avenue. There was something of *mousquetaire* in him, of actor and romancer. We were all touched with Stevenson in those days, self-conscious adventurers who slept under the stars and strewed pennies to pay for the night's lodging, and Frank thrilled to the picaresque even while he was writing of dentists and brokers. I could never see much connection between what he was and what he wrote. His talk was boyish; he argued with passion, but wound up with a despairing, "Now don't begin to agree with me or I'll think I'm wrong!"[79] Going home from joyous and noisy evenings with him, one read his works with a wondering, "How came he by that!" I remember one night when we were discussing the ultimate rewards of talent, Frank declared for going into a restaurant and having the diners elbow their neighbours with a thrilled, "That's him!" And he would greatly have loved it, but robustly, humorously. Vanity was only an endearing game, for surface things; it did not touch the deeper side, where his work was.

Never was there a writer so free from irritable resentment of criticism. He could even laugh when he was laughed at. The banquet scene in *The Octopus*, where the starving crowd huddles without, tried for a supreme splendour, and a lady's remark, "These ortolans are delicious!" struck us as funny. We were not very clear what ortolans were, but we disputed the probability *of* them and took the stilted comment for a catch phrase. "These ortolans are delicious!" one would say of a poached egg.[80] Frank stood it with flawless good humour, and worked down the scene to a less lurid and more artistic level under the jeers. And he continued to try scenes on us, which was magnanimity on the grand scale.

He had many games. When he brought his bride to South Washington Square, he had done with his Latin Quarter days and was loud against Bohemia. He loved to say: "*Je suis bon bourgeois, moi—père de famille*!"[81] with a thump on the chest. So they played Good Society in their two rooms and made a rite of dressing for dinner. One night, invited with formality, I arrived to find Jeannette cooking the dinner clad in a black evening gown of glittering scales, scant above and voluminous below, and from underneath peeping the stout tan shoes that she had not had time to change, while Frank completed his toilet in the closet. But there was never any game about the food; it was wonderful. And the talk was alive, though somewhat under control. If Frank did not like a topic or an argument, he came down on it with an "Eat, woman—eat!" that effectually settled it.

The average person would have to inherit a fortune and go round the world to get the high adventure that Frank found in moving from two to six rooms and buying a new desk. Being a parent was also a game, entered upon reluctantly, for they were having a magnificent time by themselves, but cheered by such sport as they could devise. They wanted to name the child Billy, simply because it would be such fun to call "Billy!" and then have a little girl appear. My protests finally achieved for her a normal female name to sign on checks and documents, even though it was never used. I arrived one day to find them relieving the boredom of staying in with the baby by playing Hunt the Thimble, Billy being the Thimble. Frank had hidden her so successfully that we searched all the six rooms in vain until a crow from the Thimble led us under the valance of the bed. Later Frank woke up to the pleasures of paternity. Jeannette told me how, as they sat on the grass in Golden Gate Park, the baby began to crawl over Frank, and how he lifted that astonished gaze of his to say, "You know, I kind of like the little thing!" He had only a brief time left to enjoy it.

Frank, dying in the early thirties, left an amazing volume of work. Through the romance and the realism and the massive drama of the unfinished trilogy shines the promise of what he would have written at forty, at fifty, when he had outgrown his masters and become himself a master.[82] Surely there would have been plays, dramas done on broad lines, hot with conflict, important with meaning. The high moments of his books are always pictured; the final crash in *The*

Pit, where Jadwin goes down, could be played almost without words, and there was sound theatre in the unrolling of it before the eyes of a young girl who did not quite know what it was all about. *Moran of the Lady Letty* grew out of Frank's desire to stage a physical fight between a man and a woman. He loved that fight. The struggle for sex supremacy had a thrill for one who was so consciously, so unwaveringly master in his own house. "My wife does so-and-so," he would lay down the law, and indeed she did. There was the coat that Frank considered loud, though it would be thought tame enough to-day. Jeannette's only alternative at that stage of their finances was a rain coat, but it was the rain coat that she wore.

But he had charm! Charm and beauty and a living sense of romance. Every day in their lives was a fresh adventure. I think that even a girl of this generation would submit to the rain coat for the sake of such a mate.

List of Reminiscences

Part 1. Childhood and Youth: Chicago, San Francisco, and Paris, 1870–90

Brown, Philip King. Letter to Franklin D. Walker, October 7, 1930.
Neustadter, Louis W. Letter to James D. Hart, March 22, 1954.
Norris, Charles Gilman. Interview notes by Franklin D. Walker, May 16, 1930, June 9, 1930, and July 8, 1931.
———. Letter to Jeannette Williamson Norris, [August? 1903].
Peixotto, Ernest. "Romanticist Under the Skin," 613–15.
Sloss, M. C. Letter to James D. Hart, December 3, 1952.

Part 2. College Years: Berkeley and Cambridge, 1890–95

Bacon, Thomas R. "University Loses Distinguished Son," 1, 3.
Bartlett, Louis. Letter to Franklin D. Walker, April 29, 1933.
Burgess, Gelett. Letters to Claude Fayette Bragdon, May 18, 1899, December 5, 1902.
———. Letter to Franklin D. Walker, October 18, 1930.
———. Letter to Jeannette Williamson Norris, October 29, 1902.
Davenport, Eleanor M. Letters to Franklin D. Walker, October 5, 1930, October 19, 1930.
Easton, Stanly A. Letter to James D. Hart, July 19, 1957.
Edwards, George C. "University Loses Distinguished Son," 1, 3.
Everett, Wallace W. "Frank Norris in His Chapter," 561–66.
Gibbs, George. Letter to Franklin D. Walker, June 10, 1930.
Hathorn, Ralph L. Interview notes by Franklin D. Walker, April 15, 1930.
Houston, Albert J. Interview notes by Franklin D. Walker, April 30, 1930.
———. Unpublished autobiography, 29–34.
McClaughry, H. Hull. Letter to A. Edward Newton, May 12, 1931.
Moore, Ariana. Letter to Franklin D. Walker, April 1, 1930.
Peixotto, Jessica B. Interview notes by Franklin D. Walker, May 28, 1930.
Rhodes, Harry W. Interview notes by Franklin D. Walker, April 20, 1930.
Richardson, Leon J. Interview notes by Franklin D. Walker, March 18, 1930.
Samuels, Maurice V. Letter to Franklin D. Walker, May 20, 1930.
Selfridge, Edward A. Jr. Letter to Franklin D. Walker, June 18, 1930.
Todd, Frank M. "Reminiscences of Frank Norris," March 1908.

Waterhouse, Seymour. Interview notes by Franklin D. Walker, June 5, 1930.
Weed, Benjamin. Interview notes by Franklin D. Walker, March 21, 1930.
Wright, Harry M. "In Memoriam—Frank Norris: 1870–1902," 240–45.
———. Interview notes by Franklin D. Walker, April 7, 1930.

Part 3. Apprenticeship: San Francisco and South Africa, 1895–98

Cosgrave, John O. Letter to Franklin D. Walker, June 5, 1930.
———. Letter to Jeannette Williamson Norris, [October 1902].
Garnett, Porter. Letter to Franklin D. Walker, March 26, 1931.
Irwin, Will. "Introduction," 7–11.
Millard, Bailey. "Frank Norris," 293–300.
Norris, Jeannette Williamson. Interview notes by Franklin D. Walker, May 8, 1930, May 14, 1930, May 16, 1930, and May 22, 1930.
Porter, Bruce. Letter to Franklin D. Walker, June 4, 1930.
Rickoff, Bertha. Interview notes by Franklin D. Walker, May 29, 1930.

Part. 4. Professional Years: New York, Cuba, Chicago, and San Francisco, 1898–1902

Archibald, James F. J. Interview notes by Franklin D. Walker, October 18, 1930.
———. Letter to Franklin D. Walker, October 9, 1930.
Bennett, Raine. "The Norris Who Made Life Real," 17.
Davis, Dulce Bolado. Letter to Franklin D. Walker, June 12, 1931.
———. Undated interview notes by Franklin D. Walker.
Doubleday, F. N. Letter to Franklin D. Walker, May 4, 1931.
Garland, Hamlin. Diary entries, January 29, 1900, December 15, 1901, December 20, 1901, January 17, 1902, March 5, 1902, and October 25, 1902.
———. Undated memorandum in Garland's copy of *Blix*.
Goodrich, Arthur. "Frank Norris: The Estimate and Tribute of an Associate," 14.
———. Letter to Franklin D. Walker, March 4, 1931.
Herne, Julie A. Letter to James D. Hart, September 30, 1952.
Howells, William Dean. "Frank Norris," 778.
Lanier, Henry W. Letter to Franklin D. Walker, April 30, 1931.
Lefevre, Edwin. In Maurice, Arthur Bartlett. *The New York of the Novelists*, 45–46.
Marcosson, Isaac F. "Some Recollections of Frank Norris," 4.
Moulson, George D. Letter to Franklin D. Walker, October 25, 1931.
Phillips, John S. Letter to Franklin D. Walker, April 18, 1932.
Rainsford, W. S. "Frank Norris," 3276.
Richards, Grant. *Author Hunting, by an Old Literary Sports Man*, 169–74.
Tompkins, Elizabeth Knight. Letter to Jeannette Williamson Norris, November 8, 1902.
Tompkins, Juliet Wilbor. "Foreword," vii–x.

Additional Reminiscences

Ashe, Gaston M. Letter to Franklin D. Walker, August 27, 1930, Franklin Dickerson Walker Papers, BANC MSS C-H 79, The Bancroft Library, University of California, Berkeley.

Atherton, Gertrude. Letter to David A. Munro, December 17, [1902], HM 32452, Literary File, The Huntington Library, San Marino, California.

Burgess, Gelett. "One More Tribute to Frank Norris." *Sunset* 10 (January 1903): 246.

Cosgrave, John O. Letter to Jeannette Williamson Norris, October 24, 1902, Frank Norris Collection, BANC MSS C-H 80, The Bancroft Library, University of California, Berkeley.

Garland, Hamlin. *Companions on the Trail* (New York: Macmillan, 1931), 10–11, 103–4, 117, 126–27, 166.

———. *A Daughter of the Middle Border* (New York: Macmillan, 1921), 262.

———. "Death of Frank Norris Oct. 27, 1902," in "Literary Notes," unpublished journal, 287–91, Hamlin Garland Collection, Special Collections, Doheny Library, University of Southern California.

———. Letter. *Critic* 41 (December 1902): 537.

Gibbs, George. Letter to Robert E. Burke, November 6, 1952, James D. Hart Papers, BANC MSS 81/107c, The Bancroft Library, University of California, Berkeley.

Goodrich, Arthur. "Frank Norris." *Current Literature* 33 (December 1902): 764.

———. "Norris, the Man." *Current Literature* 34 (January 1903): 105.

———. "An Unfinished Literary Career." *Literary Digest* 25 (November 8, 1902): 593.

Hammond, John Hays, to Franklin D. Walker, letter, June 2, 1930, Franklin Dickerson Walker Papers, BANC MSS C-H 79, The Bancroft Library, University of California, Berkeley.

Hathorn, Ralph L. Letter to Wallace W. Everett, September 1929, Frank Norris Collection, BANC MSS C-H 80, The Bancroft Library, University of California, Berkeley.

Howells, William Dean. Letter to Jeannette Williamson Norris, December 14, 1902, Frank Norris Collection, BANC MSS C-H 80, The Bancroft Library, University of California, Berkeley.

Howells, Mildred. Letter to Franklin D. Walker, May 3, 1931, Franklin Dickerson Walker Papers, BANC MSS C-H 79, The Bancroft Library, University of California, Berkeley.

Lanier, Henry Wysham. Letter to Jeannette Williamson Norris, November 12, 1902,

Frank Norris Collection, BANC MSS C-H 80, The Bancroft Library, University of California, Berkeley.

Light, Evelyn. Letter to Franklin D. Walker, May 5, 1931, Franklin Dickerson Walker Papers, BANC MSS C-H 79, The Bancroft Library, University of California, Berkeley.

"Lincoln Man Tells of Norris." Lincoln, Nebraska *Star*, November 22, 1902, 16.

Marcosson, Isaac F. *Adventures in Interviewing* (New York: John Lane, 1920), 232–41.

———. *Before I Forget: A Pilgrimage to the Past* (New York: Dodd, Mead, 1959), 500–508.

———. "Some Literary Friendships," *Saturday Evening Post* 192 (August 16, 1919): 8–9, 104, 107, and 110.

Millard, Bailey. *History of San Francisco Bay Region* (Chicago: American Historical Society, 1924), 1: 422–25.

———. "A Significant Literary Life." *Out West* 18 (January 1903): 49–55.

———. "Writer Was Planning to Stay in California This Winter and Complete THE WOLF when Stricken by Appendicitis." San Francisco *Examiner*, October 26, 1902, 18.

Norris, Charles G. *Frank Norris 1870–1902* (Garden City, NY: Doubleday, Page, 1914).

———. "Introduction." *The Argonaut Manuscript Limited Edition of Frank Norris's Works*. (Garden City, NY: Doubleday, Doran, 1928), X: vii–xiii.

———. Letters to Franklin D. Walker, November 1, 1930 and January 19, 1931, Franklin Dickerson Walker Papers, BANC MSS C-H 79, The Bancroft Library, University of California, Berkeley.

Osbourne, Alan. Letter to James D. Hart, August 19, 1970, James D. Hart Papers, BANC MSS 81/107c, The Bancroft Library, University of California, Berkeley.

Peixotto, Ernest C. Letter to Franklin D. Walker, June 28, 1930, Franklin Dickerson Walker Papers, BANC MSS C-H 79, The Bancroft Library, University of California, Berkeley.

Phillips, Jennie B. Letter to James D. Hart, November 23, 1952, James D. Hart Papers, BANC MSS 81/107c, The Bancroft Library, University of California, Berkeley.

Porter, Bruce. Letter to Franklin D. Walker, July 11, 1930, Franklin Dickerson Walker Papers, BANC MSS C-H 79, The Bancroft Library, University of California, Berkeley.

Rainsford, W. S. Letter to Jeannette Williamson Norris, undated fragment, Frank Norris Collection, BANC MSS C-H 80, The Bancroft Library, University of California, Berkeley.

Senger, Lucy A. Letter to Franklin D. Walker, October 14, 1930, Franklin Dickerson Walker Papers, BANC MSS C-H 79, The Bancroft Library, University of California, Berkeley.

Todd, Frank Morton. "Frank Norris—Student, Author, and Man." *University of California Magazine* 8 (November 1902): 349–56.

———. Interview notes by Franklin D. Walker, April 2, 1930, Franklin Dickerson Walker Papers, BANC MSS C-H 79, The Bancroft Library, University of California, Berkeley.

Weck, Charles A. Letter to James D. Hart, July 4, 1957, James D. Hart Papers, BANC MSS 81/107c, The Bancroft Library, University of California, Berkeley.

Wilder, Edwin M. Letter to James D. Hart, August 26, 1952, James D. Hart Papers, BANC MSS 81/107c, The Bancroft Library, University of California, Berkeley.

Wright, Harry M. Letter to Franklin D. Walker, September 11, 1931, Franklin Dickerson Walker Papers, BANC MSS C-H 79, The Bancroft Library, University of California, Berkeley.

Notes

Part 1

1. Many, though not all, members of Belmont's first class did indeed attend Harvard, graduating in 1890. Along with Brown himself, they included Summit Louis Hecht (1869–1949), who became a wool merchant in Boston; Frank Lamont DeLong (1867–1963), who returned to San Francisco where he maintained an office in the Merchants Exchange Building; and Marcus C. Sloss, who practiced law for many years in San Francisco. Although Brown neglects to mention them, Charles Hitchcock Adams (1868–1951), whom Brown mistakenly assigns to Norris's class, and Hubert Howe Bancroft (1867–?)—the A. L. Bancroft whom Brown mentions was actually Hubert's father, Albert Little Bancroft (1841–1914)—a nephew of his more famous namesake, Hubert Howe Bancroft (1832–1918), were the remaining members of Belmont's first graduating class. Adams had begun his second year at the University of California when his father's financial reverses forced him to suspend his college studies (Aitken 1951, 284), while Bancroft elected to embark on a business career immediately upon leaving Belmont.

2. Gertrude Glorvina Doggett Norris (1841–1919) was the eighth child of nine born to her parents, Samuel Wales Doggett (1800–1872) and Harriet Wotton (1804–1892). Manifesting an early penchant for the dramatic, she taught school for her brother Simeon Locke Doggett (1829–1914) in Dubuque, Iowa, and then later in Chicago, where she also enjoyed moderate success as an ingenue before marrying Benjamin Franklin (B. F.) Norris (1836–1900) in 1867. After they moved to San Francisco in 1885, Gertrude systematically established herself as a formidable society matron, not only by founding the city's famous Browning Society in 1902, before whose members she routinely gave memorable readings and for which she served as literary director (Davison 1990, 15–16), but also by becoming a member of the Century Club of California, a private women's club founded a few years earlier in 1888. B. F. had built up his wholesale jewelry business from scratch, first in Lockport and Peoria, Illinois, and then in Chicago and New York, as evidenced by census reports: the 1860 census lists his worth as $1,300 in property and personal assets, while a decade later that figure has mushroomed to a staggering $70,000 (Crisler 2002, 15); in San Francisco B. F. made another fortune in real estate, income from which, after the couple later divorced, allowed Gertrude to continue to live more than comfortably (see Davison 1988).

3. Willis Jefferson Polk (1867–1924) was already a highly successful carpenter,

draftsman, and architect in Chicago and elsewhere before 1889, when he moved to San Francisco, where he continued his career, opening his own firm, Polk & Company, in 1911. Along with several other artists and writers in the Bay Area, self-consciously calling themselves Les Jeunes, Polk contributed to *The Lark*, the group's experimental avant-garde publication, which issued twenty-four monthly numbers from May 1895 through April 1897, completed by the *Epilark*, appearing the next month. While Norris never contributed to this preciously satirical "little magazine," he was on intimate terms with its members.

4. Norris's good friend Gelett Burgess, who along with Bruce Porter founded and coedited *The Lark* (Dinnean 1980, n.p.), contributed the famous humorous poem "The Purple Cow" to its initial installment (May 1895, n.p.) as well as several subsequent pieces featuring his drawings of ghostly "goops," cartoon characters he also later incorporated into several books. In a follow-up letter to Walker on October 16, 1930, Brown enclosed not the promised menu but a photocopy of an invitation to a dinner of Les Jeunes, held at Martinelli's on May 1, 1896; those who signed the menu included Norris, Brown, Polk, Porter Garnett, Burgess, Ernest Peixotto, and John O. Cosgrave.

5. Outside the window of an office at the corner of Kearney and Geary Streets, two dentists, Mark Lawrence Libbey (1816–?) for several years and later Luther A. Teague (1850–?), displayed as an advertisement of their trade a huge gold tooth, which Norris later incorporated into his 1899 novel *McTeague* (Norris 1899e, 196). Located at 1309 Polk Street was a branch post office above which Norris placed McTeague's "dental parlors"; the "candy store on the corner" (Norris 1899e, 34) is most likely that owned by George F. Robert at 1301 Polk Street, as Neustadter suggests; a drugstore at the northeast corner of Bush and Polk Streets may have been the one sporting a "showcase full of live" snakes that the character Trina describes as "crawly and graceful" (Norris 1899e, 68). In *McTeague* Norris also situated many other actual business establishments either on Polk Street or nearby (see Crisler 1973, 39–49).

6. Charles Gilman Norris's childhood nickname derived from the physician in Chicago who delivered him, Dr. Charles Gilman Smith (1828–1894), after whom Gertrude in turn named her youngest son; earlier, Smith, eminent in national medical circles, had both attended the final illness of Thomas "Tad" Lincoln (1853–1871) and treated his mother, Mary Todd Lincoln (1818–1882), which resulted in her temporary commitment to a psychiatric hospital.

7. One of several college preparatory schools in the Bay Area, Urban Academy (also known as Urban School) was located at 1017 Hyde Street, between Pine and California, when Norris was a student there (*Circular* 1883, n.p.); here Norris prepared for his entrance examinations (see Everett, chapter 12 this volume) by undergoing special tutoring by Henry Senger.

8. Although Norris used Joe Frenna as the proprietor of a "corner grocery" with a bar in the back (Norris 1899e, 13), the real Joseph (Guiseppe) P. Frenna (1851–1914) owned a barbershop at 1201 1/2 Polk Street, while an actual grocery store, Burmeister Bros., occupied the southwest corner of Polk and Bush Streets; interestingly, after McTeague and Trina marry, McTeague perks up a despondent Trina, worried over

their finances, by informing her that he has acquired a new patient, "a barber on the next block" (Norris 1899e, 224).

9. The tale of the making and subsequent truncation of *Greed* is indeed a fascinating one, complete with increasingly fantastic rumors as time distanced players from the film (see Weinberg 1972, n.p.). The brilliant but mercurial Erich Oswald von Stroheim (1885–1957) won some notoriety as an actor, mild fame as a writer, and explosive success as a director with not just *Greed* to his credit but *The Merry Widow* (1925) and *The Wedding March* (1928).

10. Neustadter links the rather minor, though popular, American writer of romantic novels, Francis Marion Crawford (1854–1909), whose *Saracinesca* (1887), its sequel, *Don Orsino* (1892), and *Mr. Isaacs* (1882) serve as representative examples of his work, with three foremost British realists—George Eliot (1819–1880) and her important novel *Adam Bede* (1859); William Makepeace Thackeray (1811–1863); and Charles Dickens (1812–1870). John Galsworthy (1867–1933), writing a generation later, produced the mannered chronicles of the fictional Forsyte family, *The Forsyte Saga* (1922) and *A Modern Comedy* (1929).

11. In *Elsie Venner: A Romance of Destiny* (1861), Oliver Wendell Holmes Sr. (1809–1894), creates a character whose serpentine traits developed while she was still enwombed because of a snake bite her mother then received.

12. An active civic leader in San Francisco's Jewish community, Ruth Arnstein Hart (1917–1977) was Hart's first wife.

13. A probable date for this letter as sometime in August 1903 derives from the date of the celebration the previous year for Jeannette's birthday, August 12, when she, Norris, Charles, and Gertrude gathered at the Poodle Dog, a popular restaurant serving French cuisine, then located at the northeast corner of Mason and Eddy Streets.

14. Café Zinkand then occupied 923 to 929 Market Street.

15. With profits from their successful writing careers, Charles and his wife, Kathleen O'Keefe Thompson Norris (1880–1966), acquired and maintained La Estancia, a rambling ranch house in Saratoga, California.

16. Charles elsewhere refers to "Robert d'Artois" as Norris's "first novel" (C. Norris 1928, viii). Written while Norris was studying art in Paris, it was never published, and the manuscript is now lost.

17. François Fénelon (1651–1715), *Les Aventures de Télémaque* (1699).

18. Although its title page notes a publication date of 1892, *Yvernelle*, Norris's first published book, actually appeared in November 1891. While whether Norris was ever a member of California's Army National Guard has proved impossible to document, he did, like all male students at the University of California, take courses in military science in order to fulfill a two-year requirement.

19. Norris was suspended from participating in military exercises beginning on January 29, 1892, "for duty in Military Science" (Sutton 1892b). Then on April 28, 1892, James Sutton (1865–1929), the university recorder, wrote him as well as his parents (Sutton 1892a) that the Academic Council had determined to suspend him "from the University until the time of [his] first Annual Examination in June" because he

had "neglected" his "military duties, having failed to obey a direct order, although previously disciplined for neglect"; further, he was instructed "not to come on University grounds" for the duration of his suspension. Norris's university transcript confirms the faculty's decision with the notation, "April 27, 1892: Suspended till Annual Exam" (University Archives n.d.). Norris did eventually fulfill the university's two-year military science requirement, though not until he was a senior (Crisler 1990, 123, n. 17).

20. William Dallam Armes (1860–1918) was an instructor of English at the University of California in whose English XVIII course freshman Norris was a student. If Norris indeed "hated" Armes, he may have had reason, for almost all of his marks in the two-semester course on "English themes" hovered between 3 and 4, or C and D (Hart 1986, 1–2). During the second semester of his sophomore year, Norris took English XV, a course in drama, from Armes, again earning a 4. When Norris died, Armes wrote two brief estimates of him, neither very favorable: "University Loses Distinguished Son" and "Concerning the Work of the Late Frank Norris." To Joseph Le Conte (1823–1901) Norris's debt was greater. A popular lecturer, Le Conte was a professor of geology and natural history. Under Le Conte's instruction, Norris took two two-semester courses during his junior year in geology and zoology. While he received a 2 or B in the former, in the latter he only achieved a 4. Norris had more courses under Félicien Victor Paget (1833–1903) than any other professor at Berkeley, including offerings in elementary French grammar (no grade recorded) and classic French writers (1 or A both semesters) in his freshman year, a continuation of the latter as a sophomore (2 the first semester and 1 the second), nineteenth-century French poets (1 both semesters) and Victor Hugo (1 both semesters) when he was a junior, and seventeenth-century French Literature (pass) and French Realism (pass) during his senior year (see Norris's transcript, University Archives n.d.).

21. Joachim Henry Senger (1848–1928), a professor of German and Greek at the University of California, also taught at the Urban Academy; under Senger's tutelage, Norris prepared for his university entrance examinations in English, Latin, and mathematics (see Everett, chapter 12 this volume).

22. During his freshman year at the university, Norris, Maurice Samuels, and Myron Wolf were seen so often together on campus that classmates dubbed them the Three Guardsmen, referring to *The Three Musketeers* (1845) by Alexandre Dumas (1802–1870).

23. A saloon in Berkeley much frequented by students, Heagerty's was owned by J. Dennis Heagerty (1846–?). It touted its "strictly temperance" atmosphere in the 1893 *Blue and Gold*, the university's annual yearbook, but a detail given later in the advertisements belied this claim: "Strawberry Creek passes the door, but none of the Students ever pass without stopping To Get a Drink of Coffee" ("Ads" 1893, 7), a carefully worded acknowledgment of his establishment's both clandestine and public fare by Heagerty, who had been arrested, tried, found not guilty, and rearrested during the course of Norris's sophomore year for violating the university's liquor law (see untitled notes in the *Berkeley Daily Advocate* during the 1891–92 academic year).

24. Initially erected as a freshman dormitory in 1863, Grays Hall featured running

water in its basement, the first dormitory at Harvard so equipped; by the time Norris lived there it no longer housed freshman students exclusively.

25. Norris had come to Harvard specifically to study under Lewis Edward Gates (1860–1924), who offered one of only a handful of courses in creative writing then being taught in American universities. In Gates's yearlong course, English 22, Norris earned an A. However, that was not the only course in which he enrolled at Harvard: in both French 5 and 14, taught in the spring of 1895, he received a B, while in French 6, taught the previous semester in the fall of 1894, his grade was a C; he also enrolled in English 2, another two-semester course, but seems never to have attended it, since his Harvard transcript carries the notation "Abs." for this course (see copy of Norris's Harvard transcript in the Frank Norris Collection).

26. *Vandover and the Brute* was published on April 11, 1914; unfortunately, Gates neglected this opportunity to repay Norris who, besides dedicating *McTeague* to his former professor, wrote a lengthy inscription in a copy of the novel that he sent to Gates (Crisler 1986, 64–65).

27. Precisely where in the novel the "five thousand words" Charles claims to have added to *Vandover* appear has not been determined, and with the loss of its manuscript can now never be known.

28. After a protracted battle involving both money and real estate, begun in May 1892, when B. F. Norris abandoned his family to flee east, the Superior Court of California granted a divorce to B. F. and Gertrude on June 22, 1894, Gertrude to receive all their property in the city, B. F. to pay no alimony (Stronks 1991, 3; also see McElrath and Crisler 2006, 125–30, for a full discussion of the senior Norrises' tawdry divorce proceedings). The "widow" B. F. married as his third wife was Belle Bovée (1844–1921), daughter of William Henry Bovée (1822–1894), who had founded San Francisco's first coffee roasting plant in 1850. As one-time mayor of Oakland in 1859, he could well have met the Norrises at various social functions. Belle Bovée had been previously married to William Garvey (1835–?), who had died by 1880, when she and their fourteen-year-old daughter Bessie B. (1866–1939) were living with her parents on California Street in San Francisco. B. F. applied for a passport on August 19, 1892, while living at the Victoria Hotel in Chicago, noting that he planned to return to the United States "within a year"; Belle Bovée Garvey, giving her address as New York City and adjusting her birth year by eight years later than it actually was, applied for her own passport two days later, stating her intention to return "about one year hence" (Passport Applications [August 1–September 30, 1892], nos. 43877 and 44288, M-1372, National Archives, Washington, DC). When precisely the couple married has not been discovered, and it is unlikely that they first met during their trip "around the world."

29. Begun in 1890 as an organ of the Southern Pacific Railroad to promote rail travel generally but specifically to the railroad's resort, the Hotel del Monte near Monterey, *The Wave* by the time of Norris's association with it had changed its stripes, becoming a slick-paper society weekly catering to "Those in the Swim." When its first editor, Benjamin Cummings Truman (1835–1916), a correspondent who achieved

fame during the Civil War, left the magazine to begin a newspaper empire of his own, John O'Hara Cosgrave succeeded him. Cosgrave hired Norris in the spring of 1896, first as a writer and photographer and then as "subeditor." As the record of Norris's contributions to *The Wave* discloses, he was soon submitting as many as four pieces to each issue (see McElrath 1992, 216–35).

30. With Norris's assistance in late 1900, Cosgrave landed the editorship of *Everybody's Magazine*, a new periodical published by Doubleday, Page & Co. (Crisler 1986, 126–28).

31. In a letter to Walker on May 8, 1931, Viola Rodgers (1874–1944) dated her relationship with Norris to a much earlier time than Charles recalls, noting that they first met while she was still a student at the Irving Institute, a boarding school in San Francisco, from which she was graduated in 1891.

32. In September 1897 Jeannette traveled east to Godfrey, Illinois, to enroll as a "sub-senior" student in her mother's alma mater, Monticello Ladies' Seminary, founded in 1838 (*Sixtieth* 1898, 8).

33. In the late summer of 1896 Norris made the first of two visits to the Big Dipper Mine at Iowa Hill, California, owned by the father of one of his college roommates, Seymour Waterhouse, where he worked diligently on *McTeague* (Crisler 1973, 23–24); his second visit occurred over a year later in late 1897. Not long after this, in February 1898, he went on behalf of *The Wave* to New Orleans to cover Mardi Gras but then abandoned that assignment in favor of entraining to New York to assume an editorial position with *McClure's Magazine* and the S. S. McClure Newspaper Syndicate.

34. Norris most likely began *McTeague* not at the University of California but at Harvard, as surviving *McTeague*-related themes he wrote for Gates's class there indicate, the first of which is dated February 7, 1895 (see Hart 1970). Many scholars and critics have reported the murky story of both the genesis and composition of *McTeague* (see Crisler 1973, 1–32).

35. Charles Caldwell Dobie (1881–1943), a San Francisco–based writer, gathered from Charles much information about Norris's antecedents and his Chicago boyhood; unfortunately, Charles's knowledge of Norris's early life was imperfect at best, in turn hopelessly flawing Dobie's biographical interpretation, "Frank Norris, or, Up from Culture." Charles is incorrect when stating that Dobie "made up" the kindergarten incident; as with much of *McTeague*, Norris based McTeague's murder of Trina on a real-life murder that had occurred in San Francisco on October 9, 1893, when Patrick J. Collins stabbed his wife, Sarah A., to death in the cloakroom of the Felix Adler Kindergarten at the southeast corner of Second and Folsom Streets, where she worked as a scrubwoman (Crisler 1973, 49–50).

36. Students in Gates's English 22 wrote a brief theme for each class as well as a longer theme every two weeks. Herbert Vaughan Abbott (1865–1929), a newly minted assistant instructor at Harvard, served Gates as reader, in which capacity he wrote responses on the forty-five extant student themes Norris submitted during the course. (See Crisler 1973, 63, 93–94, for a discussion of how many themes students in Gates's course probably wrote.)

37. Silent film star Holbrook Blinn (1872–1928) played *McTeague* in the 1915

World Film Corporation's now lost *Life's Whirlpool*; playing Trina was Fania Marinoff (1890–1971), wife of the now better-known critic and novelist Carl Van Vechten (1880–1964).

38. Long enamored of horses, Norris, along with his friend Ernest Peixotto, drew many of them at the Presidio military reservation in San Francisco. It is thus no surprise that early in his career he praised sculptor, painter, and illustrator Frederic Sackrider Remington (1861–1909) for his skill in capturing horses in motion (see Norris 1897d).

39. What Charles must have meant is that since *Moran of the Lady Letty* (1898), Norris's first published novel, had been copyrighted by its publisher rather than Norris, his heirs received no proceeds, later selling its rights to Famous Players–Lasky Corporation for the film version, produced in 1922 and starring Dorothy Dalton (1893–1972), a celebrated silent film actress, as Moran and Rudolph Valentino (1895–1926) as Ramon Laredo, a renamed Ross Wilbur. The novel was published on September 18, 1898, by Doubleday & McClure Co., formed the previous year by F. N. Doubleday and the flamboyant, unpredictable, but highly talented Samuel Sidney McClure (1857–1949).

40. *The Pit* appeared posthumously, on January 15, 1903.

41. As captain of Berkeley's football team, Loren Edward Hunt (1870–1916) played right halfback, and, though he was graduated in 1893, he remained at the university the next academic year and continued to play. The injury that kept him from participating in the "big game" with Stanford on November 31, 1893, was a sprained ankle rather than a broken leg (Crisler 1990, 122, n. 14).

42. Walker queries the accuracy of Charles's recollection that Norris had mastered the part of Jocasta rather than the male character Creon in *Oedipus Rex* by Sophocles (496–406 BC) for a student performance at the university (see Weed, chapter 25 this volume).

43. In high school Vandover's classmates refer to him as "Skinny-seldom-fed" (Norris 1914b, 8).

44. Although John Henry "Jimmie" White (1869–?) left the University of California several years before Norris entered, taking his law degree at Hastings Law School in 1891, he continued to attend gatherings of loyal members of Norris's fraternity, Phi Gamma Delta, at which he and Norris became fast friends; indeed, Walker speculates that Norris modeled McTeague in part after White (Walker 1932, 63). White later founded and served as first headmaster of White's Preparatory School in Berkeley (Crisler 1986, 132, n. 4).

45. Delta Xi chapter of Phi Gamma Delta fraternity, chartered in 1886, leased a residence on Dana Street between Bancroft and Allston Ways as its first fraternity house; the nickname for a member of the fraternity is Fiji.

46. Maria Macapa, a "maid-of-all-work" in *McTeague*, though not as obsessive as Zerkow, manifests, like many characters in the novel, strange compulsions, including her usual response when asked her name: "Name is Maria—Miranda—Macapa. . . . Had a flying squirrel an' let him go" (Norris 1899e, 21).

47. Whether Norris ever attended San Francisco Boys' High School, founded in

1856 as Union Grammar School, but changing its name to San Francisco High School two years later and thence to Boys' High School in 1864, remains problematic, since available school records do not include his name, yet various friends say he was briefly a student there. Charles did attend this college preparatory school, by then known as Lowell High School, having changed its name for a fourth time in 1894.

48. Virgil Macey Williams (1830–1886) moved permanently to San Francisco in 1871; primarily a local color landscape artist, he became the first director and principal teacher of the California School of Design, a position he held until his death in mid-December 1886. Norris served as a pallbearer at Williams's funeral. Earlier that year, Norris entered the school, then located on Pine Street, though in 1893 it moved to a mansion on Nob Hill formerly owned by Mark Hopkins (1813–1878), at the same time changing its name to the Mark Hopkins Institute of Art (McElrath and Crisler 2006, 68).

49. Norris, 1889, "Clothes of Steel"; Norris's notes and drawings for the article are in the Frank Norris Collection.

50. Gertrude's niece, Ida Lillion Carleton (1871–1898), daughter of Gertrude's older sister, Narcissa Newton Doggett Carleton (1836–1920), lived with the Norris family for several years prior to her marriage in 1892 to Frank Thompson (?–1898), then chaplain aboard the USS *Charleston*. Norris teamed up with James F. J. Archibald in Cuba where they had both served as correspondents to cover the Spanish-American War.

51. Norris had been sent to Cuba in early May 1898 by *McClure's Magazine* as one of several journalists covering the Spanish-American War; he and Archibald, among the first to return, reached New York aboard the transport *Iroquois* on August 5, 1898.

52. Charles may be confused here. When his brother returned from South Africa in 1896, he accompanied Gertrude in late February to the Hotel del Coronado near San Diego, where he recuperated from a virulent fever he had contracted while serving as a correspondent covering unrest in South Africa for the *San Francisco Chronicle*, beginning in late 1895. The surviving guest register of the Hotel del Coronado does not show a post-Cuba visit for Norris and his mother (Special Collections, San Diego State University).

53. Possibly Félix Quatremain (ca. 1850–?).

54. Founded in 1868 by Rodolphe Julian (1839–1907) and effectively a feeder school for L'École des Beaux Arts, the Académie Julian provided its students with training in painting and other artistic media (Freher 1989, 1). The roster of students educated at the academy glitters, including, among many others, Henri Matisse (1869–1954), Robert Henri (1865–1929), John Singer Sargent (1856–1925), (Joseph) Fernand (Henri) Léger (1881–1955), and Alphonse Mucha (1860–1939). Norris studied there for two years, from July 1887 through August 1889.

55. Norris's principal instructor during his artistic foray was William-Adolphe Bouguereau (1825–1905), a major figure in nineteenth-century academic art.

56. Jules Bastien-Lepage (1848–1884) died before Norris studied in Paris. Charles may have misremembered Jules Joseph Lefebvre (1836–1911), an instructor at the Académie Julian who regularly visited Bouguereau's studio.

57. *Trilby* (1894) by illustrator, artist, and writer George Louis Palmella Busson du Maurier (1834–1896) enjoyed widespread popularity; Norris certainly read the novel but not in Paris, for it was not published until his last year at Berkeley.

58. Giacomo Meyerbeer (1791–1864) composed *Les Huguenots*, which premiered at the Paris Opéra in 1836, and *Le Prophète*, premiering at the same venue in 1849; works in five acts, both are notable examples of grand opera. Besides his best-known opera, *Faust* (1859), Charles-François Gounod (1818–1893) in his later years often conducted performances of the work of his peers.

59. A writer of imaginative children's stories, Frank Richard Stockton (1834–1902) also wrote the fable "The Lady, or the Tiger?" in 1882. Norris drew upon his apparently considerable knowledge of medieval French history for the long story he sent to Charles, naming the title character after Gaston III, Comte de Foix (1331–1391).

60. Edward George Earle Lytton Bulwer-Lytton (1803–1873) was a novelist of some repute; now little read, he enjoyed the friendship of many eminent Victorians. Norris's maternal grandmother, Harriet Doggett, owned a copy of his *Devereux* (1829), which she gave to Gertrude who in turn gave it to Norris (Crisler 1988, 2–3).

61. Norris took this detail from the closing scene of the play *Under the Gaslight* (1867) by Augustin Daly (1838–1899), in which the heroine saves the hero who had been tied fast to railroad tracks before an oncoming train.

62. Sarah "Lulu" Fargo (1871–?), daughter of wholesale liquor dealer Jerome Bonaparte Fargo (1824–?) and Martha Maria True (1834–?), appeared frequently in the society columns of San Francisco newspapers; she later married Robert Gray Bonestell (1869–1941), a Belmont School alumnus and wealthy wholesale jeweler.

63. Jean Froissart (ca. 1337–ca. 1410), *Chronicle* (1523, 1525).

64. Luke 11:11–12: "If a son shall ask bread of any of you that is a father, will he give him a stone? . . . Or if he shall ask an egg, will he offer him a scorpion?"

65. For information on Norris's banjo playing as well as a list of songs written on his own banjo, see Blues (1991); the banjo is now in the Norris collection of Phi Gamma Delta National Headquarters, Lexington, Kentucky.

66. Norris (1900c).

67. According to the 1880 Chicago census, the Norris household included a full complement of servants, of whom one was John Smith (1847–?), an African American coachman from South Carolina, where several of Norris's mother's relatives lived.

68. Originally a dry goods and clothing salesman, Augustus Eugene Bournique (1842–1926), with the help of his wife, Elizabeth Ann Corning (1846–1928), herself a dance instructor, in 1865 opened the first of a succession of dancing schools in Chicago, which immediately attracted the children of Chicago's elite.

69. Not yet born, Charles would understandably have known little about the Norris family's first trip abroad in 1878 (see McElrath and Crisler 2006, 58).

70. Supposedly said by Socrates (469–399 BC) at the time of his execution.

71. Norris owned several books by the French naturalist Émile Zola (1840–1902) (see Crisler 1988, 5, 9).

72. Norris became a Fiji on June 10, 1891, near the end of his freshman year (see Everett, chapter 12 this volume).

73. The photograph of Gertrude is now part of the Frank Norris Collection. The article by bibliophile Randolph Edgar (1884–1931) in *The Bellman* was "The Manuscript and the Man" (Edgar 1916); in 1921 Edgar gave his collection of Norris materials, including fourteen pages of the *McTeague* manuscript, to Harvard (see "Vandover and the Brute" 1921).

74. Newly arrived from Scotland, William M. Alister (1847–1921) joined B. F.'s jewelry firm in the late 1860s, becoming even more closely associated with the Norrises on December 31, 1873, when he married Ella S. Carleton (1857–1947), Ida's older sister. A change in the firm's name to B. F. Norris, Alister, and Co. recognized Alister's growing importance not only as partner but also as manager after B. F. moved his family to the Bay Area.

75. Lillian Adele Comstock (1878–?) held various positions with Doubleday, Page & Co. and its successor, Doubleday, Doran, and Co., for over four decades, before retiring in 1946. Daniel Longwell (1899–1968), then head of advertising at Doubleday, Doran, left that firm in 1934 to take up freelance journalism and editing. Every mid-July since 1878, San Francisco's all-male Bohemian Club, of which Norris had been a member, has met at the Bohemian Grove in Monte Rio, California, for an encampment of several weeks during which members present short plays and other entertainments.

76. Gertrude's eight siblings include Samuel Wales Doggett (1824–1903), Julia Harriet Doggett Wheeler (1827–1910), Simeon Locke Doggett (1829–1914), Malvina Campbell Doggett Hale (1831–?), Theophilus Melancthon Doggett (1833–62), Narcissa Newton Doggett Carleton (1836–1920), William Alfred Doggett (1839–1921), and Lawrence Bryant Doggett (1845–1864) (see McElrath and Crisler 2006, 33–36). Their father, Samuel Wales Doggett, owned no "ranch" but did purchase his father's farm in Mendon, Massachusetts, after returning there from Charleston, South Carolina, where he had met and married his wife and established the city's first free public school (Crisler 2002, 10). Aspiring journalist Denison Hailey Clift (1885–1961) was the first to state that Norris had based the character of Magnus Derrick in *The Octopus* on his maternal grandfather (Clift 1907, 320).

77. While generations of Doggetts, beginning with the immigrant Thomas (1607–1692), are buried in Massachusetts, only one, the Reverend Simeon Doggett (1765–1852), Norris's great-grandfather, ever lived in Taunton, though even he had left there by 1813; he had become a Unitarian before graduating from Rhode Island College (now Brown University) in 1788, but five years later, when he was first licensed to preach, he adopted Congregationalism, the creed of his Doggett ancestors.

78. Even though the Doggett family lived for well over a century and a half in Plymouth County, Massachusetts, they seem never to have intermarried with any Mullinses or Aldens.

79. Through several lines, including Doggetts, Waleses, Fobeses, Fullers, Hungerfords, Spragues, Fords, Eameses, Pierces, Dingleys, Chillingworths, and many others, Norris could have traced his maternal ancestry to both England and Scotland; descendants of many of these forebears, like Thomas Doggett, were New World colonists

in the early 1600s. Despite Charles's contention here, Norris could also have claimed an "aristocratic" colonial heritage from his father's family. Although efforts to extend the Norris line beyond B. F.'s own father Josiah (1803–1865) have proved fruitless, his mother, Lydia Colton (1805–1864), was born in Longmeadow, Massachusetts, and, like Samuel Wales Doggett, counted many early New England families—among them Booths, Hales, Chandlers, Abbotts, Blisses, and others—in her lineage.

80. After teaching in Chicago's public schools for four years, Gertrude embarked on a brief but apparently fulfilling stint as an actress, performing in several plays during the holiday season of 1866–67. Just a few months later, on May 27, Gertrude and B. F. married, thereby checking her dramatic aspirations; their first child, Grace Colton Norris (1868–1869), born on December 31, 1868, lived less than four months.

81. A condition of painfully swollen breasts initiated by lactation.

82. This story has not been verified; indeed, information on Gertrude's maternal progenitors is slight. Her mother, Harriet Wotton, was the daughter of James Wotton, usually identified as "Captain," and Chloe Campbell (1757–1831), who seems to have moved from Virginia to Charleston, South Carolina, as a widow prior to 1810, when she appears on the census as Chloe Woton, head of her own household. Harriet's only known sibling, John A. Wotton (?–1832), operated a public school with her husband for a time before the Doggett family moved to Massachusetts.

83. Married in Brighton, New York, in 1825, Josiah Norris and Lydia Colton by 1830 had moved to Michigan, settling first in Washtenaw County and then in Plainfield, Kent County. Their progeny numbered six: David B. (1827–1857), a daughter (name unknown) who died in infancy in 1828, James Henry (1830–1900), Sarah M. (1833–1881), B. F., and Josiah B. (1839–1922) (McElrath and Crisler 2006, 38–40).

84. Why Walker made this inquiry is not apparent, though in March 1930 the Spring Valley Water Company became a municipality-owned entity that since 1865 had enjoyed a virtual monopoly as the profitable provider of water for the city and county of San Francisco. Walker possibly had reason to speculate that B. F. had been associated in some way with the company.

85. This is possible, though they would have lived in Chicago, not Cincinnati. By the time Norris was born, his parents had recently moved from 789 Wabash Avenue to 904 Michigan Avenue, where they lived at least until 1876, when Chicago city directories list their address as 722 Michigan Avenue; their final Chicago address was 10 Lake Park Place (now Park Row).

86. Norris's younger sister, Florence Colton Norris (1871–1872) was two days shy of her first birthday when she died; both Grace and Florence were originally buried at Graceland Cemetery in Chicago, but Gertrude had their bodies moved to the family plot at Mountain View Cemetery in Oakland, California, in 1887.

87. Despite the fact that parts of Chicago were still burning on the third day the great fire raged, B. F. Norris & Co. proudly proclaimed that it had been "burnt out but not destroyed" and "like the phoenix" had risen from "ashes" to be open for business on October 10, 1871, having transferred stock to a new store at 468 Wabash Avenue (*B. F. Norris* 1872, [2–3]).

88. Charles was probably thinking of Fredrica Krocht (1836–?), who by virtue of having been born in Canada, according to the 1880 census, qualified as a "French maid." The portrait of Norris at age four is in the Frank Norris Collection.

89. Whether Gertrude, as some biographers contend, paid for the publication by J. B. Lippincott and Company of Norris's long poem with its octosyllabic couplets, a surfeit of medieval trappings, and the deathless love of Yvernelle for a wavering Sir Caverlaye is unknown, but she certainly promoted her son's maiden effort. She turned to such established artists as Will Hicock Low (1853–1932), a renowned muralist and stained glass artist, Frederick Dielman (1847–1935), a muralist and mosaicist, and illustrator Frederick Stuart Church (1842–1924), among others for contributions to the book.

90. The expression derives from a rail trip made by the fictional Eli Perkins, pen name of humorist Melville Delancey Landon (1839–1910). At each stop on his journey through Iowa at eighty miles per hour in *Eli Perkins* (1875), people gathered along the track and shouted, "Get there, Eli!"

91. Available records provide no information on where the Norrises spent the winters of 1883/84 and 1884/85, nor are city directories more helpful since that for Chicago in 1884 lists B. F.'s residence as San Francisco, while the next year's directory has him back at 10 Lake Park Place. On October 21, 1885, the family moved to 1822 Sacramento Street in San Francisco, the elegant former residence of Henry Tiffany Scott (1846–1927), co-owner with his brother, Irving Murry Scott (1837–1903), of Union Iron Works.

92. Vernon Bryson (1913–1985) was the son of Walker's mentor at the University of California Extension Division in Berkeley, the famous educator Lyman Bryson (1888–1959) to whom Walker dedicated his biography of Norris.

93. "1870," the subtitle of the first of four sketches in Norris's "Suggestions" (Norris 1897j).

94. "Grettir at Drangey" (Norris 1902e) and "Grettir at Thornhall-Stead" (Norris 1903b).

95. *La Terre* (1887); *Madame Bovary* (1857) by Gustave Flaubert (1821–80). Norris owned a copy of both novels (Crisler 1988, 5, 10).

96. While no cat appears in Norris's surviving Harvard theme for February 19, 1895, in which he first describes Trina's death, Norris does place a cat in the comparable scene in chapter XIX of *McTeague*.

97. Erected in 1870, Memorial Hall, built in honor of Harvard alumni who fought in the Civil War, functioned as Harvard's main dining hall until 1926.

98. The Hotel Harvard, owned by Bernard C. Welch (1850–?), was located at 221 Main Street—then named Massachusetts Avenue—in Cambridge. Miss Bates serves as the model for Miss Baker in *McTeague*, and Norris also used Grannis's name in the same novel.

99. Like information on the composition of *McTeague*, that for *Vandover* is equally sketchy. Charles's pronouncements regarding *Vandover* may indeed be accurate, though others suggest that Norris had not completed it by the time he left Harvard in 1895; at any rate, he did not submit the novel for publication until several years later,

when it was rejected by both Doubleday, Page & Co. and William Heinemann (1863–1920), the intrepid British publisher (see Phillips, chapter 46 this volume). Meanwhile, *Blix,* his third published novel, appeared on September 15, 1899. The description of the Bessemer family's parlor is part of chapter II in *Blix*; the wreck of the *Mazatlan*, on which Vandover is a second-class passenger, occurs in chapter 9 of *Vandover and the Brute.*

100. Charles is possibly referring to President Herbert Clark Hoover (1874–1964), who on March 19, 1892, at the first "big game" between the University of California and Stanford, was the manager of Stanford's then fledgling football team.

101. A sister of John O. Cosgrave, Millicent M. Cosgrave (1875–1939), a physician in San Francisco, was a faculty member of both Stanford and Finch Junior College in New York City.

102. Svengali was a hypnotist in George du Maurier's *Trilby.* Paul Meredith Potter (1853–1921) wrote a dramatic adaptation of the novel, which premiered at the Park Theatre in Boston on March 11, 1895, starring Virginia Harned (1872–1946) in the title role and, as Svengali, Wilton Lackaye (1862–1932), about whom Norris later wrote in "Lackaye 'Making Up'" (Norris 1896c), and who himself starred as Jadwin in the stage adaptation of *The Pit* (Norris 1903d).

103. What survives of the *McTeague* manuscript, about a third of the original, shows that Norris was a skillful reviser.

104. "Moran of the 'Lady Letty': A Story of Adventure off the California Coast" (Norris 1898b) ran in thirteen weekly installments in *The Wave*, from January 8, 1898, through April 9.

105. John S. Phillips, a partner in the S. S. McClure Company, wrote Norris on February 11 to offer him a position with the McClure syndicate, which he and McClure, who had met as students at Knox College, cofounded in 1882. While Norris officially responded on February 14 (McElrath and Noto 1990, 61; McElrath and Crisler 2006, 256), he had proudly confided his fortuitous news to a college chum, Eleanor M. Davenport, two days earlier (Crisler 1986, 45), confirming a visit to New York where he discussed possible employment with the firm.

106. *McTeague* appeared on February 25, 1899; its third printing, published on June 10, contained revisions Norris made primarily on p. 106, but on other pages as well to delete the famous pants-wetting scene, substituting instead McTeague's search for his misplaced hat (McElrath 1992, 30, 323). Neither Doubleday, then head of Doubleday & McClure Co., nor his wife, was responsible for the altered text; instead, British publishing phenomenon Grant Richards, who had just published Norris's *Moran* as *Shanghaied* (Norris 1899f), worried over the reception a British audience might accord the Zolaesque *McTeague*, insisted that Norris rewrite the offensive scene (McElrath and Crisler 1989).

107. In 1930 San Francisco bibliographer and publisher Harvey Taylor brought out a keepsake volume, *Frank Norris: Two Poems and "Kim" Reviewed*, accompanied by a bibliography that he had compiled, of which Charles said, "This is the most accurate bibliography of the first editions of my brother's writings" (qtd. in Taylor 1930, n.p.).

108. When McClure opted not to publish any of Norris's Spanish-American War

articles, Norris turned to Paul Revere Reynolds (1864–1944), founder of America's first literary agency, for assistance in placing them. Reynolds successfully sold "With Lawton at El Caney" (Norris 1899g) to *Century* (Crisler 1986, 55–56). Why Walker wrote "Nothing" is not determinable.

109. For the complicated story of Norris's involvement in the publication of *Sister Carrie* (1900), the first novel Theodore Dreiser (1871–1945) wrote, see McElrath and Crisler (2006, 373–76).

110. Cattle magnates Henry Miller (1826–1916) and Charles Lux (1823–1887), both immigrant German butchers in San Francisco, formed a partnership in 1858 to supply beef to the city. By the 1890s, their firm owned nearly a million and a half acres in California with additional holdings in Nevada and Oregon (Igler 2001, 201); almost half of their California acreage comprised a ranch in the San Joaquin Valley. Although Norris visited the San Joaquin Valley during his research for *The Octopus* (see McClaughry, chapter 16 this volume, and Millard, chapter 30 this volume), he also spent much of his time at the Santa Anita Ranch near Tres Piños to the west of the San Joaquin.

111. Bruce Porter notes that Norris "twice 'did'" him in print, intimating that the second was as Sheldon Corthell in *The Pit* (Norris 1903d); Norris's earlier rendition of Porter evidently was as Vanamee in *The Octopus* (Norris 1901c).

112. Leo Tolstoy (1828–1910), *Anna Karenina* (1877); Alphonse Daudet (1840–1897), *Jacques* (1876), quotation from chapter XIII.

113. By the end of 1931, both hardcover and paperback sales of *The Octopus*, published on March 30, 1901, would number almost 60,000 copies, making it Norris's third largest selling book after *The Pit* at nearly 190,000 and *McTeague* at 68,000 (see "Frank Norris Sales," Frank Norris Collection n.d.).

114. Norris and Jeannette purchased a single-room cabin, naming it Quien Sabe, in the coastal range above Gilroy, California, from Fanny Stevenson, widow of Robert Louis Stevenson, when they resided in San Francisco in the summer and fall of 1902.

115. At the time of Norris's death, his last novel, *The Pit*, was running serially in the *Saturday Evening Post*; twenty installments appeared between September 20, 1902, and January 31, 1903 (Norris 1902–3).

116. "The Passing of Cock-Eye Blacklock" appeared in *Century* nearly eight months after Norris died (Norris 1902g).

117. "Bibliography, Essays, Articles, Letters" accompanied Norris's literary essays, which Charles compiled as *The Responsibilities of the Novelist* (Norris 1903e), published by Doubleday, Page & Co. in 1903. For assistance on the project Jeannette turned to her good friend, Isobel Stewart Osbourne Strong Field (1858–1953), daughter of Fanny Stevenson and widow of artist Joseph Dwight Strong Jr. (1852–1900).

118. As Peixotto earlier recalled in a letter to Walker on June 28, 1930, one reason he and Norris spent a good deal of time together was that Norris then "had few friends . . . being of a retiring and quiet disposition" (Peixotto 1930).

119. No. 1 Rue de Lille, not far from the present Musée D'Orsay (McElrath and Crisler 2006, 100).

120. The battle at Crécy during the Hundred Years' War occurred on August 26, 1346.

121. Like both Norris and Peixotto, Guy Orlando Rose (1867–1925), later characterized as an American impressionist, was a student at the California School of Design before continuing his artistic study at the Académie Julian in 1888.

122. Norris actually published four stories before "The Jongleur of Taillebois" (Norris 1891b) appeared in *The Wave*, the first of which was "The Coverfield Sweepstakes" (Norris 1890b), which came out in the *Occident*, a student periodical, during the first semester of his freshman year at Berkeley; his first story to appear in a nonstudent journal was "The Son of the Sheik" (Norris 1891c), published in the *Argonaut* in 1891.

123. Sir Walter Scott (1771–1832).

124. Walter Shirlaw (1838–1909) specialized in murals, stained glass, and magazine illustration.

125. *Yvernelle*, Canto III (ll. 453–56) (Norris 1892c).

126. Not Berkeley's college paper but its yearbook, the *Blue and Gold*, produced by each successive junior class, actually included material for the academic year prior to its yearly appearance; thus, Norris's freshman year at the University of California, 1890–91, was captured in the 1892 edition of the annual. The 1894 *Blue and Gold* lists him as an assistant editor, one of two "artists" for this volume of the yearbook (*Blue and Gold* 1893 [1894], 4).

127. Although Charles Norris had gathered a few of Norris's *Wave* selections for the tenth volume of the *Argonaut Manuscript Limited Edition of Frank Norris's Works* (C. Norris 1928) and others had appeared in *The Third Circle* (1909), *Frank Norris of "The Wave"* (Norris 1931), edited by Oscar Lewis (1893–1992), included thirty examples of Norris's work from the weekly.

128. The "sea-dog" to whom Peixotto refers here is Joseph Hodgson (1858–?), who served as Keeper of the Fort Point Life Saving Station at the southern side of Golden Gate on the Presidio Reservation for over a decade, 1892–1903 (Abbott 2004). While the Fort Point Station did not open until 1889, a lighthouse had existed there since 1853; the station operated for over a century, not closing until 1990. Norris met Hodgson during the summer of 1897, introduced the crusty seaman to Jeannette, included material about him in "Life-Line and Surf Boat" (Norris 1897e), used him as the original of Jack Hoskins in *Blix* (Norris 1899b), and dedicated *Moran of the Lady Letty* (Norris 1898b) to him.

129. James F. J. Archibald and Norris were fellow correspondents in Cuba, covering the Spanish-American War.

130. See Norris (1899e, 4).

131. See "A New American Author," a four-page encomium appearing at the end of the first printing of the first edition of *McTeague* (1899e).

132. *McTeague* was published in England on October 24, 1899.

133. One contentedly makes his own little way forward.

134. *A Man's Woman* (Norris 1900b) appeared on February 3, 1900 (McElrath 1992, 61).

135. Norris was actually fifteen when Belmont opened in the fall of 1885.

136. William Henry Chickering (?–1915) with William Thomas (1853–?) formed

Chickering and Thomas in 1875, which became Olney, Chickering, and Thomas in 1885 when Warren Olney (1841–1921) joined the firm, and thence Chickering, Thomas, and Gregory in 1893 with the addition of Warren Gregory (1864–1927).

137. An older brother of Ernest C. Peixotto, Sidney (or sometimes "Sydney") Salzado Peixotto (1866–1925) was very young when his family moved from New York to San Francisco. Usually referred to as Major Peixotto by virtue of his honorary rank in the California National Guard, he devoted his life to improving the lot of young boys in San Francisco, founding the Columbia Park Boys' Club in 1894 and the Public School Athletic League and City Boys Baseball League in 1921, pioneering walking tours for boys as summer vacations, and volunteering with the Boy Scouts.

138. Ella Spencer Reid Harrison (1857–1922) was the second wife of Ralph Chandler Harrison (1833–1918), who, like Sloss, had been a California Supreme Court justice. Robert Waite Harrison (1872–1969), for a time assistant district attorney in San Francisco, was the youngest of his three sons by his first wife, Juliet Lathrop Waite Harrison (1845–1890).

139. While Hart did publish *A Novelist in the Making* (1970), an important book on Norris, the "work" Sloss mentions here was the project Hart had recently initiated to acquire Norris manuscripts and other material for what would eventually become the Frank Norris Collection at the University of California's Bancroft Library.

Part 2

1. Bacon quotes from *Colasterion* (1645), a tract John Milton (1608–1674) wrote in response to an anonymously published pamphlet that attacked Milton's earlier defense of divorce: "Since my fate extorts from me a talent of sport, which I had thought to hide in a napkin, he shall be my Batrachomuomachia, my Bavius, my Calandrino, the common adagy of ignorance and overweening," one of many insults Milton formulated to impugn the abilities of the pamphlet's author rather than the arguments advanced in the pamphlet itself.

2. Older than Norris but a member of the same college fraternity, Frederic Augustus Juilliard (1868–1937) served as student body president during his senior year (1890–91) at Berkeley. After his graduation Juilliard moved to New York, where he worked for Juilliard Dry Goods Company, owned by his uncle, Augustus D. Juilliard (1836–1919), and enthusiastically entered New York's social whirl. With another fraternity brother, Edward A. Selfridge Jr., he socialized with Norris during his first few months in New York (Crisler 1986, 51, n. 6).

3. *L'Assommoir* (1877) and *Nana* (1880) by Zola; *Salammbô* (1862) by Flaubert.

4. Burgess probably met architect Claude Fayette Bragdon (1866–1946) through their mutual friend Bruce Porter, for whom Bragdon had briefly worked in New York in 1890.

5. A typically capricious reference by Burgess to *The Lark*.

6. "Blix" first appeared in six installments in the *Puritan* from March through August 1899 (Norris 1899b).

7. Then one of several daily newspapers published in San Francisco, the *Chronicle* had moved in 1890 to a ten-story building at the corner of Market and Geary Streets.

8. Lotta's Fountain at the intersection of Market, Kearney, and Geary Streets has enjoyed its status as a famous San Francisco landmark since it was built in 1875 with money donated by "The Nation's Darling," actress Lotta Crabtree (1847–1924); the fountain, diagonally across from the dental offices of Luther A. Teague, which sported the gold tooth McTeague envies, figures in *Blix* as a possible locale at which Condy and Travis propose to stage an arranged meeting between the characters Captain Jack and K. D. B. (Norris 1899b, 119).

9. This was Norris's second collection of stories. The first, title unknown, was accepted in the fall of 1895, but never published by Lovell, Coryell, and Company (McElrath and Crisler 2006, 169; 451, n. 26). Eleanor M. Davenport, Norris's Berkeley classmate, described the second, "Ways That Are Dark": "Mr. Norris's readers are looking forward to the book, now in press" (Davenport 1897, 281). It, too, did not see print. Burgess was correct in surmising that Doubleday, Page & Co. would opt to publish a collection of Norris's stories; *A Deal in Wheat and Other Stories of the New and Old West* (Norris 1903a) appeared in September 1903.

10. Frances "Fanny" Matilda Van de Grift (1840–1914) was the widow of Robert Louis Stevenson, her second husband. Leaving her first husband, Samuel Osbourne (1837–1887), one-time private secretary to the governor of Indiana, in 1875, she traveled from Oakland, California, to Paris, where she and her daughter, Isobel "Belle" Osbourne, studied art for a time at the Académie Julian. While there, she met Stevenson, who followed her back to California, where they eventually married in San Francisco in 1880. She and Stevenson led a peripatetic life in Scotland, New York, California, Honolulu, and eventually Samoa, where Stevenson died at Vailima, the house they built on Upolo. Fanny then returned to California, settling near Gilroy at Vanumanutagi ("Flight of the Mourning Dove"), her house there, but with frequent trips to New York, where she, Belle, and her son, Lloyd Osbourne, became intimate friends of Norris and Jeannette. Following Norris's death, she commissioned Burgess to erect a fitting memorial to him on the road to the cabin the Norrises had purchased from her during their final stay in California en route to research "The Wolf."

11. Burgess adapted the inscription for his memorial to Norris from lines in the dedicatory poem of *Barrack-Room Ballads and Other Verses* (1892) by Rudyard Kipling (1865–1936): "In simpleness, and gentleness, and honor and clean mirth" (l. 21). Kipling's good friend Charles Wolcott Balestier (1861–1891), who had moved from New York to London in 1888 in order to solicit work by English authors for American journals, secured publication rights of Kipling's *Departmental Ditties: Barrack-Room Ballads and Other Verses* for the United States Publishing Company in 1890; when Balestier abruptly died of typhoid fever the next year, Kipling dedicated his next volume of verse to him, married his sister, Carrie Starr Balestier (1862–1939), moved to the Balestiers' hometown of Brattleboro, Vermont, and published *The Naulahka* (1892), a novel on which he and Balestier had collaborated before the latter died.

12. All members of Les Jeunes and several of their associates, including Norris, in

lieu of a standard signature sometimes used an individualized chop mark. While Burgess's was predictably complicated and distinctive, Norris's was a triquetra.

13. Located at 80 Washington Square East, the Benedick Building still exists as Paul Goddard Hall, a dormitory for New York University students. Other friends of Norris's who lived there at one time or another included Bruce Porter and John F. "Jack" Harrold (see Jeannette Norris, chapter 31 this volume).

14. Opened in 1887 on the south side of O'Farrell Street, the Orpheum Opera House, sometimes termed the O'Farrell Street Orpheum, was the brainchild of impresario Gustave Walter (1848–1899) who had envisioned a theater patterned after the great opera houses of Europe. The theater seated 3,500 and featured a mixture of vaudeville and more legitimate acts to appeal to a cross-section of spectators. Walter also opened theaters in Los Angeles, Sacramento, and Denver; all four specialized in precisely the kind of variety show the bumbling McTeague so thoroughly enjoys on his outing with Trina, her mother, and her brother Owgooste, which culminates in the boy's unfortunate accident.

15. These and other notes are now in the Frank Norris Collection (n.d.).

16. Although Burgess was fired from the University of California, Edward Rowland Sill (1841–1887), a poet of some repute who preceded him as a faculty member at Berkeley, was not.

17. Burgess is particularly generous here, for not only does Norris chastise Les Jeunes generally for a lack of virility in their pieces published in *The Lark*, but he also specifically, if anonymously, targets Burgess by demanding instead "stories" with "men, strong, brutal men, with red-hot blood in 'em, with unleashed passions rampant in 'em, blood and bones and viscera in 'em, and women, too, who move and have their being, people who love and hate, something better now than Vivettes and Perillas and Goops" (Norris 1897h, 7). Vivette, Perilla, and Goops were Burgess's creations.

18. During his time as editor of *The Wave* John O. Cosgrave assembled not just a stable of trusted writers but a capable staff as well. James "Jimmie" Marie Hopper (1876–1956) was fresh from the University of California, where he had won the hearts of his classmates as both football star and budding writer. He edited the student journal, the *Occident*, and one of his early stories, "The Proud Dig and the Lazy Student," was published in *Under the Berkeley Oaks* (1901), which also included Norris's "Travis Hallett's Half-Back" (Norris 1894b). Hopper joined *The Wave*'s staff in 1900, the same year he completed a law degree at Hastings College of Law; in later years he became a popular, though minor, writer of short stories and novels as well as a founding member of the famous writer's colony at Carmel, California. Geraldine Bonner (1870–1930), a transplanted Californian from New York, moved from the *Argonaut* to *The Wave*, eventually returning to New York where she published stories in *Harper's Weekly, Collier's Weekly*, and other periodicals (McElrath and Crisler 2006, 218) before striking out on her own as a novelist. Even so, she did not forget her ties to California, as indicated by the inclusion of her story, "A Californian," in *The Spinner's Book of Fiction* (1907), which also reprinted Norris's "A Lost Story" (Norris 1903c).

19. Charles Norris had informed Walker that Cosgrave had fired Norris.

20. That Burgess asks Walker not to use his name, should he decide to get in touch with Rodgers, adumbrates the possibly unsavory link between her and Norris that Charles Norris also suggests. A Bay Area socialite with scanty journalistic training, Rodgers became the society editor in 1904 for the San Francisco *Examiner* and by 1906 had moved to a position as featured reporter for the New York *American*, both owned by William Randolph Hearst (1863–1915). In her response to Walker on May 8, 1931, Rodgers mentioned a cache of "many letters" from Norris preserved in a trunk, which she "wouldn't think of having" published.

21. Although Mildred Howells (1872–1966) met Norris, she left only a cursory comment concerning him (see Part 4, n. 56, this volume).

22. Burgess's memory appears hazy here and rightly so, for no Walter Doubleday seems to have been a relative of F. N. Doubleday.

23. Why Burgess would have recommended William Morrow (1872–1931), who founded the publishing firm of William Morrow and Company in 1926, to Walker as someone who might have remembered Norris is a mystery: anything Morrow might have published of Norris's remains unknown.

24. Despite the persistence of this provocative tidbit of gossip among Norris scholars and critics, it is false: that B. F. and Gertrude's niece, Ida Carleton, might have had an affair is not beyond the realm of possibility, given comments made to Charles in a letter from his fiancée, Kathleen Thompson, dated November 26, 1908 (Davison 1993, 104), but they did not elope. McElrath and Crisler discuss in detail the situation between Norris's parents during the months just prior to Ida's marriage and their own subsequent divorce (McElrath and Crisler 2006, 25–30).

25. Less than four months after she and Charles returned from Paris, Gertrude established the Lester Norris Memorial Kindergarten at 1231 Pacific Street on December 12, 1888, as a tribute to her middle son, Lester, who had died a year earlier (McElrath and Crisler 2006, 83).

26. See her second letter to Walker below in which she enclosed five letters she and her mother had received from Norris and a typed transcription of a sixth.

27. In his July 4, 1957, response to Hart's solicitation for information regarding Norris, Charles Albert Weck (1871–1959) had suggested that he get in touch with Easton; though Weck was also a classmate of Norris's at Berkeley, he confessed that he knew Norris "less than some of the others" in their class.

28. Easton possibly means "Two Pair," the farce Norris wrote for his class's Junior Day activities on December 10, 1892 (Norris 1893b).

29. Six weeks earlier, on September 12, 1902, Norris had given a public reading of his then unpublished short story, "Two Hearts That Beat as One" (Norris 1903f) at the university's Harmon Gymnasium, sharing the stage with Jacob Voorsanger (1852–1908), a prominent Bay Area rabbi (McElrath and Crisler 2006, 423).

30. A slang expression used to characterize a student committed only to his coursework, that is, one who "dug" incessantly in the soil of academe. Elmer Ellsworth Brown (1861–1934), chancellor of New York University, greeted the incoming freshman class there in 1913 by accusing typical college students of both "dilettantism" and

"mental flabbiness," while simultaneously emphasizing that he did not intend to suggest that they should spend "too much of strenuous drudgery" in "the occupation of the college dig" ("Are Our Colleges" 1913, 4).

31. William Penn Humphreys (1871–1947) graduated two years before Norris but, as a law student at Harvard during the year Norris studied there and as a practicing lawyer in San Francisco after 1896, continued his association with him.

32. Built in 1863 as an imposing, multistoried, mid-Victorian extravaganza, the Cliff House, perched on a rocky bluff at San Francisco's extreme western end, by the 1890s had become a favorite haunt of a cross-section of the city's populace. Norris knew the site well: on one of their lengthy rambles to less frequented outposts of San Francisco, which ends at the restaurant where they enjoyed their beers, McTeague first reveals his growing feelings for Trina to his pal, Marcus Schouler (Norris 1899e, 50–56), initiating the central conflict in the novel.

33. When it opened in 1875 at the southwest corner of Market and Montgomery Streets, the Palace Hotel boasted that it was the largest hotel in the world; the original building, lost to the San Francisco fire in 1906, was replaced three years later by another structure, sometimes now referred to as the New Palace Hotel.

34. Like Norris, Jonathan Monroe Gilmore (1871–1954) entered Berkeley as an "at large" or "special student" but graduated on track in 1894.

35. Besides his contribution, as both coauthor and actor in a minor role in "Vehmegericht" (Norris 1913), performed at Class Day exercises in 1894, Norris also wrote his class's Junior Day farce, "Two Pair" (1893b), an unstaged play titled *The President's Address*, the lyrics for *Minstrels*, presented on November 30, 1893, and a parody of *Romeo and Juliet* (1597) in March 1894; as for acting credits, Norris had roles in 1891 in *The Jenkinses* (1830) by James Robinson Planché (1796–1880), Henry J. Byron's *Our Boys* in 1893, and W. S. Gilbert's *Engaged* the next year (McElrath and Crisler 2006, 115; Crisler 1990, 118–19). For Norris's stage career after leaving college see Graham (1976).

36. Beginning with "Football in Town," which appeared in *The Wave* on October 10, 1896 (Norris 1896b), Norris wrote weekly unsigned articles covering football games played by the University of California, Stanford, the Olympic Athletic Club, and the Reliance Club through the end of the year. Never a college athlete himself, Norris ironically delighted in robust physical activity, as evidenced by two articles, "College Athletics" (Norris 1896a) and "The U.C. Track Team" (1897l), he later wrote for *The Wave* chronicling the 1896–97 season of the university's track team.

37. Harvey Wiley Corbett (1873–1954), a member of Phi Gamma Delta, graduated from the University of California in 1895; continuing his study at L'École des Beaux Arts in Paris, from which he was graduated in 1900, Corbett soon became a distinguished architect with the George Washington National Masonic Memorial in Washington, DC, and other such structures to his credit. Norris inscribed his own copy of the English edition of *McTeague* to Corbett during a visit he made to the Norrises in early February 1901 (Crisler 1986, 217, 221).

38. Norris did not graduate from Harvard, where he spent only a single academic year.

39. Years later, on November 6, 1952, Gibbs confirmed his memory here in a letter to Robert Eugene Burke (1921–1998), then head of manuscripts at The Bancroft Library: "We were together a great deal while he was writing *The Pit* and I spent hours with him trying to explain how one could sell wheat *short* and he always answered, 'But one simply can't sell anything when he does not own it.'"

40. Norris departed for South Africa as a correspondent for the *San Francisco Chronicle* on October 28, 1895 (Crisler 1987, 4), several years before the outbreak of the Boer War (1899–1902). Possibly, he did write "constantly" to Gertrude while he was away from San Francisco, but news articles in the *Chronicle* in late December 1895 note that he had been unable to cable either his arrival or whereabouts to her; then in mid-February 1896, she finally received a letter, six weeks in transit, in which he explained his circumstances (see Crisler 1989). Unfortunately, neither this letter nor any other to his mother survives.

41. Although Gibbs was busy with his career in Chicago and later in Milwaukee, he made frequent visits to California both before and after Norris's death.

42. John Alfred Marsh (1871–?), another member of Phi Gamma Delta, played on the university tennis team with Hathorn. In 1893, a year after his graduation from college, he completed a law degree at Hastings College of Law. Later shifting his interest to automobiles, Marsh eventually became president of Pierce-Arrow Sales Company in San Francisco as well as of the Motor Car Dealer's Association of California (see Jeannette Norris, chapter 31 this volume). The episode of the "goop" in the beds of Norris and Waterhouse in time assumed near legendary character among Fijis of Norris's era (see Houston, chapter 15 this volume, and Wright, chapter 26 this volume). Norris later incorporated the episode in Chapter III of Book One of *The Octopus* when Annixter discovers what he calls "sloop" between the sheets of his bed (Norris 1901c, 121).

43. Attending the World's Columbian Exposition (see Gibbs, chapter 13 this volume).

44. A popular brand, Knapsack Tobacco took its name from the tin in which it was marketed, which was shaped like a miniature backpack with the word "knapsack" printed diagonally in block letters across its front.

45. One of America's premier actors, William Hooker Gillette (1853–1937) played Sherlock Holmes in the play of the same name, which he had adapted from several works by Arthur Conan Doyle (1859–1930) for the stage; *Sherlock Holmes* debuted in New York on November 6, 1899, and he performed the role at home and abroad for many years.

46. Norris never received a degree, honorary or otherwise.

47. Sir Walter Scott, *The Lady of the Lake* (1810).

48. A pioneer in merchandising clothing affordable to the middle and lower classes, Scottish immigrant Alexander Nicholl (1821–1895) had founded a haberdashery empire in a number of key American cities, including San Francisco, where his store,

Nicoll the Tailor, located at 719 Market Street, advertised "fashionable tailoring at moderate prices" with "thousands of styles to select from."

49. As Hathorn (chapter 14 this volume) also recalled, Norris loved to play blackjack.

50. The University of California established its Botanical Garden in 1890 near the middle of the Berkeley campus.

51. Houston is the only one of Norris's many friends who mentions Oscar Sutro (1872–1935) in connection with Norris. A year behind Norris at the University of California, Sutro later became a lawyer, cofounded the firm of Pillsbury, Madison, and Sutro, and was legal counsel for Standard Oil of California, for which he also served as vice president. Pages of the *McTeague* manuscript once owned by either Houston or Sutro have never surfaced.

52. Either Houston confuses his chronology here, confirming Walker's surmise regarding his faulty memory, or there were at least two Louise Boyds on San Francisco's social circuit, for Louise Arner Boyd (1887–1972), society matron, hostess, and Arctic explorer, was too young to have consorted with Ida Carleton, Norris's cousin, and other young women who frequented Gertrude's home when Norris was in college.

53. Having negotiated an amended contract with Doubleday, Page & Co. on September 6, 1900, one of the provisions of which allowed him a four-day block of time to devote to personal writing (Crisler 1986, 120–21), Norris was better able to enjoy the house in Roselle, New Jersey, that he and Jeannette had rented earlier in the summer.

54. Houston is mistaken here. Norris's college transcript reveals that he failed both of the courses in mathematics he took at Berkeley (University Archives n.d.).

55. Like the pages of the *McTeague* manuscript Houston claims to have owned, Norris's copy of Horace, also subsequently in Houston's possession, is not now extant. If it were, Norris's possible marginalia in it might support the comment to Walker by Leon J. Richardson, a faculty member at Berkeley, that Horace was Norris's "favorite Latin writer" (see Richardson, chapter 20 this volume).

56. McElrath and Crisler address the nature of Norris's religious commitment, sophistication, and affiliation with the Episcopal church (McElrath and Crisler 2006, 365–70; McElrath 2001); Houston's comments here differ from those by Jeannette and another fraternity brother, Harry M. Wright.

57. Ida Carleton, Gertrude's niece who lived with the family, married naval chaplain Frank Thompson in 1892, moving to Vallejo in November 1893 ("Personal Mention" 1893).

58. The firm Martin J. Madison and Frank H. Burke (1848–1910) owned was located at 626 Market Street.

59. The huge fires following the San Francisco earthquake that struck the city on April 18, 1906, were actually more destructive than the earthquake itself, burning for three days, consuming nearly five hundred city blocks and twenty-five thousand buildings, and resulting in over $300 million in property loss.

60. Houston refers to the Southern Pacific Railroad Company which, augmented by government subsidies, had made huge fortunes for its owners by the 1890s.

61. The so-called T-D pipe was named for its maker, London craftsman Thomas

Dormer, who flourished as a pipe maker for over two decades (1748–70) and introduced this particular variety around 1755.

62. Vandover introduces two friends to Crème Violette in chapter sixteen of *Vandover* (Norris 1914b, 291), while the stove appears earlier in the novel at the beginning of chapter twelve (176).

63. Possibly the Yo Semite House Hotel, where Norris stayed temporarily while researching *The Octopus*, as confirmed by a letter he wrote to Chicago publisher Herbert Stuart Stone (1871–1915) (Crisler 1986, 85). Located at 335 and 337 E. Main Street in Stockton, California, the lavishly appointed hotel opened for business on July 5, 1869, continuing in uninterrupted operation until fire destroyed it half a century later on July 23, 1923 (Rayman 1977, 166, 169).

64. Jerusha Pauline Hull McClaughry (1834–1911).

65. Harry M. Wright, medalist for the university's class of 1894, delivered the primary student address at commencement exercises that year.

66. Armed with Moore's comments regarding the possible compatibility between Norris and Louis Du Pont Syle (1857–1903), Walker concluded that during his senior year Norris had taken English 19, Literature of the Eighteenth Century, from Syle, earning a 2 or B in the course. But this course, covering the best English comedies, was actually taught by Charles Mills Gayley (1858–1932). Syle, born in Shanghai, the son of missionary parents, and Norris possibly did have a friendship of sorts after the former came to Berkeley as an assistant professor of English in 1892, for he considered himself primarily a specialist in drama, directing student productions (*Blue and Gold* 1893 [1900], 6–7), though Norris acted in none of them. Like Syle, Gayley was also born in Shanghai to a missionary family; he assumed a faculty position at the university in 1889, thereafter enjoying a long and distinguished career as scholar, orator, critic, author, and teacher (Academic Senate 1935, n.p.). Gayley taught Norris in four courses during his senior year—the aforementioned English 19, English 15 (Literary Criticism), and English 18a and 18b (Nineteenth-Century British Poets); Norris's mark in English 15 was another 2, while his transcript shows a "pass" for English 18a and a 1 or A in English 18b, one of only two he earned in English courses at the university (University Archives n.d.).

67. Norris wrote "Two Pair" (1893b) as the Junior Day Farce; besides Harry M. Wright and Jessica B. Peixotto, it also starred Annie Cecilia Haehnlen (1870–?) and William Denman (1872–1959), the latter a class officer at Berkeley, later a graduate of Harvard Law School in 1897, and eventually a federal circuit judge.

68. Although Peixotto admits an acquaintance with Norris prior to their college days, her interview properly belongs during the latter period of his life because of their closer association as students in the same university class.

69. Norris had long esteemed Kipling as the beau ideal of the writer who could seamlessly transfer his exciting life in exotic locales to the printed page. In some of his earliest tales an eagerly precocious Norris mimicked Kipling's penchant for technical jargon and realistic dialect (McElrath and Crisler 2006, 139–41). Jeannette told Walker that Norris often read from Kipling to her. Condy Rivers, the hero of *Blix*,

happily suffers from "an inoculation of the Kipling virus" (Norris 1899b, 19). The Norrises' library included Kipling's *Many Inventions* (1893), his *Plain Tales from the Hills* (1899), inscribed to "Miss Jeannette Black | Rudyard Kipling," and, according to Lars Åhnebrink (1950, 461), a "set" of Kipling's works (Crisler 1988, 5, 8, and 10).

70. Norris's design for the new student weekly, *The Berkeleyan*, did not grace the periodical's cover until its eighth installment on March 24, 1893, continuing in use until the issue appearing on December 6, 1894, after which the magazine altered both its format and frequency of publication to four times per week (Crisler 1990, 124, n. 41). The 1894 *Blue and Gold* reproduced Norris's cover as well (*Blue and Gold* 1893, 104). As for written contributions to *The Berkeleyan* by Norris only one of his stories, "Unequally Yoked" (Norris 1893c), appeared in it, nor did he ever join its editorial staff.

71. *Trilby*.

72. That in Peixotto's recollection Norris "admired" Cornelius Beach Bradley (1843–1936) "very much" comes as no surprise, since for the course Norris took under him, English XIII, Poets of the 14th and 15th Centuries, which included Geoffrey Chaucer (1343?–1400), Norris received a 1 or A, definitely not a grade he customarily earned and the only A he garnered as a sophomore, save in the second term of a French class (see his transcript, University Archives n.d.). A son of missionary parents, Bradley, born in Bangkok, attended both Oberlin and Yale Divinity School and served as a missionary himself in Siam and then as vice principal at Oakland High School before his appointment to the Berkeley faculty in 1882 (Academic Senate 1935 [*In Memoriam 1937*], n.p.).

73. Unlike Norris and Peixotto, their classmate Maida Castelhun (1872–1940), daughter of the German poet and surgeon Friedrich Karl Castelhun (1828–1905), had served on the editorial staff of *The Berkeleyan*. A member of Kappa Alpha Theta, a fraternity for women, she also played on the university's women's tennis team, delivered a reading at Junior Day on December 10, 1892, cowrote with Gelett Burgess and Norris the Senior Extravaganza "Vehmegericht," and was selected but declined to present a student address at commencement. She married Charles M. Darnton (1869–1950), a theater critic and screenplay writer, in 1906; they divorced a year before her death.

74. Norris did not understand that using a sextant involves sighting the horizon from an upright position.

75. Norris's poem "Brunehilde" (1890a) appeared in 1890 in the *Occident*, a student publication, with no accompanying illustration; nearly two years later, however, it was reprinted as "Brunhilde" in *California Illustrated Magazine* (1892a), and this time Norris supplied two drawings for the text, one of which, though untitled, is most likely the sketch about which Rhodes "joshed" Norris.

76. Norris's signed but untitled pen-and-ink sketch of Monk, the fraternity chapter's mascot, was first published by Charles in his "intimate sketch" of his brother in 1914 (C. Norris 1914, 3).

77. As historian of his class during its sophomore year, Norris recounted in "The Class of '94" (1892b) the story of the successful rout by sophomores on February 14, 1892 of freshmen who had attempted to continue a Berkeley tradition by painting

their class's anticipated graduation year on the backstop; he also illustrated the incident with a drawing in the 1893 *Blue and Gold* (50).

78. Although a year older than Norris, Frederic Orson Johnson (1869–1943) entered the University of California in the class behind him. Johnson apparently never graduated, nor did he and Norris seem to have had any lasting relationship. A hotelier, Johnson owned the grand Hotel Westminster in Los Angeles.

79. Walter Benjamin Rountree (1872–1949), like Fred Johnson, was an accomplished tennis player in college, teaming with their fraternity brother George Gibbs in doubles; a mining student, he also left the university without graduating.

80. A good friend of Norris's during his sophomore year at Berkeley was George Deroy Blood (1870–1944), another member of Phi Gamma Delta, known to his fraternity brothers as "Dusty." Following his graduation in 1892, he and Norris remained in contact through their mutual pal and fraternity brother, Seymour Waterhouse, whose father, Columbus Waterhouse (1828–1898), employed Blood as superintendent of the family's Big Dipper Mine at Iowa Hill, California (Crawford 1896, 274). When Norris visited Hathorn, Waterhouse, and Blood at the Big Dipper in the late summer of 1896, he inscribed to Blood a drawing he titled "P. Portrait de Mlle. X" (Crisler 1986, 212–13).

81. Norris's earliest surviving letter, dated November 1891, is a petition to the faculty of the university to change his student status from "at large" to "special," a ploy on his part to obviate his taking certain required courses such as those in mathematics and Latin. George M. Richardson, ironically Norris's Latin teacher at the time, brought the petition before the Academic Council, which body predictably declined to grant the request (Crisler 1986, 23–27).

82. While one cannot now know whom among Norris's uncles Richardson means, the most likely is Gertrude's oldest brother, Samuel, a successful realtor who lived in San Francisco and to whom she seems to have been closest among her male siblings. Precisely who paid for the publication of *Yvernelle*—not during Norris's junior year, as Richardson implies, but in November 1891, when he was a sophomore—remains moot, though some evidence suggests that the firm of Lippincott itself covered the cost of the lavish production (see Charles Norris, chapter 3 this volume, and Wright, chapter 26 this volume).

83. Clinton Ralza "Brick" Morse (1872–1942) was a member of Norris's class at Berkeley. Secretary of the Athletic Association, he played in the first "big game" against Stanford. His "knock" in the "Temple of Fame" in the 1894 *Blue and Gold* was "I will roar you as gently as any suckling dove; I will roar you an' 'twere any nightingale" (*Blue and Gold* 1893 [1895], 251) from *A Midsummer Night's Dream* (I.ii.85–86). A singer and pianist, Morse later composed two school songs, "Sons of California" in 1905 and "Hail to California" in 1907.

84. The first installment of *Smiles*, described by the *Occident* as a "humorous paper," appeared during Norris's sophomore year on October 15, 1891, with both Norris and Samuels listed among its staff. Although the paper lasted only five issues, Norris was somewhat more involved in its contents than Samuels recalls: his story "The

Great Szarrattar Opal" (Norris 1891a) with his own illustrations ran in the issue for November 18, 1891; he provided the cover art for that same issue; and an untitled but signed series of cartoons was part of the December 7, 1891, issue (Crisler 2003, 114).

85. A native Californian, Emanuel Myron Wolf (1871–1918) pledged Sigma Nu, played in the university's marching band, managed the baseball team for a time, was a member of the Durant-Neolean Student Congress, a mock legislative assembly, was on the staff of the 1894 *Blue and Gold* with Norris and Samuels, and entered Hastings College of Law upon his graduation in 1894.

86. *Elaine* (1919), a play in three acts, based on the story of Elaine and Lancelot.

87. Samuels mixes fact and fiction in this complicated series of memories. Norris's time in South Africa preceded the Boer War; the "epic of Grain" refers to Norris's unfinished Trilogy of the Wheat; Dr. Teague's dental office was located at the intersection of Kearney and Geary Streets, not Larkin Street; and the final sequences in *McTeague* occur in Death Valley.

88. Guiseppe Mazzini (1805–1872), revolutionary, patriot, and reformer, who diligently worked for Italian unification.

89. The Mint Saloon and Restaurant near Montgomery Street at 605 Commercial Street was across the street from San Francisco's original mint at 608–10.

90. That is, Prohibition, which began with the passage of the Eighteenth Amendment to the Constitution on January 16, 1919, and ended with the ratification of the Twenty-First on December 5, 1933.

91. Walter Edmund Magee (1860–1932) served first as instructor and then as director of Physical Culture during Norris's time at the University of California. While Norris was notoriously opposed to physical exercise, he did manage to secure a pass in Magee's courses each semester of his freshman and sophomore years, thereby fulfilling the university requirement. How he fared in Military Science under Benjamin Harrison Randolph (1850–?) is an altogether different story. On leave from the United States Army, Randolph taught at the university for three years (1890–93), succeeded by Frank Long Winn (1864–1941). As with Physical Culture, Norris received a pass both semesters in Military Science during his freshman year, but as a sophomore he received no mark at all, a situation repeated in his junior year; then as a senior, while he earned a 2 or B the first semester, he failed the second (Crisler 1990, 123, n. 17; see also Norris's transcript, University Archives n.d.).

92. Mellen Woodman Haskell (1863–1948), a faculty member in mathematics, seems never to have taught Norris; Armin Otto Leuschner (1868–1953), though he came to the university to teach in the department of mathematics, by Norris's senior year had migrated to astronomy, teaching Norris three courses in his senior year in none of which he actually received a grade (see Norris's transcript, University Archives n.d.).

93. Erected in 1910, many years after Norris left Berkeley, Sather Gate at one time marked the south entrance to campus; the two oldest fraternities at the University of California are Chi Phi and Zeta Psi (Zetes), established in 1876 and 1870, respectively.

94. When he first arrived in New York, Norris took an apartment at 10 West

Thirty-Third Street, across from the Waldorf-Astoria Hotel, where, as he confirms in a letter to their mutual friend, Harry M. Wright, he and Selfridge often dined (Crisler 1986, 49–50).

95. A year ahead of Norris, Henry Frederick Rethers (1870–1941) was another fraternity brother. Principal musician in the university band in which he played the drum, he enlisted in the army as an officer immediately following his graduation in 1893. Promoted to brigadier general in 1926, he had previously served in both the Spanish-American War and World War I.

96. The Bourdon Burial was a tradition begun at the University of California in 1875 by the class of 1878, then completing its freshman year, to burn the mathematics and literature textbooks it had labored through during the preceding academic year. By 1891, when Norris participated in it, the ritual had become increasingly grandiose with the freshman class burning the two textbooks it considered particularly obnoxious—*Elements of Algebra: On the Basis of M. Bourdon, Embracing Sturm's and Horner's Theorems* (1873) and Minto's *A Manual of English Prose Literature, Biographical and Critical, Designed Mainly to Show Characteristics of Style* (1872)—while the sophomore class, having successfully consigned their books to a conflagration a year earlier, courageously strove to thwart them. Louis Pierre Marie Bourdon (1779–1854), inspector general of studies at Académie de Paris, had first published his textbook, the nemesis of generations of mathematics students, in 1848; William Minto (1845–1893) taught at the University of Aberdeen, publishing works of literary criticism on a variety of subjects. The principal participants in the annual ceremony were the Damnator, Maledictor, and Laudator; Norris, famed already for his difficulties in mathematics and parodies of prominent English prose writers in the student periodical, *Occident*, was a logical choice for the role of Pontifex Maximus, who would introduce the three speakers. But as Wright clarifies, Norris in the event was unable to preside over the ceremonies, having been abducted by members of the rival sophomore class (McElrath and Crisler 2006, 118–19).

97. Ambroise Thomas (1811–1896), *Mignon* (1866); the Opéra Comique fire at the second Salle Favart in Paris occurred on May 25, 1887.

98. Prior to his investment in mining operations in northern California, Seymour Waterhouse's father, Columbus, had established the carriage firm of Waterhouse and Lester in 1851; his partner, J. W. Lester managed its New York office, while the Waterhouse family oversaw the San Francisco end of the trade until 1915, when the firm ceased production.

99. See Houston, chapter 15 this volume.

100. Line 126 of *Andria* by the Roman playwright Terence (ca. 184–159 BC).

101. Norris did write the ritual for Skull and Keys but not the play *Our Boys* (see Everett, chapter 12 this volume).

102. The Berkeley chapter of Delta Kappa Epsilon (Dekes), Todd's fraternity, the third established at the university, was founded in 1876.

103. Frank's Rotisserie opened in 1878 at 419 Pine Street. Located at the corner of Vallejo and Dupont Streets in the heart of San Francisco's famed Mexican Quarter,

Luna's featured quaint but authentic Mexican fare; it unfortunately was a casualty of the 1906 earthquake and subsequent fire. Luna's figures prominently in *Blix* as the site Condy and Travis utilize for the introductory meeting between Captain Jack and K. D. B. in chapter VII; Norris also described it in "Cosmopolitan San Francisco."

104. Dr. William Martin Lawlor (1845–1907) replaced Antrim Edgar Osborne (1856–1935) in 1901 as superintendent of the California Home for the Care and Training of Feeble-Minded Children in Glen Ellen. Over the course of the next year he was accused, unjustly in the opinion of Norris, who visited the facility in order to form his own conclusions, of a multitude of offenses against his charges. Resigning on July 12, 1902, Lawlor continued to be vilified in major San Francisco newspapers; the culmination took place on August 3, when Norris himself dramatically saved Lawlor from being fired upon in a meeting room in San Francisco's Grand Hotel by single-handedly apprehending Lawlor's would-be assassin. Outraged over both Lawlor's treatment and this harrowing attempt on his life, Norris wrote a scathing denunciation of the San Francisco press, which the *Argonaut* published as a letter to the editor, "Frank Norris Defends Dr. Lawlor" (McElrath and Crisler 2006, 418–22).

105. From Kipling's "Dedication" to his *Barrack-Room Ballads and Other Verses*: "And they rise to their feet as He passes by, gentlemen unafraid" (l. 15).

106. Among other mementos of his time in South Africa, Norris returned with an Uitlander uniform that he wore in support of the English cause during the Boer-British hostilities of 1895–96.

107. John Hays Hammond (1855–1936), a geologist and mining engineer, had assumed supervision of the considerable South African interests of Cecil Rhodes (1853–1902) in 1894; Norris and his wife later became good friends of the Hammonds in New York (see Jeannette Norris, chapter 31 this volume).

108. Why Waterhouse held such a negative opinion of Fiji Lowell Albion Eugley (1867–1940) is not clear. Entering with the class of 1892, Eugley pledged Phi Gamma Delta in 1889 at the end of his freshman year, withdrew from the university that same year, entered Hastings College of Law in 1890, for entrance to which students could qualify by graduating from either high school or college, and completed his studies there three years later. Norris inscribed a photograph of himself to "mon ami Lowell Eugley" while they were in college (Crisler 1986, 208, 210–11).

109. Alexis Frederick Lange (1862–1924), as an assistant professor of English, taught Norris in three courses during his sophomore year, in all of which, save in the second semester of a two-semester course, Norris fared dismally: in English XVI (English Literature to the Restoration) he received a 4 or D; in the first half of English XXV (Themes) he earned another 4, while in the second a 2 or B; and in English XVII (English Literature from the Restoration) his mark was yet another 4 (see Norris's transcript, University Archives n.d.).

110. Norris did take Military Science as a senior, having been suspended from it as a sophomore.

111. Begun as a semimonthly student literary journal in 1881, the *Occident* was the oldest college literary magazine on the west coast. If Weed were suggesting that

Norris was unsympathetic to the older *Occident* rather than the newer *Berkeleyan*, then his conclusion was unwarranted, since eight of Norris's pieces—poetry, stories, and parodies—appeared in it during his freshman year.

112. British clergyman Edward Hayes Plumptre (1821–1891) included his translation of *Oedipus* in his 1865 collection, *The Tragedies of Sophocles*. Charles Norris and others allude to Norris's memorizing a part for a student production of the play, but only Weed suggests that the reason it may never have been mounted was that Berkeley faculty and administrators intervened. These Victorian moralists included Norris's erstwhile Latin professor George M. Richardson, the university's president and former Congregationalist minister Martin Kellogg (1827–1903), professor of Greek Edward Bull Clapp (1856–1919), and military band director David Webster Loring (1836–1904).

113. In contrast, Rhodes recalls that Norris was not a devotee of hiking and camping.

114. Charles Augustus Keeler (1871–1937) entered the University of California with the class of 1893, pledged Beta Theta Pi fraternity, but did not graduate; something of a polymath, Keeler was a poet, many of whose verses were published during his lifetime, a naturalist who recorded bird songs, an armchair architect who devised a number of new ideas in *The Simple Home* (1904), an adventurer, joining with others to chart Alaska's coast, and a biologist who taught at the California Academy of Sciences in San Francisco. Norris could have known him both at Berkeley and later, since both were members of the Bohemian Club.

115. At various times in the mid-1890s San Francisco could count as many as three different restaurants denominated the Louvre or some variation of that name: the New Louvre at O'Farrell and Bagley Streets, the Original Louvre at 8–14 O'Farrell Street, and the Louvre at the intersection of Eddy and Powell. In a note at the bottom of the typescript of his interview with Weed, Walker specified the "Portola-Louvre Restaurant, corner of Powell and Market streets"; there was indeed a restaurant by that name at that intersection when Walker was collecting information for his dissertation, but it did not exist until 1910, when the Louvre at Powell and Eddy consolidated with the Portola Café as the new Portola-Louvre Restaurant (Kastler 1908, 6–7).

116. While *The Wasp*, founded as a weekly in 1876, attracted many writers associated with bohemian San Francisco, Norris seems never to have published anything in it.

117. On March 5, 1912, Skull and Keys held a meeting in memory of Norris, one of the society's founders, at which Frank M. Todd spoke, most likely giving the tribute to Norris he wrote in 1908 (see program in the Frank Norris Collection n.d.). Another speaker was noted Scottish historian Henry Morse Stephens (1857–1919), who addressed Norris's place in literature. Along with Weed and current members of Skull and Keys, Stephens sponsored the dinner, which seems surprising, since his having joined the faculty of the University of California only in 1902 precluded his having known Norris save by reputation, a fact that did not, however, inhibit him from penning an estimate of Norris's achievement a year later: "The Work of Frank Norris: An Appreciation" (Stephens 1903).

118. The *Overland Monthly* short story, demonstrating Norris's boyish enthusiasm for all things French, was "Lauth," published in 1893 (Norris 1893a). Norris's illustrations appear in three successive volumes of the *Blue and Gold*, beginning in 1893. He also illustrated "The Great Szarrattar Opal" (Norris 1891a) in the short-lived campus periodical *Smiles* in 1891, and "Travis Hallett's Half-Back" (Norris 1894b) and a five-part series, "Outward and Visible Signs," in the *Overland Monthly* between March 1893 and February 1895 (Norris 1894–95).

119. See Todd, chapter 23 this volume, and n. 96 above.

120. In the seven courses in French Norris took under Félicien V. Paget, he never earned less than a 2 or B, and that only once; by contrast in the single French class taught him by the university's only other French instructor, Samuel David Huntington (1869–1914), he barely passed with a 4 or D (see Norris's transcript, University Archives n.d.).

121. Richard Harding Davis (1864–1916) was a journalist, short story writer, and novelist who influenced not only Norris's own early shorter efforts but also his first published novel, *Moran of the Lady Letty* (Norris 1898b); Norris owned copies of Davis's *Van Bibber and Others* (1893) and *The West from a Car-Window* (1892) (Crisler 1988, 4). The two would eventually meet in Cuba when they were both correspondents (see Archibald, chapter 34 this volume, and Jeannette Norris, chapter 31 this volume).

122. See Norris's letter to newspaper book reviewer Isaac F. Marcosson (Crisler 1986, 57–58).

123. Gaston Mears Ashe (1864–?), a San Francisco lawyer, was the first husband of Dulce Bolado Davis, owner of a ranch in San Benito County, California, where Norris spent time researching *The Octopus*.

124. Norris not only interviewed the president of the Southern Pacific Railroad corporation, Collis Potter Huntington (1821–1900), in the course of his research on *The Octopus*, but, according to Jeannette, the two became "good friends."

125. That is, Wright, not Norris went to Alaska as an attorney for a mining concern.

126. Founded in 1860 to promote amateur athletics and young men's physical fitness, San Francisco's Olympic Club is now the oldest athletic club in the country.

127. While as a senior Norris was a member of the Society for the Study of Ethics and Religion, Wright was not.

128. "Gallegher: A Newspaper Story," featuring a newsboy as young detective and cub reporter in New York City, was the title story of Davis's 1891 collection.

129. Frederick Augustus Hyde (1848–?), San Francisco lawyer and financier, was convicted of land fraud in 1908 ("Two Years for F. A. Hyde" 1908, 9).

130. The most likely place for Norris to have met Josephine Lippincott (1874–?) in Paris would have been at the Académie Julian, but she is not known to have studied there; Craige Lippincott (1847–1911), who succeeded his father, founder Joseph Ballinger Lippincott (1813–1886), as president of the family publishing house, also had a second daughter, Constance (1883–?), who, thirteen years Norris's junior, would have been too young to have known him either in Paris or elsewhere. Wright possibly confused his memory of "Lippincott's daughter" with Josephine Lippincott Hoffman

(1880–1966), a resident of San Francisco, who though also related to the publishing family, was not the current president's daughter. At any rate, Wright here confirms what others have suggested, that is, that Gertrude most likely did not pay to have *Yvernelle* published.

131. As the Norris family physician, Julius Rosenstirn (1850–1926) operated successfully on Jeannette for appendicitis but could not save Norris himself from a fatal attack of the same condition a few days later (McElrath and Crisler 2006, 424, 428–29).

132. Ida Hart Houston (1855–?) came to San Francisco from St. Louis with her husband and two sons in the 1880s.

133. A year behind Norris, Morton Raymond Gibbons (1873–1949) was a fellow Fiji; after his graduation from college in 1895, he attended Cooper Medical College in San Francisco, taking his degree there in 1897, after which he became a prominent physician and faculty member at Stanford.

Part 3

1. Norris died at 9:15 a.m. on Saturday, October 25, 1902 (McElrath and Crisler 2006, 429).

2. Cosgrave's mother, Mary McHugh Cosgrave (1844–1892), died in early September 1892 in San Francisco.

3. Justin Sturgis was a pseudonym used by Norris, Gelett Burgess, and others in *The Wave* (see McElrath 1988).

4. The attention to chilling detail in *A Man's Woman* perhaps confused Garnett's recollections of Norris, who never traveled farther north than southern Ireland.

5. In *The Octopus* Norris alters this comical statement to "How long have you known you had this power?" Mrs. Cedarquist poses this question in turn to each of several artists (Norris 1901c, 315).

6. The men-only Bohemian Club was founded in 1872 by a group of San Francisco journalists, many of them then working for the *San Francisco Chronicle*. By the time Norris and several of his friends, college chums, and associates, including Garnett, joined it, membership had extended to musicians and artists as well as to businessmen, military personnel, and entrepreneurs, in time transforming the original image of the club to a gathering place for San Francisco's wealthy elite.

7. While carefree and whimsical dramatic extravaganzas, termed either Low or High Jinks, had been performed by Bohemian Club members in the redwood groves north of San Francisco since 1878, only in 1902 did members exclusively begin composing these plays, including any accompanying music. Will Irwin was the author of *The Hamadryads: A Masque of Apollo* (1904), while Garnett himself wrote the 1911 Grove play, *The Green Knight: A Vision*. Irwin's dedication includes the well-known line from the Prologue to Chaucer's *Canterbury Tales* that characterizes the knight (l. 72).

8. Walter Aaron Yelton (1867–1913), a local compositor, was foreman of *The Wave* during Irwin's time with it.

9. That is, Norris produced both photographs and written material as copy for *The Wave*; his camera also accompanied him to Cuba during the Spanish-American War, where his were the only photographs taken of the surrender at Santiago (McElrath and Crisler 2006, 319–20).

10. The actual title of the three sketches was "Little Dramas of the Curbstone."

11. This oft-quoted phrase was apparently uttered by Burgess to Irwin at some point after Irwin had become employed by *The Wave*, for which Burgess himself had also once worked.

12. Irwin here recalls Norris's four memorable sketches collected as "Suggestions" (1897j) in *The Wave*: "1870," "A Hotel Bedroom," "Brute," and "The Dental Parlors."

13. Not only a bohemian crowd frequented Keens Chop House at the corner of 36th Street and Sixth Avenue in New York in the 1890s; it also hosted more established groups such as civic clubs and chapters of college fraternities at Columbia University.

14. California native Morrison Frank Pixley (1865–1959) could well have been an expert on the events at Mussel Slough in 1880 that Norris incorporated into *The Octopus*, especially since his uncle, Frank Morrison Pixley (1824–1895), an attorney general of California, founder in April 1877 of the *Argonaut* with Frederick M. Somers (1850–1894), and its publisher from then until his death, was active in both politics and journalism in the early 1880s. Pixley, California, in Tulare County not far from Mussel Slough, which Norris also used in his novel, was named for him.

15. Norris (1899a).

16. Through the character of Presley and his poem "The Toilers" in *The Octopus*, Norris thinly satirizes both "The Man with the Hoe" and its author, Charles Edwin Anson Markham (1852–1940), who catapulted to considerable, though not lasting, fame because of the poem's popularity. Millard published the poem in the San Francisco *Examiner* on January 15, 1899.

17. At a meeting in San Francisco's Grand Hotel of the trustees of the California Home for the Care and Training of Feeble-Minded Children on August 2, 1902, one of the trustees, Colonel John T. Harrington (1843–1921), who had been highly critical of the home's administration under Norris's friend Dr. William M. Lawlor, became so offended by remarks made by both Lawlor and his son, Theodore Stuart Lawlor (1875–1947), that he brandished a revolver in Lawlor's face, whereupon Norris pinned Harrington's arm to his side, thereby saving his friend (McElrath and Crisler 2006, 419–20).

18. At its conclusion the anonymous *Sun* review observes that the final paragraph of *The Octopus* "is probably a confession that the subject had overwhelmed the author" ("Books and Their Makers" 1901).

19. After his journalistic work in San Francisco, Herbert Bashford (1863–1951) moved to Tacoma, Washington, continuing his career as a poet.

20. The Hotel Pleasanton, which Norris's mother made her permanent residence for a time after her divorce, stood at the northwest corner of Sutter and Jones Streets.

21. See "Writer Was Planning to Stay in California," in Additional Reminiscences.

22. English novelist and poet Thomas Hardy (1840–1928).

23. Millard here quotes parts of two lines from the first stanza of Sidney Lanier's poem "To Bayard Taylor" (1879): "And hear the beating of the hearts of trees, / And think the thoughts that lilies speak in white" (ll. 4–5).

24. From "Rabbi Ben Ezra" (ll. 39–40) by Robert Browning (1812–1889).

25. Thomas Beer (1889–1940), biographer of Stephen Crane and Mark Hanna (1837–1904); Van Wyck Brooks (1886–1963), literary historian.

26. James A. Herne (1840–1901), the "American Ibsen," a celebrated actor and playwright best known for *Shore Acres* (1891), had died before Norris met his wife, Katherine Corcoran Herne (1856–1943), herself an actress, and their daughters, Julie A. Herne and Katherine Chrystal Herne (1883–1950), who were also actresses.

27. Fanny Osbourne Stevenson, widow of Robert Louis Stevenson, had three children by her first marriage, two of whom, Isobel and Lloyd, lived to maturity. Isobel married her second husband, Edward Salisbury Field (1878–1936), her mother's private secretary, soon after Fanny died; Austin Strong (1881–1952), Isobel's son by her first marriage to Joseph D. Strong Jr., wrote the play *Seventh Heaven* (1922). Samuel Lloyd Osbourne (1868–1947) collaborated with his stepfather on three novels, including *The Ebb-Tide* (1894) and *The Wrecker* (1892), as well as on plays with his nephew, Austin Strong.

28. The "note" appears in full as the memoir of Juliet Wilbor Tompkins, chapter 50 this volume.

29. In March 1901, the Norrises, initially ensconced at the Hotel Newberry at 225 Dearborn Avenue in Chicago, could have easily become the center of a heady whirl of social activities, led by newspaper editor and book reviewer Wallace de Groot Cecil Rice (1859–1939) and his wife, the former Minna Needham; novelist George van R. Horton (1859–1942); and the Chatfield-Taylors. Hobart Chatfield Chatfield-Taylor (1865–1945), who through an unexpected inheritance in 1892 had become extremely wealthy, was a popular novelist; he and his first wife, Rose Farwell (1870–1918), formed a social circle in Chicago, centering on the "Little Room," an exclusive club where the city's bohemian crowd frequently gathered to host visiting artists such as the Norrises.

30. Jeannette here refers to the second time the Norrises spent part of their summer vacation at Greenwood Lake, near West Milford, New Jersey, where they lived at the Lakeside Hotel (Crisler 1986, 154–55), a fashionable getaway for New Yorkers.

31. Returned from their New Jersey idyll, the Norrises took an uptown apartment in New York at The Riverview, located at 3605 Broadway and 148th Street.

32. Born on February 9, 1902, six months after the Norrises had taken residence at what would be their final New York address, Jeannette Williamson Norris, nicknamed "Billy," was christened five months later on July 13 at St. Andrew's Dune Church on Long Island (St. Andrew's Dune Record of Baptisms, St. John's Episcopal Church, Southampton, New York), not far from the estate of James A. Herne, where the Nor-

rises were spending the summer. The sponsors at her baptism were Katherine Herne and George D. Moulson (McElrath and Crisler 2006, 415). Billy died from an overdose of barbiturates in 1942.

33. Located at 1921 Broderick Street (Crisler 1986, 200).

34. Jeannette's address when she and Norris first met was 1324 Octavia Street. Purchased by her father, Robert McGee Black (1830–1900), an Irish immigrant from Rathmullan in County Donegal, with money he had made as a forty-niner and then later in Virginia City, Nevada, the house was not as chic as the Norrises' on Sacramento, though it was still located in a fashionable San Francisco neighborhood. Jeannette had an older brother, Francis (1871–?), and a younger sister, Edna A. (1893–?). Norris describes the living room of the fictional Bessemer family, complete with decorated sewer pipe, early in *Blix* (1899b, 26), while Condy Rivers later complains about Travis Bessemer's lack of vocal talent (1899b, 77); Norris also adapted for the novel several other events to which Jeannette refers in her interviews with Walker.

35. The popular guidebooks issued by the German publishing firm Verlag Karl Baedeker, which Karl Baedeker (1801–59) founded in 1827, were considered indispensable by veteran European travelers.

36. An example of one such inscription survives in a copy of *The Octopus* Norris presented to his wife in August 1901 (Crisler 1986, 226).

37. In *Blix* Travis convinces Condy to visit San Francisco's waterfront and see the *City of Everett* (Norris 1899b, 48), a relief ship with a cargo of grain it will soon be transporting to starving villagers in India, which Norris describes as a "whaleback" in both the novel and his article "A Strange Relief-Ship" (Norris 1897i).

38. Dick or Ricardo was locally famous during his days of waiting on tables at Luna's in San Francisco (Edwords 1914, 31).

39. Jeannette here refers to "Outward and Visible Signs," a series of five stories published in the *Overland Monthly* (Norris 1894–95). Although Norris could have been friends with the famous prizefighter James John "Gentleman Jim" Corbett (1866–1930), an encounter with whom he jokingly refers to in his untitled poem published in the 1895 *Blue and Gold* (Crisler 1990, 122, n. 12), Jeannette most likely meant Norris's fraternity brother, Harvey W. Corbett. Like Norris, James Guilford Swinnerton (1875–1974) had studied at the California School of Design; moving to New York in 1896 as a result of his success as a cartoonist for the San Francisco *Examiner*, he was one of a long line of Norris's acquaintances to whom a degree of national prominence came before it befell Norris himself. Like Norris, Fred Allen Greenwood (1872–?), an electrical engineer, was a member of San Francisco's Bohemian Club.

40. Condy comes down with ptomaine poisoning at the beginning of chapter VI of *Blix* (1899b, 124).

41. The Norrises owned a copy of *Harvard Episodes* (1897) by Charles Macomb Flandrau (1871–1938) (Crisler 1988, 4).

42. This was John Alfred Marsh, who took his law degree at Hastings Law School in San Francisco rather than at Harvard (see Rhodes, chapter 19 this volume).

43. M[arcosson] (1899).

44. *Cousin Kate*, by British playwright and journalist Hugh Henry Davies (1869–1917), was first performed in London in 1903 and a year later in New York. Among many other friends, Davies, on November 17, 1902, sent Jeannette a letter of condolence when Norris died.

45. John F. Harrold (1864–?), though several years older than Norris, ran in his social circle in both San Francisco, where Harrold had graduated from Boys' High School in 1882, and New York. Norris probably met Harrold through their mutual friend Gelett Burgess, with whom Harrold shared a humanitarian interest in boys' clubs (see "The Boys' Clubs" 1894) and settlement house work; Burgess and Harrold later roomed together at the Benedick on Washington Square East, where Harrold, employed by Tiffany's and a director of Allied Arts Company (*Trow* 1901, 8), frequently visited the Norrises (McElrath and Crisler 2006, 377).

46. Sir Frederick Sleigh Roberts (1832–1914), a career British officer who fought in the Indian Rebellion of 1857, as well as skirmishes in Abyssinia and Afghanistan, commanded all British troops during the Boer War.

47. Norris owned copies of Crane's *The Red Badge of Courage* (1896), *George's Mother* (1896), and *Wounds in the Rain* (1900) (Crisler 1988, 4, 9).

48. Vice president of Doubleday, Page & Co., Walter Hines Page (1855–1918) had left Doubleday & McClure Co. with F. N. Doubleday and others in 1900 to found the new publishing house. A man of great energy, Page later drew upon his experience as an editor of *Atlantic Monthly* to found and edit *The World's Work*, which Doubleday, Page & Co. published (Crisler 1986, 138, n. 2). Although he was initially enthusiastic regarding the publication of Dreiser's novel (Page to Dreiser, June 9, 1900, Dreiser Papers, Van Pelt Library, University of Pennsylvania), Page eventually withdrew his support.

49. Norris (1902f).

50. In chapter VIII of Book Two of *The Octopus* Norris counterpoints the plight of the starving Mrs. Hooven and her daughter Hilda against scenes of a sumptuous feast that Presley attends at the Cedarquists' mansion.

51. See n. 42 above.

52. Although Jeannette's mother, Carolina Virginia Williamson Black (1851–?), was herself a California native, her parents had come there about the time of the gold rush. Mills Seminary was founded in 1852 in Benicia, California, as Young Ladies Seminary. Susan Lincoln Tolman Mills (1825–1912) and her husband, the Reverend Cyrus Taggart Mills (1819–84), bought and renamed it in 1865, moving it to Oakland in 1871. In 1885 it became Mills College. Completing her studies at Mills, Carolina then went to Monticello Ladies' Seminary in Godfrey, Illinois. When widowed, she became a vocal instructor.

53. C. N. is Norris's brother, Charles.

54. Jeannette and her second husband, Frank Preston, from whom she was by this time divorced, had lived in Medford, Oregon.

55. Telephone number in San Francisco for Norris's daughter, married in April 1924 to Gerald Francis Herrmann (1891–1943), a liquor importer.

56. This pen-and-ink drawing is now part of the Frank Norris Collection.

57. Gertrude was baptized at Trinity Episcopal Church in Chicago on October 18, 1868, over a year after her marriage to B. F. (Trinity Parish Register, St. James Cathedral, Chicago), who transferred his own membership to Chicago's Second Presbyterian Church several years later on May 15, 1876, as did his mother-in-law, Harriet W. Doggett (Second Presbyterian Church Register, Chicago). Later in San Francisco, B. F. continued his Presbyterian affiliation by attending Old First, though he did not join it until November 11, 1887 (Old First Church Register, San Francisco), two years after the family had relocated to San Francisco; meanwhile, Gertrude remained a staunch Episcopalian, as the confirmation of her oldest son on April 6, 1886, at St. Luke's in San Francisco attests (St. Luke's Parish Register, San Francisco).

58. "Salt and Sincerity," a series of seven articles, appeared in *The Critic* in successive months from April through October 1902 (Norris 1902i).

59. The English translation of *Farthest North*, the record of a failed attempt to reach the North Pole by Fridtjof Wedel-Jarlsberg Nansen (1861–1930), appeared in 1897, while *The Voyage of the Jeannette*, comprising the journals of George Washington DeLong (1844–1881) during his earlier venture to find a route to the North Pole by way of the Bering Strait, was published posthumously in 1883. Robert Louis Balfour Stevenson (1850–1894) played a significant role in molding Norris the writer: more than once he praises Stevenson's work in print; he especially enjoyed *The Wrecker*, which Stevenson wrote with his stepson, Lloyd Osbourne; and he had a copy of *The Ebb-Tide* with him at Harvard (Crisler 1988, 2). To their library Norris and Jeannette later added a set of Stevenson's works (Åhnebrink 1950, 461), *St. Ives* (1897), and probably the first volume of a 1901 edition of Stevenson's letters (Crisler 1988, 10).

60. The brothers Goncourt, Edmond (1822–1896) and Jules (1830–1870), wrote six novels together; Marcel Prévost (1862–1941) published *Lettres de Femmes* in 1892; Henri René Albert Guy de Maupassant (1850–93) is known primarily for his ironic short stories; *The Turn of the Screw* by Henry James (1843–1916) appeared in 1898; the novel by Joseph Conrad (1857–1924) that Norris discovered while a reader for Doubleday & McClure Co. was *Lord Jim* (1900); like Norris, his character Curtis Jadwin, protagonist in *The Pit*, also disliked the novels of George Meredith (1828–1909).

61. William S. Rainsford, *The Reasonableness of Faith and Other Addresses* (1902).

62. In March 1900, a month after her marriage, Jeannette became a member of St. George's Episcopal Church; Norris had transferred his membership to St. George's over a year earlier in February 1899 (St. George's Parish Register, New York).

63. Norris based the famous scene in *McTeague* in which McTeague kills Trina on an actual murder that occurred at the Felix Adler Kindergarten in San Francisco in October 1893 (see Charles Norris, chapter 3 this volume).

64. Norris modeled the dress and carriage of young women in many of his drawings on the "Gibson girl," popularized in the work of New York illustrator Charles Dana Gibson (1867–1944); Richard Harding Davis's *Soldiers of Fortune*, illustrated

by Gibson, appeared in 1897. Davis's heroine is an unconventional young woman like Norris's in *Blix*.

65. Having since acquired both a new name—Hospital for Children and a Training School for Nurses—and stately new quarters at the corner of California and Maple Streets, the former San Francisco Children's Hospital instituted its two-year course in nursing education in 1887.

66. Charles G. Norris, *Zelda Marsh* (1927).

67. *Travels with a Donkey* (1879).

68. While researching material for *The Pit* in Chicago in March 1901, Norris turned to his new friend Wallace Rice for a letter of introduction to the young financier, Joseph Leiter (1868–1932), who attempted to maintain a corner of Chicago's wheat market in 1897–98 (McElrath and Crisler 2006, 388–90).

69. Either Jeannette misremembered or Walker misrecorded the title of Kipling's *Stalky & Co.* (1899).

70. Norris (1901a).

71. Head of the major New York publishing firm, Frederick A. Stokes Company, which had published Stephen Crane's *War Is Kind* and *Active Service* in 1899, Frederick Abbott Stokes (1857–1939) married Ellen Rebecca Colby (1861–?) in 1885.

72. Gertrude may well have been aware of Mary Antoinette Anderson (1859–1940), an actress known to audiences by the sobriquet "Our Mary," but she could hardly have patterned her own brief stage career on the younger actress who did not debut until 1877; instead, Jeannette most likely means that both approached their acting with a more serious purpose than motivated the typical popular actress of the day.

73. Mark Twain (1835–1910), *Personal Recollections of Joan of Arc* (1896).

74. Gilbert Emery Bensley Pottle (1875–1945) was originally a writer who worked for several New York newspapers and periodicals, including *Criterion*; he later turned to acting, performing in small roles in nearly ninety films. He and Juliet Wilbor Tompkins did not marry until November 1903, over a year after Norris's death. Norris satirizes the self-important members of literary coteries in his late story, "Dying Fires" (1902c). Juliet's sister was Elizabeth Knight Tompkins.

75. Jeannette Leonard Gilder (1849–1916) was a member of an important New York literary family: her older brother, Richard Watson Gilder (1844–1909), first edited *Scribner's Monthly* and then, from 1881 to his death, *Century*, which published four Norris pieces, "With Lawton at El Caney" (1899g), "The Passing of Cock-Eye Blacklock" (1902g), "The Wife of Chino" (1903g), and "A Lost Story" (1903c); Jeannette's younger brother, Joseph Benson Gilder (1858–1936), served as literary advisor to *Century* and with Jeannette cofounded *Critic*, which published Norris's "Salt and Sincerity" series (1902i) as well as "The Responsibilities of the Novelist" (1902h); Jeannette herself worked with brother Richard at *Scribner's* before coediting *Critic* with brother Joseph.

76. Precisely which stories Norris sold in order to earn money for Jeannette's Christmas present cannot be determined with any accuracy. The illustrated "Miracle Joyeux" appeared in *McClure's Magazine* (1897g).

77. Neltje B. Doubleday.

78. Known during his life as much for his musical prowess as a flautist as for his literary achievement, Sidney Lanier (1842–1881) is today remembered for his lyrical and musical verses such as "The Marshes of Glynn," which commemorated the salt marsh seacoast of his native Georgia.

79. François de la Rochefoucauld (1613–1680) is the urbane, witty, literate, informed, intellectual author of *Maximes* (1665), a volume that would have appealed to Norris, who delighted in producing trenchant essays. Among other collector's items the Norrises owned were a four-volume set of *Oeuvres* by Jean-Baptiste Racine (1639–99), published in Paris in 1829, and a French edition of Sappho (?–570 BC), *Poésie de Sapho*, published in Amsterdam in 1777 (Crisler 1988, 3–4).

80. A reference to the explanation given by Samuel Taylor Coleridge (1772–1834) for his inability to complete perhaps his most characteristic poem, "Kubla Khan" (1816), upon being roused from a deep and lengthy sleep by a "person on business from Porlock," where the poet was then living.

81. Norris had been the colleague at *McClure's* of two writers who later led the muckraking parade: Ida Minerva Tarbell (1857–1944) was a discriminating editor for *McClure's* until 1906 when, with Ray Stannard Baker (1870–1946) and other *McClure's* writers, she founded the *American Magazine* under the editorship of McClure's former partner, John S. Phillips.

82. Since both were members of the Bohemian Club, Norris and Ambrose Gwinnett Bierce (1842–1913) quite possibly encountered each other in San Francisco, where the latter flourished as columnist for both the *Wasp* and the *Examiner*; Bierce's collection of eerie and surrealistic stories, *Tales of Soldiers and Civilians*, appeared in 1891. Artist and writer Robert William Chambers (1865–1933) had studied at Académie Julian for several years (1886–90), where Norris might have met him; one of the stories in Chambers's best-known collection, *The King in Yellow* (1895), was "The Yellow Sign," which may be the tale Jeannette recalls Norris having admired.

83. Like Gelett Burgess, Jimmy Swinnerton, Geraldine Bonner, and various other writers, Edward Waterman Townsend (1855–1942) had joined the seemingly endless caravan of those leaving San Francisco to graze in the greener literary pastures New York offered; Norris's comment in a letter to Elizabeth H. Davenport when he first arrived in New York that Townsend's Bowery stories featuring Chimmie Fadden as protagonist were "very ordinary" confirms Jeannette's memory of Norris's estimate of the older writer (Crisler 1986, 48–49).

84. *Way Down East* (1897) was instead written by actress, playwright, and composer Charlotte Blair Parker (1858–1937).

85. In 1914 Chrystal married Harold Stanley Pollard (1878–1953), editor of the New York *Evening World*.

86. Commissioned by the *San Francisco Chronicle* to report on unrest in South Africa, Norris arrived in time to take part in the ill-fated raid on the Boer colony in the Transvaal, led by Sir Leander Starr Jameson (1853–1917) on December 29, 1895, in an effort to secure a strong British foothold there (McElrath and Crisler 2006, 188–

89, 197–98). As a young physician in Kimberley, South Africa, Jameson met Cecil Rhodes, who had founded in 1888 what later became De Beers Consolidated Mines; Rhodes appointed him administrator over Matabeleland in 1891. Popularly known as the Jameson raid, the abortive attack resulted in Jameson's capture and, as a sidelight, Norris's exile from the colony.

87. In a letter to Walker on June 2, 1930, John H. Hammond confirmed that his wife, Natalie Harris Lum Hammond (1862–1931), did act as temporary nurse to Norris, then suffering from fever contracted while he was reporting on events before and during the Jameson raid (see McElrath and Crisler 2006, 194–95). When the Norrises were living in New York, Hammond was teaching at Yale; his sister, Mary Elizabeth (Betty) Hammond (1865–?), traveled and eventually lived with him and his wife.

88. Leila Burton, a San Francisco debutante, took the minor role of Esther Eccles in *Caste*, a venerable play by Anglo-Irish playwright Thomas William Robertson (1829–1871), when it was performed in San Francisco in March 1897; Norris played Sam Gerridge in the same production ("Strange Fatality Has Pursued Them" 1897).

89. Norris left New York to research *The Octopus* in California on May 10, 1899, two months after *Blix* had begun appearing in the *Puritan* (Crisler 1986, 75–76); he was in California "about three months," according to Jeannette later in this interview, meaning that he and Gertrude would have been able to read at least three of the six installments of *Blix* to each other.

90. Colonel, later President, Theodore Roosevelt (1858–1919).

91. Gertrude was then living at 1322 Washington Street, between Jones and Leavenworth Streets.

92. "Comida!" (Norris 1899c) was one of the articles Norris wrote based on his experiences in Cuba; others included "Untold Thrilling Account of Santiago's Surrender" (1917), "With Lawton at El Caney" (1899g), and "On the Cuban Blockade" (1914a). His hope that *McClure's* would publish all or any of them was ultimately thwarted when none appeared in that periodical. During his recovery in San Francisco from the fever he contracted in Cuba, he gave two interviews, published as "A California Author" (1898a) and "Witnessed the Fall of Caney" (1898c) in Bay Area newspapers.

93. San Francisco's Mechanics' Institute Library was founded in 1854 to provide vocational material for the city's many out-of-work gold miners.

94. Helen Manchester Gates (1868–1950) was the first wife of Archer Milton Huntington (1870–1955), her step-cousin, whose adoptive father, Collis P. Huntington, was the brother of her mother, Helen Maria Huntington Gates (1835–1920); both daughter and mother were poets of minor reputation.

95. The famous incident to which Jeannette here refers occurs at the end of *La Bête Humaine* (1890); in that novel as well the mentally unstable Jacques Lantier is monomaniacally driven to kill a woman.

96. Norris incorporated many of Dulce B. Davis's mannerisms in the character of Annie Derrick in *The Octopus*.

97. At 53 Washington Square South, just a few doors away from where Norris was

then living, was the six-story tower of the Judson Hotel. Added to the elegant Judson Memorial Church in 1895, it was originally conceived as housing for the poor in the neighborhood immediately west of the wealthier Washington Square district.

98. See n. 76 above.

99. *The Virginian* (1902) remains the most popular novel of Owen Wister (1860–1938); Newton Booth Tarkington (1869–1946), who later twice won the Pulitzer Prize for fiction, published *The Gentleman from Indiana* in 1899, a copy of which Norris inscribed "to my wife | Jeannette" (Crisler 1988, 5); O. Henry was the pseudonym that William Sydney Porter (1862–1910) used for his many ironic short stories; British novelist Stanley John Weyman (1855–1928) wrote a number of highly popular historical romances.

100. Norris uses the collective name, the Three Black Crows, for three characters in four separate stories, three of which were published posthumously: "The Dual Personality of Slick Dick Nickerson" (Norris 1902b), "The Ship That Saw a Ghost" (1902j), and "Two Hearts That Beat as One" (1903f); "A Bargain with Peg-Leg" (1902a) had appeared earlier in 1902.

101. Charles was graduated from the University of California in 1903.

102. Porter and Norris had known each other for several years prior to November 1898, when Cosgrave and his wife, Helen Anna Borden Cosgrave (1868–1931), married.

103. Norris never actually wrote a story with the plot Porter here remembers, but he did offer what he terms a possible "idea" for such a story in "Fiction Is Selection": "A Jew sweats old clothes in a sordid basement . . . in front of his shop stands a poplar tree—tall, very beautiful . . . the starved poetry of the man's life is centered about the tree. One day the tree is suddenly cut down . . . something gone out of the Jew's life . . . becomes morose . . . develops latent melancholia—insanity perhaps . . . kills the sordid wife without knowing why—is adjudged insane and straight-jacketed in a sanitarium—would it all have happened if the tree had been left standing?" (Norris 1897b, 3).

104. Porter could have had any of several men surnamed Blum in mind, but no one of that name appears in *The Octopus*. He may have misremembered the character S. Behrman.

105. French novelist Honoré de Balzac (1799–1850).

106. Besides using some of Porter's mystical traits in Vanamee, Norris also more negatively portrayed him in Sheldon Corthell, Laura Dearborn's would-be lover in *The Pit*. Still, Porter respected Norris's art, as his comment on what he imagined Norris's "method" of composition to have been in a subsequent letter to Walker on July 11, 1930, reveals: "a process . . . of setting him self on fire & smouldering till the flame burst forth."

107. Rickoff rebutted Norris's 1896 article three weeks after it appeared in *The Wave* with "Realism and Naturalism" (Rickoff 1896). She posits *A Summer in Arcady* (1896) by James Lane Allen (1849–1925) as an example of "pure" realism as opposed to that of not only Zola but also of Howells and Tolstoy.

108. In a letter to fraternity brother Harry M. Wright, Norris sympathizes with him for having suffered Rickoff's "talent for the inappropriate that at times amounts to positive genius" (Crisler 1986, 74–75).

109. Rickoff's father, Andrew Jackson Rickoff (1824–1899), a well-known Ohio educator, was elected third president of the National Education Association in 1859. Before moving his family to Berkeley in 1882, he had coauthored, with William Torrey Harris (1835–1909) and Mark Bailey (1822–1904), a series of readers published not by Applegate, but by D. Appleton and Company, in the late 1870s.

110. Rickoff contributed at least two articles to the *North American Review* in 1893, "A Reply to Amélie Rives" (1893a) and "The Women of the World" (1893b).

111. Sir Thomas Henry Hall Caine (1853–1931), British novelist and playwright.

112. *Quo Vadis* (1896), historical novel set in ancient Rome, by Nobel laureate Henryk Adam Aleksander Pius Sienkiewicz (1846–1916).

113. John Pierpont Morgan (1837–1913), financier, banker, and philanthropist, hired and paid the salary of W. S. Rainsford and gave $300,000 to St. George's for a new parish house and rectory as well as another $1,350,000 for a maternity hospital near the New York City church of which he was a member.

114. No verification that one of Gertrude's brothers made his livelihood as a gambler has been discovered.

115. The feeling was apparently mutual: Norris also admired Keith's work, as he noted in "The Winter Exhibition" (Norris 1896d). Although born in Scotland, Keith (1838–1911) is known chiefly for his many realistic paintings of California, where he moved in 1859. A copy of his *A Memory of Berkeley* serves as the frontispiece of *Under the Berkeley Oaks* (1900), a collection of student pieces, which includes Norris's "Travis Hallett's Half-Back" (1894b).

Part 4

1. Major General William Rufus Shafter (1835–1906) commanded the US Army Fifth Corps in Cuba during the Spanish-American War.

2. As Archibald acknowledged in a subsequent letter to Walker on March 1, 1931, Norris instead arrived in Tampa, Florida, from New York City, not from San Francisco. Archibald also misremembered the conditions under which Norris and he returned to the United States: departing after other ships had already begun returning soldiers to the United States, the *Iroquois* did not change course but sailed directly from Santiago de Cuba, arriving at New York on August 5, 1898—a week *before* the signing of the peace protocol.

3. The record of the interview commences with Archibald's commentary on the wartime presence of literary celebrity Richard Harding Davis in Tampa and then Cuba following the declaration of war on Spain.

4. Rear Admiral William Thomas Sampson (1840–1902) commanded the US North Atlantic Squadron during the Spanish-American War. Davis repeatedly criticized Sampson's conduct in his publications during and immediately after the war.

5. Volume 10 of the *Argonaut Edition* of Norris's works, which included two of Norris's war publications: "Comida!" (1899c) and "With Lawton at El Caney" (1899g).

6. Norris was not a well-known correspondent such as Stephen Bonsal (1865–1951), whose war articles were published in *McClure's Magazine*, while Norris's were not.

7. The *Gussie* expedition was the war's first American landing on the Cuban shore. Its purpose was to supply munitions to Cuban insurrectionists. Norris did not participate. During the landing, Archibald became the first American wounded by the Spanish.

8. While in Key West, Florida, Norris sailed on this New York *World* press boat to observe action off the Cuban shore in the company of fellow correspondents Henry Sylvester Scovel (1869–1905) and Stephen Crane.

9. Charles Dudley Rhodes (1865–1948), "Diary of a Lieutenant," *The Santiago Campaign* (1927); the volume collects numerous reminiscences of the kind. Norris and Archibald visited the American Army's headquarters on July 14, where Rhodes records meeting them.

10. The comical allusion is to Stephen Crane's collection of stories titled *Wounds in the Rain*.

11. Howard Chandler Christy (1873–1952) was the artist whose drawing of the Cuban girl appeared in Archibald's article "What I Saw in the War: No. 1."

12. Norris and Archibald were present on July 1, 1898, at the taking of El Caney, while to the west the better-known attack on the San Juan Heights was commencing. After the Spanish surrender they returned to El Caney to help the Red Cross distribute food to Cuban civilians (McElrath and Crisler 2006, 290–91, 303–4).

13. Brigadier General Chambers McKibben (1841–1913); Brigadier General and Military Governor of Santiago in 1898 Leonard Wood (1860–1927); Colonel Theodore Roosevelt.

14. See n. 2 above.

15. On June 20, 1898, Norris and other journalists went ashore at Asseraderos, Cuba, with Admiral Sampson and General Shafter. There the Americans met with General Calixto García e Iñiguez (1839–98) to discuss the part that the insurrectionists he led would play in the Santiago campaign (McElrath and Crisler 2006, 286).

16. William Randolph Hearst, publisher of the San Francisco *Examiner* and the *New York Journal*.

17. Frederic Remington, painter and sculptor, much admired by Norris for his equine portraits.

18. That is, handsome.

19. Archibald had shown Walker a letter in which Norris refuted charges that they had obtained in disreputable ways the military medals they collected while in Cuba (see Crisler 1986, 168–69). Archibald here alleges that unflattering rumors about how they obtained the decorations had been spread by other correspondents who were jealous of him.

20. William Burr McIntosh (1862–1942), photojournalist for *Leslie's Weekly*; Caspar Whitney (1863–1929), correspondent for *Harper's Monthly*; Edward Mar-

shall (1869–1933) and James Creelman (1859–1915), correspondents for the *New York Journal.*

21. Clarissa Harlowe "Clara" Barton (1821–1912) founded the Red Cross organization that, for the first time in Cuba, provided aid to soldiers and civilians during a war. C. C. Bangs (1847–1898) was a Red Cross staff member whom Norris and Archibald assisted in distributing food to civilians at El Caney.

22. The heroine of Norris's novel *Blix* (1899b).

23. Patterned after The Lambs, a London club established in honor of British Romantic Charles Lamb (1775–1834) and his sister, Mary Ann (1764–1847), in 1869, the American version, also called The Lambs, was founded in 1874. America's oldest professional theatrical club, it moved to its first permanent quarters at 132 West 44th Street in 1905.

24. Novelist, playwright, actor, screenwriter, and director Dan Totheroh (1894–1976) is best known for writing the screenplay for the film version of the one-act opera *The Devil and Daniel Webster* (1939) by Stephen Vincent Benét (1898–1943) and Douglas Stuart Moore (1893–1969). Like Bennett, Totheroh was born in California.

25. Often associated with both the pre-Raphaelites and aestheticism, Walter Horatio Pater (1839–1894) is best known for his historical novel *Marius the Epicurean* (1885).

26. Davis was twenty-six when Norris visited her ranch.

27. As a fellow member of the Bohemian Club, Peixotto knew Dulce's first husband, Gaston Ashe, who himself had joined the club in 1888. Ashe later recalled to Walker on August 27, 1930, that Norris "was a most delightful comrade and full of personality and magnetism."

28. Juan Batista Valentin Alvarado y Vallejo (1809–1882), twice colonial governor of Alta California, was an older half-brother of Davis's maternal grandmother, Maria Josefa Casilda Aniceta Estrada de Abrego (1814–1897). In *The Octopus* (Norris 1901c) Presley hears the story to which Walker alludes not from Alvarado but from an old man who claims to have known the governor (21).

29. Walker here confuses discrete turn-of-the-century flower and vegetable seed producers—the D. M. Ferry Seed Company, founded by Dexter Mason Ferry (1833–1907) in Rochester, Michigan, and the C. C. Morse Company, established by Charles Copeland Morse (1842–1900), the "American Seed King," in Santa Clara, California, in 1877. The two firms did not merge until 1930 as the consolidated Ferry-Morse Seed Company.

30. Neltje Blanchan de Graff Doubleday (1865–1918).

31. Norris himself rewrote the scene having to do with Auguste Sieppe's incontinence at the Orpheum Theatre in chapter 6, in response to publisher Grant Richards's stipulation that he do so for publication of the novel in England (see McElrath and Crisler 1989).

32. Zulime Taft Garland (1870–1942) was a painter. She married Garland in 1899.

33. Earnest Evan Seton Thompson (1860–1946), who changed his name to Ernest Thompson Seton in 1901, was a Canadian naturalist, author, and illustrator who in 1902 founded the Woodcraft League of America—which merged with the Boy Scouts

of America upon its establishment in 1910. He was, as Norris became when in South Africa in 1895–96, hostile toward the Boer government, and, like Norris, he was supportive during the Boer War (1899–1902) of the ultimately successful effort of the British to topple it.

34. Julie Herne and her mother Katherine who lived on the Upper West Side of Manhattan near Frank and Jeannette.

35. Garland refers to his interest in the American West rather than residence. He instead hailed from the Midwest, Wisconsin, and only much later lived in California.

36. John Wanamaker (1838–1922), most famous for his invention of the modern department store, was also a publisher. His monthly magazine, *Everybody's*, was a property edited and marketed by Doubleday, Page & Co. John O. Cosgrave became its editor in late 1900 through Norris's intervention on his behalf.

37. The same day Garland keened at length in a five-page manuscript titled "Death of Frank Norris" ("Literary Notes," Special Collections, Doheny Library, University of Southern California, transcribed in Crisler 1986, 227–28).

38. Goodrich, that is, fancifully wishes that it were possible to bring Norris back to life. The inconsolable Vanamee in *The Octopus* enjoys the delusion that he has done just that with his deceased lover Angéle.

39. Norris was fifteen years old when, in 1885, he began his residence in San Francisco. He departed for art study in Europe in June 1887.

40. The play, "Two Pair," was performed on December 10, 1892. Scenes 4–7 appeared in the 1894 *Blue and Gold*.

41. Norris studied at Harvard in 1894–95. He received a degree from neither the University of California nor Harvard.

42. Goodrich quotes from "The True Reward of the Novelist" (1901d). He previously alludes to the sincerity theme central to Norris's "Salt and Sincerity" series of essays that appeared in *The Critic* in April–October 1902.

43. Goodrich is quoting from the "Dedication" (l. 24) to *The Idylls of the King* (1891) by Alfred, Lord Tennyson (1809–1892).

44. Paraphrase of "Fra Lippo Lippi" (l. 314) by Robert Browning; the poem first appeared in Browning's collection *Men and Women* (1855).

45. Possibly a paraphrase of 1 John 2:17 which declares in more overtly Christian terms the notion that some individuals and the outcomes of their actions transcend the effects of nature's mutability.

46. Both letters deal with Norris's contributions of articles to *The World's Work* (see Crisler 1986, 195–96).

47. Ruth Frederic Keen (1878–?); Harold Frederic (1856–1898), novelist and journalist; Hamilton Wright Mabie (1846–1916), essayist, magazine editor, and cultural critic; Julian Ralph (1853–1903), journalist; Addison Irving Bacheller (1859–1950), journalist, newspaper syndicate proprietor, and novelist whose *Eben Holden* was a best seller in both 1900 and 1901; Ellen Anderson Gholson Glasgow (1873–1945), novelist.

48. See Crisler 1986, 170, 172.

49. Montrose James Moses (1919–?), then professor emeritus of medical education at Duke University Medical Center.

50. Mary Isabel Garland Lord (1903–1988) and Constance Hamlin Garland Doyle (1907–1988).

51. By mid-October 1901, the Norrises had taken up residence at The Riverview apartment building at 3605 Broadway.

52. Herbert Joseph Edwards (1890–1960) was a professor of English at the University of Maine. With Herne he coauthored the posthumously published *James A. Herne: Rise of Realism in the American Drama* (1964).

53. Lars Åhnebrink, *The Beginnings of Naturalism in American Fiction: A Study of the Works of Hamlin Garland, Stephen Crane, and Frank Norris, with Special Reference to Some European Influences, 1891–1903* (1950).

54. "Herne, the Unconventional" (Norris 1897c).

55. *The Oxford Companion to American Literature* (1941).

56. In a letter to Walker on May 3, 1931, Mildred Howells wrote, "I only saw Mr. Norris once when he first came to see my father in New York, and was only just introduced to him—a tall, dark young man, with a beautiful profile. My father was enthusiastic about *McTeague*, and was much interested in meeting Mr. Norris. I suppose he must have had various literary talks with him,—but I can't tell you anything of them, because I was young and engrossed in my own affairs."

57. John Leslie Thompson (1860–?), treasurer and head of sales at Doubleday, Page & Co., and Samuel Alexander Everitt (1871–1953), business head of the firm, had also both been at Scribner's with Doubleday and Lanier.

58. Norris recommended *Sister Carrie* for publication by Doubleday, Page & Co. The "mix-up" involved the company's acceptance of Norris's recommendation, subsequent attempt to avoid publishing it, and decision not to promote its sale once it was published.

59. That is, the railroad corporation represented in the novel.

60. Marcosson visited the recently wed Norrises on Washington Square South in the summer of 1900 (see Jeannette Norris, chapter 31 this volume).

61. *Moran* was published in September 1898; Norris, however, did not begin referring to his conceptualization of the trilogy in his known correspondence until March 1899. Marcosson's enthusiastic review of *Moran* (1898b) was titled "A Splendid Story of the Sea" (1898).

62. Bret Harte (1836–1902) was a short story writer and novelist associated with the Local Color school of western American fictional writers.

63. Norris actually wrote to Marcosson in early December 1898 (see Crisler 1986, 57–58; other letters by Norris from which Marcosson later quotes are also reprinted in Crisler 1986 [160, 67, 173]).

64. George Douglas Brown (1869–1902) offered in his 1901 novel a realist's portrait of the less than picturesque characteristics of Scottish village life.

65. Lamentation of the brevity of one's youth in the *Rubáiyáat of Omar Khayyám* (1859), translated by Edward Fitzgerald (1809–1883).

66. Charles G. Norris.

67. That is, Walker had stated to Phillips that Norris finished writing *Moran* and initiated *Blix* after beginning his employment with the McClure firm.

68. The novel published in 1914 as *Vandover and the Brute*.

69. While there are multiple contemporaneous references to "The Squid" as an alternate working title for *The Octopus* (1901c), this is the single known citation of "Bread" as an alternate for the never composed "The Wolf."

70. William James Glackens (1870–1938), illustrator and painter known after 1908 as a member of the Ashcan School of Realist art.

71. Henry Chalmers Roberts (1870–1949), first an editor for Doubleday & McClure Co. and then for Doubleday, Page & Co.

72. In his letter to Walker, Doubleday denied that his wife did anything of the kind with regard to the manuscript of *Sister Carrie* or any other submitted to the publishing firm (see Doubleday, chapter 37, this volume).

73. This recollection is anachronistic: the publication of *Sister Carrie* occurred in November of the previous year.

74. When Walker wrote to Dreiser for information concerning his relationship with Norris, Dreiser did not reply; instead, his personal secretary, Evelyn Light, responded on May 5, 1931: "Mr. Dreiser has talked with me about your letter of April 22nd, and while he would be very glad to help you out, there is little he can tell you beyond what you have already found in *McTeague* [Norris 1899e] and the account in the *Colophon*. He visited Frank Norris when he and Mrs. Norris were living on the south side of Washington Square, and also when he was living at Doubleday's house, and a third time when Norris had moved to a small town in New Jersey. He said that he considers Norris by far the best of the American realistic writers."

75. When Norris met with Richards in May 1901, he was not "to write *The Octopus*" at some future time. The novel had already been available for sale for a month.

76. She refers to the winter of 1898/99.

77. James Russell Lowell (1819–1891), "After the Burial" (ll. 37–40), published in 1869.

78. Her brother, playwright and music publisher Gilbert Tompkins (1863–?).

79. In her last interview with Walker (May 16, 1930), Jeannette Norris attributes a similar statement to Cosgrave (see Chapter 37, this volume).

80. Ortolan buntings are small birds legendary among students of French cuisine: captured, force-fed, roasted, and consumed whole, they are treasured by some gourmets. In chapter VIII of the second book of *The Octopus* (1901c), Norris refers to them as served in patties as hors d'oeuvres—a comic touch given the number of the tiny creatures (approximately six inches in length) that it would take to do so. The phrase in question did not have to do with ortolans: one of the characters in the same chapter instead declares, "These stuffed artichokes are delicious" (1901c, 611).

81. "I am a fine middle-class fellow, I—the father of a family." The point risibly intended is that he has settled down and is no longer associated with the bohemian lifestyle of the artistic set.

82. By then married to Gilbert Pottle, Tompkins echoed this observation in a letter to James D. Hart on September 4, 1952: "It was a great pity that Frank did not live long enough to outgrow his Zola craze and to strike a note more distinctively his own. I always felt that his talent was greater than his work."

Works Cited

Abbott, Susan. 2004. Letter to Jesse S. Crisler, October 12.

Academic Senate, University of California. 1935. *In Memoriam 1935*. Berkeley: Academic Senate (and subsequent years).

"Ads." *Blue and Gold, '93*. 1893. Berkeley: Junior Class of the University of California, 1893, 1–31.

Åhnebrink, Lars. 1950. *The Beginnings of Naturalism in American Fiction, 1891–1903*. Cambridge: Harvard University Press.

Aitken, R. G. 1951. "In Memoriam, Charles Hitchcock Adams, 1868–1951." *Publications of the Astronomical Society of the Pacific* 63: 283–85.

Archibald, James J. 1898. "What I Saw in the War: No. 1." *Leslie's Weekly* 87 (October 20): 314.

———. 1931. Letter to Franklin D. Walker, March 1. Franklin Dickerson Walker Papers, BANC MSS C-H 79, The Bancroft Library, University of California, Berkeley.

"Are Our Colleges Creating too Many Dilettantes?" 1913. *New York Times Sunday Magazine*, October 5, 4.

Armes, William Dallam. 1902. "Concerning the Work of the Late Frank Norris." *Sunset* 10 (December): 165–67.

———. 1902. "University Loses Distinguished Son." *Daily Californian*, October 27, 1, 3.

Ashe, Gaston M. 1930. Letter to Franklin D. Walker, August 27. Franklin Dickerson Walker Papers, BANC MSS C-H 79, The Bancroft Library, University of California, Berkeley.

B. F. Norris & Co.'s Thirteenth Annual Price-List for 1872, Watches, Clocks & Jewelry. 1872. Chicago, J. J. Spalding.

Bacon, Thomas R. 1903. "The Last Book of Frank Norris." *Impressions Quarterly* 4 (March): 12.

Blue and Gold, '93. 1893. Berkeley: Junior Class of the University of California (and subsequent years).

Blues, Thomas. 1991. "A Note on Frank Norris's Banjo." *Frank Norris Studies* 12 (Autumn): 6–10.

"Books and Their Makers." 1901. *New York Evening Sun*, March 30, 5 (see McElrath and Knight 1981, 112–14).

"The Boys' Clubs." 1894. San Francisco *Morning Call*, May 7, 10.

Brown, Philip King. 1930. Letter to Franklin D. Walker, October 16. Franklin Dickerson Walker Papers, BANC MSS C-H 79, The Bancroft Library, University of California, Berkeley.

Burgess, Gelett. N.d. Diaries, Gelett Burgess Papers, BANC MSS C-H 52, The Bancroft Library, University of California, Berkeley.

Circular of the Urban School. 1883. San Francisco: Dodge Bros., and Shreve.

Clift, Denison Hailey. 1907. "The Artist in Frank Norris." *Pacific Monthly* 17 (March): 313–22.

C[osgrave, John O.]. 1897. "November Magazines." *The Wave* 16 (November 6): 12.

Crawford, J. J. 1896. *Thirteenth Report of the State Mineralogist for Two Years Ending September 15, 1896.* Sacramento: A. J. Johnston.

Crisler, Jesse S. 1973. "A Critical and Textual Study of Frank Norris's *McTeague.*" Diss., University of South Carolina.

———. 1986. *Frank Norris: Collected Letters.* San Francisco: Book Club of California.

———. 1987. "Norris's Departure for Johannesburg." *Frank Norris Studies* 3 (Spring): 4–5.

———. 1988. "Norris's 'Library.'" *Frank Norris Studies* 5 (Spring): 1–11.

———. 1989. "Norris in South Africa." *Frank Norris Studies* 7 (Spring): 4–7.

———. 1990. "Norris and the *Blue and Gold.*" *Analytical and Enumerative Bibliography* n.s. 4: 110–28.

———. 1997. "A Note on Frank Norris' Death: Berkeley Faculty Members Pay Tribute." *American Literary Realism* 29 (Winter): 81–87.

———. 2002. "Norris's Parents: Not a Marriage of 'True Minds.'" *Frank Norris Studies* n.s. 2: 8–21.

———. 2003. "Frank Norris: College Man." *Resources for American Literary Study* 28: 111–20.

Davenport, Eleanor M. 1897. "Some Younger California Writers." *University of California Magazine* 3 (November): 280–82.

Davies, Hugh H. 1902. Letter to Jeannette Williamson Norris, November 17. Frank Norris Collection, BANC MSS C-H 80, The Bancroft Library, University of California, Berkeley.

Davison, Richard Allan. 1988. "Some Light on Gertrude Doggett Norris's 1894 Divorce Suit." *Frank Norris Studies* 6 (Autumn): 3–4.

———. 1990. "Gertrude Doggett Norris: Professional Actress, Dramatic Reader, and Mother of Novelists." *Book Club of California Quarterly News-Letter* 56 (Winter): 8–19.

———. 1993. *Charles and Kathleen Norris: The Courtship Year.* San Francisco: Book Club of California.

Dillon, Richard H. 1960. *Gelett Burgess and His Lark.* Balboa Island, CA: Paisano Press.

Dinnean, Lawrence. 1980. *Les Jeunes: An Account of Some Fin de Siècle San Francisco Authors and Artists.* Berkeley: Friends of the Bancroft Library.

Dobie, Charles Caldwell. 1928. "Frank Norris, or, Up from Culture." *American Mercury* 13 (April): 412–24.

Edgar, Randolph. 1916. "The Manuscript and the Man." *Bellman* 20 (May 27): 602–3.

Edwords, Clarence E. 1914. *Bohemian San Francisco: Its Restaurants and Their Most Famous Recipes.* San Francisco: Paul Elder.

Frank Norris Collection. N.d. BANC MSS C-H 80, The Bancroft Library, University of California, Berkeley.

Franklin Dickerson Walker Papers, BANC MSS C-H 79, The Bancroft Library, University of California, Berkeley.

Freher, Catherine. 1989. *The Julian Academy, Paris, 1868–1939.* New York: Shepherd Gallery.

Graham, D. B. 1976. "Frank Norris, Actor." Book Club of California *Quarterly News-Letter* 41 (Spring): 38–40.

Gibbs, George. 1952. Letter to Robert E. Burke, November 6. James D. Hart Papers, BANC MSS 81/107c, The Bancroft Library, University of California, Berkeley.

Hammond, John Hays. 1930. Letter to Franklin D. Walker, June 2. Franklin Dickerson Walker Papers, BANC MSS C-H 79, The Bancroft Library, University of California, Berkeley.

Hart, James D. 1986. "The Freshman Themes of Frank Norris." *Frank Norris Studies* 2 (Autumn): 1–2.

Hart, James D., ed. 1970. *A Novelist in the Making: A Collection of Student Themes and the Novels "Blix" and "Vandover and the Brute." Cambridge,* MA: Harvard University Press.

Howells, William Dean. 1902. Letter to Jeannette Williamson Norris, December 14. Frank Norris Collection, BANC MSS C-H 80, The Bancroft Library, University of California, Berkeley.

Howells, Mildred. 1931. Letter to Franklin D. Walker, May 3. Franklin Dickerson Walker Papers, BANC MSS C-H 79, The Bancroft Library, University of California, Berkeley.

Igler, David. 2001. *Industrial Cowboys: Miller and Lux and the Transformation of the Far West, 1850–1920.* Berkeley: University of California Press.

Irwin, Will. n.d. Letter to Jeannette Williamson Norris, undated. Frank Norris Collection, BANC MSS C-H 80, The Bancroft Library, University of California, Berkeley.

Jackson, Donald C. 1995. *Building the Ultimate Dam: John S. Eastwood and the Control of Water in the West.* Topeka: University Press of Kansas.

James D. Hart Papers, BANC MSS 81/107c, The Bancroft Library, University of California, Berkeley.

Jones, William Craig. 1895. *Illustrated History of the University of California.* San Francisco: Frank H. Dukesmith.

Kastler, Deanna. 1908. "The Portola-Louvre Restaurant." *San Francisco Bay Area Post Card Club* 23, no. 1 (January): 6–9.

Lanier, Henry Wysham. 1902. Letter to Jeannette Williamson Norris, November 12. Frank Norris Collection, BANC MSS C-H 80, The Bancroft Library, University of California, Berkeley.

Light, Evelyn. 1931. Letter to Franklin D. Walker, May 5. Franklin Dickerson Walker Papers, BANC MSS C-H 79, The Bancroft Library, University of California, Berkeley.

"Lincoln Man Tells of Norris." 1902. Lincoln, Nebraska *Star,* November 22, 16.

McElrath, Joseph R., Jr. 1988. "The Deconstruction of a Bibliography: The Frank Norris Canon." *South Central Review* 5 (Summer): 51–61.

———. 1992. *Frank Norris: A Descriptive Bibliography*. Pittsburgh: University of Pittsburgh Press.

———. 2001. "'One Thing One Did Not Question': The Christian Perspective of Novelist Frank Norris." *Literature and Belief* 21 (Winter): 1–25.

McElrath, Joseph R., Jr., and Jesse S. Crisler. 1989. "The Bowdlerization of *McTeague*." *American Literature* 61 (March): 97–101.

———. 2006. *Frank Norris: A Life*. Urbana: University of Illinois Press.

McElrath, Joseph R., Jr., and Katherine Knight. 1981. *Frank Norris: The Critical Reception*. New York: Burt Franklin.

McElrath, Joseph R., Jr., and Sal Noto. 1990. "An Important Letter in the Career of Frank Norris." *Book Club of California Quarterly News-Letter* 55 (Summer): 59–61.

M[arcosson], I[saac]. F. 1898. "A Splendid Story of the Sea." *Louisville Times*, November 26, 7 (see McElrath and Knight 1981, 17–18).

———. 1899. "The Story of McTeague." *Louisville Times*, March 13, 8 (see McElrath and Knight 1981, 33–35).

Millard, F[rank]. B[ailey]. 1897. "Last Word from the Essayist." San Francisco *Examiner*, January 17, 30.

Noble, Dennis L. 1997. *Lighthouses and Keepers: The U.S. Lighthouse Service and Its Legacy*. Annapolis, MD: Naval Institute Press.

"Norris." 1902. St. Paul *Dispatch*, October 27, 6.

Norris, Charles. 1914. *Frank Norris, 1870–1902*. Garden City, NY: Doubleday, Page.

———. 1928. "Introduction." *Collected Writings Hitherto Unpublished in Book Form. The Argonaut Manuscript Limited Edition of Frank Norris's Works*. 10 vols. Garden City, NY: Doubleday, Doran. Vol. 10: vii–xiii.

Norris, Frank. 1889. "Clothes of Steel." *San Francisco Chronicle*, March 31, 6.

———. 1890a. "Brunehilde." *Occident* 19 (November 21): 110.

———. 1890b. "The Coverfield Sweepstakes." *Occident* 19 (December 19): 145–47.

———. 1891a. "The Great Szarrattar Opal." *Smiles* 1 (November 18): 6.

———. 1891b. "The Jongleur of Taillebois." *The Wave* 7 (December 19): 6–9.

———. 1891c. "The Son of the Sheik." *Argonaut* 28 (June 1): 6.

———. 1892a. "Brunhilde." *California Illustrated Magazine* 2 (June): 61–63.

———. 1892b. "The Class of '94." *Blue and Gold*. Berkeley: Junior Class of the University of California, 46–49.

———. 1892c. *Yvernelle: A Legend of Feudal France*. Philadelphia: J. B. Lippincott.

———. 1893a. "Lauth." *Overland Monthly* 21 (March): 241–60.

———. 1893b. "Two Pair." *Blue and Gold*. Berkeley: Junior Class of the University of California, 183–92.

———. 1893c. "Unequally Yoked." *Berkeleyan* 2 (September 22): 43–48.

———. 1894a. "I took my girl to Schuetzen Park" (untitled poem). *Blue and Gold*. Berkeley: Junior Class of the University of California, 250–52.

———. 1894b. "Travis Hallett's Half-Back." *Overland Monthly* 23 (January): 20–27.

———. 1894–95. "Outward and Visible Signs." *Overland Monthly* 23 (March 1894): 241–46; 23 (May 1894): 502–6; 24 (July 1894): 82–86; 24 (October 1894): 375–79; and 25 (February 1895): 196–201.
———. 1896a. "College Athletics." *The Wave* 15 (December 12): 13.
———. 1896b. "Football in Town." *The Wave* 15 (October 10): 9.
———. 1896c. "Lackaye 'Making Up.'" *The Wave* 15 (December 5): 4.
———. 1896d. "The Winter Exhibition." *The Wave* 15 (December 12): 4.
———. 1896e. "Zola as a Romantic Writer." *The Wave* 15 (June 27): 3.
———. 1897a. "Cosmopolitan San Francisco." *The Wave* 16 (December 18): 14.
———. 1897b. "Fiction Is Selection." *The Wave* 16 (September 11): 3.
———. 1897c. "Herne, the Unconventional." *The Wave* 16 (February 27): 9.
———. 1897d. "Holiday Literature." *The Wave* 16 (December 11): 8.
———. 1897e. "Life-Line and Surf Boat." *The Wave* 16 (September 18): 9.
———. 1897f. "Little Dramas of the Curbstone." *The Wave* 16 (June 26): 5.
———. 1897g. "Miracle Joyeux." *McClure's Magazine* 12 (December): 4; original version, 1897. *The Wave* 16 (October 9): 4.
———. 1897h. "An Opening for Novelists." *The Wave* 16 (May 22): 7.
———. 1897i. "A Strange Relief-Ship." *The Wave* 16 (June 12): 7.
———. 1897j. "Suggestions." *The Wave* 16 (March 13): 7.
———. 1897k. "The Third Circle." *The Wave* 16 (August 28): 5.
———. 1897l. "The U.C. Track Team." *The Wave* 16 (February 16): 4.
———. 1897m. "What Is Our Greatest Piece of Fiction?" San Francisco *Examiner*, January 17, 30.
———. 1898a. "A California Author." *Oakland Enquirer*, August 29, 4.
———. 1898b. *Moran of the Lady Letty*. Doubleday and McClure; and 1898. "Moran of the 'Lady Letty.'" *The Wave* 17 (January 8– April 9).
———. 1898c. "Witnessed the Fall of Caney." *San Francisco Chronicle*, August 28, 8.
———. 1899a. "'As Long as Ye Both Shall Live.'" *Sunday Examiner Magazine*, June 4, 32.
———. 1899b. *Blix*. New York: Doubleday and McClure; *Puritan* 5 (March–May) and 6 (June–August).
———. 1899c. "Comida!" *Atlantic Monthly* 83 (March): 343–48.
———. 1899d. "A Man's Woman." *San Francisco Chronicle*, July 23–October 8.
———. 1899e. *McTeague*. New York: Doubleday and McClure.
———. 1899f. *Shanghaied*. London: Grant Richards.
———. 1899g. "With Lawton at El Caney." *Century* 58 (June): 304–9.
———. 1900a. "A Reply." *Blue and Gold*. Berkeley: Junior Class of the University of California, 174.
———. 1900b. *A Man's Woman*. Doubleday and McClure.
———. 1900c. "Student Life in Paris." *Collier's Weekly* 25 (May 12): 33.
———. 1901a. "Frank Norris' Weekly Letter: [9]." *American Art and Literary Review* (Chicago *American*), August 3, 5.
———. 1901b. "The Need of a Literary Conscience." *World's Work* 3 (December): 1559–60.

———. 1901c. *The Octopus*. New York: Doubleday, Page.

———. 1901d. "The True Reward of the Novelist." *World's Work* 2 (October): 1337–39.

———. 1902a. "A Bargain with Peg-Leg." *Collier's Weekly* 28 (March 1): 13, 16.

———. 1902b. "The Dual Personality of Slick Dick Nickerson." *Collier's Weekly* 30 (November 22): 8–9, 22–23.

———. 1902c. "Dying Fires." *Smart Set* 7 (July): 95–101.

———. 1902d. "Frank Norris Defends Dr. Lawlor." *Argonaut* 51 (August 11): 87.

———. 1902e. "Grettir at Drangey." *Everybody's Magazine* 6 (March): 257–65.

———. 1902f. "Life in the Mining Region." *Everybody's Magazine* 7 (September): 241–48.

———. 1902g. "The Passing of Cock-Eye Blacklock." *Century* 64 (July): 385–91.

———. 1902h. "The Responsibilities of the Novelist." *Critic* 41 (December): 537–40.

———. 1902i. "Salt and Sincerity." *Critic* 40 (April): 307; 40 (May): 447–50; 40 (June): 550–55; 41 (July): 77–81; 41 (August): 178–82; 41 (September): 267–70; 41 (October): 363–67.

———. 1902j. "The Ship That Saw a Ghost." *New England Magazine* 27 (December): 439–49.

———. 1902–3. "The Pit." *Saturday Evening Post* 175 (September 20–January 31).

———. 1903a. *A Deal in Wheat and Other Stories of the New and Old West*. New York: Doubleday, Page.

———. 1903b. "Grettir at Thornhall-Stead." *Everybody's Magazine* 8 (April): 311–19.

———. 1903c. "A Lost Story." *Century* 66 (July): 371–79.

———. 1903d. *The Pit*. New York: Doubleday, Page.

———. 1903e. *The Responsibilities of the Novelist*. New York: Doubleday, Page.

———. 1903f. "Two Hearts That Beat as One." *Ainslee's* 10 (January): 52–58.

———. 1903g. "The Wife of Chino." *Century* 65 (January): 369–78.

———. 1907. "The Exile's Toast." *Reader* 9 (May): 684.

———. 1909. *The Third Circle*. New York: John Lane.

———. 1913. "Vehmegericht." *California Play and Pageant*. [Berkeley]: English Club of the University of California. N.p.

———. 1914a. "On the Cuban Blockade." New York *Evening Post*, Final Edition, April 11, Part 3, 6.

———. 1914b. *Vandover and the Brute*. New York: Doubleday, Page.

———. 1917. "Untold Thrilling Account of Santiago's Surrender." New York *Sun*, July 13, Section 7, 1–2.

———. 1931. *Frank Norris of "The Wave."* San Francisco: Westgate Press.

"Ode on a Grecian Yearn: Norris's Salute to Distant Fijis Becomes Classic." 1963. *Phi Gamma Delta* 86 (October): 16–17.

Peixotto, Ernest C. 1930. Letter to Franklin D. Walker, June 28. Franklin Dickerson Walker Papers, BANC MSS C-H 79, The Bancroft Library, University of California, Berkeley.

"Personal Mention." 1893. San Francisco *Morning Call*, November 27, 7.

Phillips, Jennie B. 1952. Letter to James D. Hart, November 23. James D. Hart Papers, BANC MSS 81/107c, The Bancroft Library, University of California, Berkeley.

Porter, Bruce. 1930. Letter to Franklin D. Walker, July 11. Franklin Dickerson Walker Papers, BANC MSS C-H 79, The Bancroft Library, University of California, Berkeley.

Rayman, Ronald. 1977. "Stockton's Yo Semite House Hotel, 1869–1923." *California Historical Quarterly* 54 (Summer): 164–69.

Rickoff, Bertha M. 1893a. "A Reply to Amélie Rives." *North American Review* 156 (March): 377–79.

———. 1893b. "The Women of the World." *North American Review* 157 (October): 451–56.

———. 1896. "Realism and Naturalism." *The Wave* 15 (July 18): 3.

Rodgers, Viola. 1931. Letter to Franklin D. Walker, May 8. Franklin Dickerson Walker Papers, BANC MSS C-H 79, The Bancroft Library, University of California, Berkeley.

Senger, Lucy A. 1930. Letter to Franklin D. Walker, October 14. Franklin Dickerson Walker Papers, BANC MSS C-H 79, The Bancroft Library, University of California, Berkeley.

Sixtieth Annual Catalogue of the Officers, Instructors and Students of the Monticello Ladies' Seminary, Godfrey, Madison County, Ill., for the Year Ending June 14th, 1898. 1898. St. Louis: Woodward and Tiernan.

Stephens, Henry Morse. 1903. "The Work of Frank Norris: An Appreciation." *University of California Chronicle* 5 (January): 324–31.

"Strange Fatality Has Pursued Them." 1897. San Francisco *Call*, March 1, 11.

Stronks, James B. 1991. "B. F. Norris (Senior) in Probate Court, with New Light on Frank Norris as Son." *Frank Norris Studies* 12 (Autumn): 3–5.

Sutton, James. 1892a. Letter to B. F. Norris, April 28. University Archives, CU-10, The Bancroft Library, University of California, Berkley.

———. 1892b. Letters to Frank Norris, January 29 and April 28. University Archives, CU-10, The Bancroft Library, University of California, Berkeley.

Taylor, Harvey, comp. 1930. *Frank Norris: Two Poems and "Kim" Reviewed.* San Francisco: Harvey Taylor.

Tompkins, Juliet Wilbor. 1952. Letter to James D. Hart, September 4. James D. Hart Papers, BANC 81/107c, The Bancroft Library, University of California, Berkeley.

The Trow Copartnership and Corporation Directory. 1901. New York: Trow.

"Two Years for F. A. Hyde." 1908. *New York Times*, October 9, 9.

University Archives. N.d. CU-10, The Bancroft Library, University of California, Berkeley.

Untitled notes in *Berkeley Daily Advocate*, 17 September 1891: 3; 29 October 1891: 3; 23 May 1892: 3; 24 May 1892: 3; 25 May 1892: 3; 26 May 1892: 3; and 28 May 1892: 3.

"Vandover and the Brute." 1921. *New York Times*, February 27, 30.

Walker, Franklin D. 1932. *Frank Norris: A Biography*. Garden City, NY: Doubleday, Doran.

———. Letter to W. John Bauer. 1972. September [17]. Franklin Dickerson Walker Papers, BANC MSS C-H 79, The Bancroft Library, University of California, Berkeley.

Weck, Charles A. 1957. Letter to James D. Hart, July 4. James D. Hart Papers, BANC MSS 81/107c, The Bancroft Library, University of California, Berkeley.

Weed, Benjamin. 1913. "The Genesis of the Greek Theater." *California Play and Pageant*. [Berkeley]: English Club of the University of California. N.p.

Weinberg, Herman G., comp. 1972 [1973]. *The Complete Greed of Erich von Stroheim*. New York: Dutton.

Wilder, Edwin M. 1952. Letter to James D. Hart, August 26. James D. Hart Papers, BANC MSS 81/107c, The Bancroft Library, University of California, Berkeley.

Wright, Harry M. 1931. Letter to Franklin D. Walker, September 11. Franklin Dickerson Walker Papers, BANC MSS C-H 79, The Bancroft Library, University of California, Berkeley.

Index

FN in index refers to Frank Norris.
Italicized page numbers refer to photographs.